International Politics

The rules of the game

Raymond Cohen

Longman
London and New York

Longman Group Limited
Longman House
Burnt Mill, Harlow, Essex, UK

Published in the United States of America
by Longman Inc., New York

© Longman Group Limited 1981

First published 1981
Second impression 1982

British Library Cataloguing in Publication Data

Cohen, Raymond
   International politics.
   1. International relations
   I. Title
   327   JX1391   80–41594

ISBN 0–582–29558–0

Set in Malaysia by Syarikat Seng Teik Sdn. Bhd.
Printed in Singapore by Huntsmen Offset Printing Pte Ltd

Contents

Introduction

In recent years the concept of 'rules of the game' has found increasing expression in the literature of international politics. It is sometimes used in a minimal sense to refer to the informal understandings which supplement the formal agreements and practices by which the United States and the Soviet Union regulate their relationship. Just as frequently authors use the term to refer, in a general sense, to the overall network of ties, formal and informal, between the two superpowers. Equivalent phrases are 'ground rules' or 'code of détente'. In this book I intend to take the liberty of applying the term 'rules of the game' in the latter broader sense to international politics in general.

My point of departure is the proposition that it is both feasible and useful to examine within a common framework the whole range of normative restraints by which states, not only the superpowers, regulate their conduct. The term 'rules of the game' provides a convenient and expressive appellation for this inclusive concept. Such regulatory principles are taken to include general norms of behaviour, aspects of international law, and rules which are created by formal and informal understanding, or are contained in the 'spirit' of agreements, verbal 'gentlemen's' agreements and different kinds of tacit understanding. Their shared feature is that they guide the conduct of states in their relations with each other and thereby prevent, or at least mitigate, conflict and facilitate cooperation. The advantage of an integrated approach to their analysis is that it permits an insight into what I believe to be the significant point that these various normative principles function, evolve, decay, are maintained and communicated in analogous ways. Without overlooking differences in scope, formulation, generality, solemnity and so on between various kinds of rules, it seems to me as logical to consider them as a single genus as it is so to consider social norms or linguistic conventions. I shall argue, for instance, that the consequences of their infringement are surprisingly uniform. Indeed I agree with Hedley Bull's view in *The Anarchical Society* that treating them in separate compartments obscures the working of one of the central elements in the maintenance of international order.

This book is not intended as a general introduction to international politics and I do not intend to give a general account of the concepts, procedures and institutions appropriate to such a wider study. However, one of the convictions that stimulated the writing of this book was that research into international politics has, with the decline in general acceptance of the power politics theory, lost its former focus and that the community of scholars in the field has begun to lack a common language of discourse. The teaching of the subject has therefore become correspondingly more difficult, with students confused by contradictory assumptions and orientations. Research into international law, diplomatic history, the behaviour of groups and individuals engaged in the making of foreign policy, communications between states and regional affairs, has proceeded as though there were no common factors linking together these different areas of emphasis. One of the advantages of studying international politics from the perspective of rules of the game is that it enables one to draw on these diverging specializations and integrate aspects of them within a common framework. Moreover the analysis of those normative limits within which states have conducted their political relationships, at different times and in different places, is surely one of the recurrent and shared problems to which scholars throughout the field have addressed themselves. This book is an attempt to emphasize one of the unifying concerns of an otherwise increasingly fragmented discipline.

Part one

The theory of rules of the game

Chapter one

Rules as a mechanism of international order

In a twentieth century which has seen two world wars with tens of millions of casualties and which faces the awful prospect of nuclear holocaust, it is natural that the very highest priority in the study of international politics has been given to the related questions of how conflict can be regulated, war avoided and cooperation facilitated. Isaiah's vision of a universal harmony in which 'Nation shall not lift up sword against nation, neither shall they learn war any more' has an empty quality for modern man. More authentic has seemed to be Yeats's prospect of a universal chaos in which 'things fall apart; the centre cannot hold; mere anarchy is loosed upon the world'.

In contrast to the dark pessimism with which international affairs is so often viewed, a less sombre and more balanced picture may equally be suggested. Absolute peace, unflawed by disagreement and unblemished by the shadow of weapons of mass destruction, may be nothing more than a messianic ideal. Equally, war, though a hideous and too frequent scourge of the human condition, has still been an exceptional event, signalling the breakdown of order rather than the customary state of things. Most of the time states do somehow succeed in maintaining a *modus vivendi* – more or less effective – in their relations. Occasionally working relationships break down; occasionally cooperation of a high order is achieved. Usually disagreements are lived with or patched up, cooperation gives way to periodic dissension, states converge and diverge. Nevertheless, and this is surely a remarkable thing, only exceptionally, in a world of competing interests, scarce resources and endemic suspicions and hatreds, does disagreement make way for armed conflict.

In this respect wars can be compared to traffic accidents: collisions and fatalities draw a disproportionate, if unsurprising, amount of attention. In the general run of things cars – and states – manage to avoid colliding with each other with an unusual degree of success. A recent statistical survey on the frequency of war, based on the number of months states were at war over the 150 years 1816–1965, finds that overall war was in progress only 5 per cent of the total time available.[1] Without overemphasizing the precision of this kind of exercise or wishing to minimize the horror of war, it would seem reasonable to conclude that a major task of the historian is not simply to account for the incidence of war but also for its unexpectedly frequent absence.

The question of the avoidance of war has usually been conceived in the larger context of a study of international order, since it is this latter condition of the international system which is generally assumed to permit the consistent and effective preservation of peace. A recent definition of 'international order' which has received wide approbation is that of Hedley Bull. He sees it as 'a pattern or disposition of international activity that sustains those goals of the society of states that are elementary, primary or universal'. Such goals include:

1. the preservation of the system and society of states itself ;
2. the maintenance of the independence or external sovereignty of individual states;
3. peace;
4. the common goals of all social life: limitation of violence resulting in death or bodily harm, the keeping of promises and the stabilization of possession by rules of property[2]

Other writers, such as Richard Falk, have taken a more modest position, viewing international order as a state of affairs in which conflict is confined 'within tolerable limits' and 'the risk of large-scale irreversible violence occurring in the relations among principal states' is minimized.[3] The view to be adopted by this book is closer to that of Hedley Bull and accepts that an element of positive cooperation is a necessary component of international order. Furthermore, the existence of a substantial body of social-like norms in relations between states rather than mere minimal curbs on violence, does suggest the aptness of considering the international system as a sort of society or constellation of societies, albeit of a rudimentary kind.

At various times philosophers have put forward a range of theories to account for or to promote the preservation of international order. The balance of power, the primacy of international law and the operation of a directorate of great powers have been among the most popular candidates for this role. However, each of these theories, taken in isolation, has come under telling criticism.

The working of the balance of power has been the classic realist answer to the problem of maintaining international order. According to the most prevalent version of the theory (and writers have imputed to it a confusingly broad spectrum of meanings) order is maintained in the international system, or its constituent subsystems, by preventing, through the construction of countervailing power by armament or coalition, the emergence of a single predominant state or alliance. The theoretical and descriptive limitations of this doctrine have been pointed out by, among others, Hans Morgenthau and Raymond Aron.

For his part Morgenthau demonstrates that the 'uncertainty of all power calculations not only makes the balance of power incapable of practical application but leads to its very negation in practice'. Since power can never be quantified in any precise manner states can never know whether or not a 'balance' of power actually exists. Worse, the attempt 'to make sure' that the opponent will not be tempted to miscalculate his own superiority leads inevitably to a process of escalation in which each side seeks to steal an edge on the other. In the end wars which are the very negation of international order are fought in the name of international order.[4] In the nuclear age, moreover, the 'small' wars which were a feature of the working of the balance of power in previous eras, are no longer a tempting proposition.

Aron, in his turn, argues convincingly that it is simply not true that safeguarding the equilibrium of the system is either the sole or the predominant concern of states.[5] Under the Bismarckian aegis Europe was preserved from general war for a generation by a series of remarkable devices, some of which did correspond to the prescriptions of the balance of power (the principle of 'compensation', great power intervention in 1875 to prevent German interference in internal French affairs) but others of which were quite peculiar to the period. These included the diversion of the competitive energies of the great powers to the accumulation of colonies outside Europe and Bismarck's unusual contrivance of, on the one hand, reining in Austria-Hungary by a treaty of alliance and, on the other hand, restraining Austria's most likely opponent, Russia, by a converse treaty of 'reinsurance'. Great Britain, which during the terms in office of foreign secretaries such as Castlereagh and Canning, had indeed conceived of its role as a 'balancer', ready to shift its weight as needed from one scale of the balance to the other, increasingly withdrew, after the neutralization of Belgium in the 1830s, from Continental affairs. In 1870 British policy was less concerned about the outcome of a Franco-Prussian War which was decisively to shift the distribution of power in Europe, as with obtaining renewed assurances about Belgian neutrality. Following Bismarck's downfall a balance of power system eventually emerged in its classic sense: the concentration of the great powers around two opposing poles. In fact the rigidity and hostility engendered by these alliances proved fatal for the stability of the system and the balance of power was widely blamed at the time as one of the underlying causes of the First World War.

A similar critique could be made of the inapplicability of the theory of the balance of power to the period between the two world wars. Utter French military predominance on the Continent in the 1920s was succeeded by a decade of increasing instability as German power moved menacingly into balance.

The concept of international law as a custodian of international order has fared no better in recent years. Hedley Bull, while paying due regard to important functions performed by international law, points out its major limitations in the task of maintaining international order. First, he argues that past international societies have existed without a concept of international law and that therefore this cannot be 'a necessary or essential condition of international order'. Second, he believes that while international law can express existing assumptions about international society, it 'is not by itself sufficient to bring about international order'.

Third, Bull emphasizes the sometimes conflicting requirements of international law and measures to maintain international order. The political necessities of alliance may require turning a blind eye to one's ally's infringements of the law. Fourth, 'legal instrumentalities' used to promote concepts of justice may also conflict with requirements of international order.[6]

To these reservations it is worth adding one other: that with the passing of a previous ideological consensus in world affairs the 'Law of Nations' has ceased to be sufficiently uniform, comprehensive or determinate to perform a decisive role. Edward McWhinney, for one, sees international law at the present time not as a 'single, comprehensive or overarching, body of authoritative rules or propositions, but rather a congeries of separate and distinct bodies of more or less authoritative rules'. These include classical international law, United Nations-based law, regional law, 'Socialist' international law and interbloc law. In these circumstances it is not sufficient for the lawyer to give a legal opinion. He must also make some kind of judgement of priority between the different bodies of rules.[7]

Turning to the idea of a great power 'directorate' as the prop of international order, there is no doubt that the great powers, by mere virtue of their preponderant position, must necessarily play a central role in the international system – whether this be constructive or not. The question is whether there is or has been an identifiable and effective mechanism of the great powers purposively working together to ensure the preservation of international order. It is this which must be in doubt. The nineteenth-century Concert of Europe, which is usually considered the paradigm of a directorate of great powers, was far from being a permanent institution continuously functioning to regulate the major questions of the age, but rather a spasmodic and *ad hoc* style of diplomacy by conference which actually came into effect extremely infrequently – on no more than a handful of occasions throughout the entire period.[8] Issues which crucially affected the distribution of power throughout the system – Italian unification, the three Prussian wars with Denmark, Austria and France that precipitated German unification, the Baghdad Railway and other momentous questions – were settled outside the framework of great power cooperation. Similarly, in the twentieth century, the League of Nations and the United Nations conspicuously failed to resolve most major international disputes and in some cases actually hindered the resolution of conflict. The reasons for this failure are well known: an absence of consensus and ideological rivalry conspired to prevent either decision or action. Great power cooperation outside these organizations was no more fruitful. In the interwar period this failure was marked by the forcible dismantlement of the order set up by the victors after the First World War; after 1945, most conspicuously, by the absence of an agreed settlement of the status of Germany, the central issue which more than anything else was a touchstone of the ability of the great powers to work together.

If neither the balance of power, international law nor great power cooperation provides adequate explanations for the maintenance of international order, what then can be put in their place? One answer, implicit in the Hedley Bull account, is that *all these mechanisms* can be thought of as contributing, separately but cumulatively, towards the preservation of international society. In other words, though each individual device possesses its own limitations, taken together they constitute a more effective regulatory system. Precisely how these various components interrelate in an overall synthesis is not made explicit; nor is any scale of priority elaborated. This seems to me to be a serious drawback to the Bull approach since, for his case to be demonstrated, he would surely have to explain how individually flawed mechanisms work any better if taken in the aggregate. Indeed Bull himself points out that they actually work, on occasion, at cross-purposes.

The thesis proposed in this book is as follows: *rules of the game* perform the same function for international society as norms in domestic society; they indicate the limits on permissible conduct, thereby permitting conflict to be contained, and act as guidelines for desirable behaviour, thereby facilitating active cooperation. They should not be thought of as excluding provisions of *international law* which contribute to international order, but rather as a wider concept than law, which they subsume. Rules are prior to law; the latter is a special case of the former. When they come into conflict rules, not law, are the operative guide to conduct. Laws are not inherently different from rules, they are simply those rules which have achieved a degree of solemnity and permanence. It is for this very reason that, as circumstances change, they may fall into disuse and be replaced by less formal and more flexible provisions.

International and regional organizations are also not excluded by the concept of rules of the game from a role in maintaining order. They do this by providing frameworks within which rules, and especially international and regional norms, are given expression, legitimized and sometimes enforced, if only by the exercise of communal opinion.

Finally, and most importantly, there is an organic connection between rules of the game and *power*. First, as Richard Falk points out, rules 'clarify and sustain established patterns of power that are generally acceptable, or at least tolerated, by the relevant political community'.[9] Rules which cease to reflect the distribution of power sooner or later fall into redundancy (assuming that the change is appreciated and that rival states possess an interest in altering the rules). Conversely, power enforces and defines the scope of rules of the game. A concrete example will help here. The Chinese attack on Vietnam in 1979 was designed to maintain Cambodian independence and curb Vietnamese expansion within an area which China saw as its special sphere of interest. However, power relations in the arena – specifically Chinese awareness of Soviet strength and the revelation of a Vietnamese capacity to stand firm – exerted decisive constraints on Chinese objectives. It is not the balance of power, in the sense of a mechanical system of equilibrium, that is a crucial component of international order. Rather it is the relative distribution of power throughout the international system which provides the sub-structure upon which the network of rules of the game is supported. An equilibrium of force is not an end in itself, as it has been too frequently viewed, for even if obtained, it cannot by itself ensure peace. But it is a condition of the construction of an order regulated by rules of conduct. The ideas sketched out here will be further developed during the course of this book.

How and why rules function to maintain order will be taken up in chapter three. At this stage it will suffice to clarify why there is a necessary and not merely contingent link between rules and order. According to communications theory the 'amount of order' in a system is related to the 'amount of information' in that system, indeed the latter is equivalent to the former. 'The more disordered a portion of the world is', Anatol Rapoport points out, 'the more information is *required* to describe it completely, that is, to make it known. Thus the process of obtaining knowledge is quantitatively equated to the process of ordering portions of the world.'[10]

This can be exemplified by considering the information required to describe an orderly as opposed to random arrangement of a pack of cards. In the first case one lays down the principle of arrangement, the ordinal relationship between different cards of a single suit and the instruction that this same principle applies in the case of the other three suits. In the second case the location of each individual card must be described. Thus it can be seen that since a rule is the most parsimonious way of imparting information about a recurrent event or state of affairs, an orderly pack of cards is describable by a single set of rules repeatedly applied.

In an analogous way, to the extent that states manage their relations by rules of conduct and not by unpredictable and spasmodic improvization, one will be able to describe the international system as in a state of relative order. To order the universe of international relations is to subject it to rules of behaviour. International order, therefore, is not only facilitated by rules of the game; it is in fact synonymous with their existence.

Chapter two

The nature of rules

An essential first step in analysing the working of rules of the game is a theoretical clarification of the concept. Fortunately there have been several useful investigations of rules, especially in the fields of philosophy and the social sciences. Much of the stimulus for this interest, it should be noted, has derived, directly or indirectly from the reflections of Ludwig Wittgenstein. In the following chapter I shall consider some of the salient features of rules, partly by the method of contrasting them with other related but distinct concepts, and go on to suggest three criteria by which the presence of rules of the game can be detected.

Our interest in rules stems from their impact on conduct. Behaviour can obviously either be in a conformity with rules or it can diverge from them. What is important to emphasize at the very outset is that rules as such are not actions but items of information about actions; they are *expectations of right conduct in defined circumstances*. Even when rules are not articulated, as in the case of tacit understandings and unstated norms, they are still necessarily articulable. Otherwise we should hardly be able to discuss them. The point of this distinction is that a given action, taken in isolation, could exemplify any number of rules or no rule at all.[1] A car may halt at a zebra crossing to allow pedestrians to cross over the road. It may also stop because of engine failure, to avoid a collision or to back into a parking space. In this example the ostensible intentions of the subject appeared deceptively self-evident to an observer. In other cases stated intentions may be no less misleading. The description assigned to an act of state by its government ('legitimate self-defence', 'protection of democratic rights' and so on) may be no more than a rhetorical justification. Furthermore the potency of a rule may lie precisely in its effective discouragement of action. It would be a mistake to overlook the possibility that inaction as much as action may indicate rule-conforming behaviour.

An additional implication of the distinction between rule and act is that observed regularities may 'often alert us to the existence of rules' and 'when regularities present themselves we would do well to look for the guiding rules'.[2] However a recurrent event or pattern of behaviour need not logically indicate an underlying rule. It may simply reflect a policy position, an ideological stance or the expression of a domestic norm.

Similarly, consistent avoidance of a course of action may indicate a lack of capability or internal opposition rather than considered self-restraint grounded in rule-conforming conduct. These points have to be borne in mind when it comes to identifying the supposed working of a tacit rule.

Just as an act is an exemplification of a rule and not the rule itself, entities such as boundaries and declarations, though they may function as rules, are not rules but *signs* of. rules.[3] A state boundary imparts vital information about the limits of jurisdiction and should warn others about those restrictions on ingress and interference which are central to accepted principles of sovereignty. But the prohibitions and permissions associated with boundaries are items of information standing by themselves. Marks on a map or on the ground are reminders of the geographical outer limits of the state they contain, but their existence is not essential. A boundary is like a stop sign; it tells you what to do while deriving its meaning from a prior convention.

Other kinds of signs perform an analogous function. Warnings, doctrines such as the so-called Brezhnev Doctrine, and even treaties (for example Soviet friendship treaties) are intended to dramatize òr draw attention to an existing rule of the game – in the two latter cases to a tacitly recognized sphere of influence. They may also be aimed at setting up an agreed restraint on action, but here their validity will depend, as I shall later argue, on some subsequent process of assent, tacit or formal.

The use of the term 'rule' may give rise to misconceptions which should also be removed. A rule, in the sense to be used here, is not a law describing a behavioural regularity, as in the phrase 'the law of diminishing returns'. It is a prescription (or proscription) of behaviour. In the former case the law describes the necessary link between cause and effect; in the latter the rule works as a contingent motive for action. Thus, while a law in its descriptive sense can be falsified by counterexample, a prescriptive rule is neither true nor false, though it can be given up or changed.[4] (This does not mean that one cannot provide a descriptive account of the working of a prescriptive rule.) A related distinction to be drawn is that between 'norm' in the statistical sense of denoting average or typical behaviour and 'norm' in its prescriptive, sociological sense.[5] It is in the second sense that I am interested.

Since a prescriptive rule is quite different from a law of behaviour it follows that identifying a rule will not necessarily permit one to predict a future course of action. One can only predict that subject S will behave in accordance with rule R in the future by assuming, circularly, that S will continue to follow R.[6] It is precisely this assumption which most discussions of rules call into question. On the contrary, the consensus of opinion is, paradoxically, that 'rules are made to be broken'. In the words of Wittgenstein's well-known aphorism: 'A rule stands there like a signpost. Does the sign-post leave no doubt about the way I have to go?'[7] Later followers of Wittgenstein have developed this point, arguing that the grammar of 'following a rule' also implies 'making a mistake' or 'violating a rule'. What this means, to put it very simply, is that the notion of rule only makes sense if the subject in question possesses some choice in the matter. Otherwise what would be the point of the instruction? And to possess choice necessarily entails the possibility of violation.[8]

Empirical studies into the sociology of sport have tended to bear out this linguistic argument. In basketball and soccer occasional rule-breaking to gain an advantage is by no means inconsistent with knowledge of the rules and commitment to the game. In fact cheating is effective only because of the prior existence of known rules.[9] Handling the ball in soccer in a goal-mouth mêlée with the referee unsighted obtains advantage because other players are restricted by the non-handling rule. However, persistent or blatant cheating may call the very game itself into question. (Occasional cheating which would be penalized if found out should not be confused with institutionalized rule-breaking. In ice hockey illegitimate tactics, such as the use of physical violence, are considered occupationally essential skills and are built into the normative framework of the game. At one and the same time there is a two-tier system of constitutive rules, found in the rule book, and normative rules which are not, but are winked at by trainers, players and officials.)[10]

If this course of argument is accepted then it follows that rules possess at best not only a limited predictive value but also that they provide less than foolproof guarantees of orderly conduct. This does not mean that rules are invariably violated: as we have seen the cheat benefits because the majority maintain the rules most of the time. It means merely that certain limitations are inherent in the very concept of a rule. The practical effect of these limitations varies from case to case. In the United Kingdom knowledge of the Highway Code enables the road user to go about his business with a high degree of confidence in the conduct of other drivers. Elsewhere a rather greater degree of caution is required.

In international politics, as in more complex schemes of social behaviour, whether or not rules are maintained depends on surrounding circumstances. Expectations can always be contradicted by reality. Although rules of the game may define the limits of the permissible, they cannot in themselves be relied upon to hold back the ambitions of an adversary unless they are reinforced by a perceived capability and willingness to oppose intrusions – a 'balance of power' in the sense that I understand it. A warning notice is not a substitute for a guard system; rather it is a way of drawing attention to the latter and announcing its purpose. Similarly, agreements to cooperate cannot ensure ultimate cooperation. If a relationship fails to fulfil its initial promise, agreements will be reduced to dead letters. What agreements can do is to make available guidelines for coordinating behaviour should this be desired.

A further useful distinction to draw is that between a rule and an order. In one way rules and orders do have certain features in common. Both convey instructions about behaviour which is either required or forbidden. The first difference between them is that a rule, unlike an order, can define behaviour which is neither mandatory nor prohibited, but simply permitted. This supplies a further reason why rules do not necessarily permit prediction. Rule-conforming conduct does not have to be determinate. The rules of chess leave open an infinite range of possible progressions. 'You may trade with whomsoever you choose' and 'you are not obliged to impose sanctions on an aggressor' are feasible rules of the game which leave a state with broad leeway for preferred action.

A second difference between a rule and an order lies in the scope of the instruction. 'An order is like a shot fired at a poacher, a regulation is like a fence to keep anybody off the grounds.'[11] In other words, the application of an order (but not a 'standing order') is limited to its immediate context; it is a 'one-off' instruction. A rule, like a regulation, has general application to future instances of the defined pattern of behaviour.

Because of the contingent nature of rules and the inherent risk of their violation, the possibility of sanctions has usually been considered to be a characteristic feature of the concept. As with other aspects of rules whether or not the sanction will actually be imposed cannot be predicted with certainty. The same freedom of choice which one party brings to the performance of a rule will be brought by others concerned to the imposition of sanctions. Nevertheless the expectation of sanctions of some kind is thought to be a necessary incentive for conformity with a prohibition or an obligation (but not with a permission). The converse of this expectation is that imposition of sanctions for rule-breaking is considered a legitimate act of the community.[12]

So far as the nature of sanctions is concerned, Kjell Goldmann has suggested classifying them as internal or external, and individual or collective.[13] By 'internal' sanctions Goldmann refers to 'deprivations of value' imposed on the delinquent government by other members of the same society. 'External' sanctions are imposed by other members of the international community. He further suggests that such external measures may be publicly or privately organized. Goldmann does well to raise the eventuality that sanctions may be imposed, or governments fear that they may be imposed, by the public of the offending state or by branches of its own authorities. Certainly fear of judicial, parliamentary or public criticism is an observably powerful influence on the western conduct of foreign policy. Dr Kissinger also argued in 1972 that the groundrules of détente might provide incentives for restraint *within* the Soviet Government that might not otherwise exist.[14]

External sanctions, Goldmann continues, may be either individual or collective, the difference being a matter of degree. For historical reasons (Abyssinia, Rhodesia) the notion of collective sanctions comes most readily to mind. If, however, as I shall go on to argue, rules of the game may be just as validly of bilateral rather than of regional or universal application, then the possibility of individual sanctions may well turn out to be the relevant incentive for orderly behaviour. That is, of course, not to make any judgement about the efficacy of any such sanctions. But it should be noted in passing that the argument heard at the time of the

Soviet invasion of Afghanistan namely, that sanctions, such as an Olympic boycott, could not induce a Soviet withdrawal, was beside the point. The purpose of sanctions is to penalize an infringement of the rules in order (*a*) to emphasize the consensus of the community that a breach of international order has taken place and (*b*) to discourage such action in the future. Symbolic disapproval, such as the withdrawal of an ambassador or a suspension of cultural ties, has rarely been conceived of as a lever to undo an act already committed.

Alongside the idea of sanctions in the negative sense of 'a deprivation of value', positive 'sanctions' or rewards should be recognized as an equally material motive for rule conformity. David Hume, in his classic account of the origin of social norms and conventions, saw them as operating even in cases where no need for reinforcement arises. On the contrary, conventions arose out of interactions that had proved mutually beneficial. It is the 'common sense of interest' which 'mutually expressed and . . . known to both . . . produces a suitable resolution and behaviour'.[15] Without entering, at this stage, into a discussion of the positive factors that are at the basis of rule-observance. Hume is surely correct to shift the emphasis from deprivation to benefit. The penalties for breaking rules are far from negligible, if often uncertain, but if there were not substantial interests at stake in their working states at least would be unlikely to maintain them.

On the basis of our discussion in this chapter the following cluster of factors may be thought to provide reasonable indicators of the existence of rules of the game. None of these conditions are either necessary or sufficient. Some may be present without the existence of a rule; others may be absent and yet the rule exists. It is the presence of a general pattern of evidence which points to an underlying rule. International politics is not an exact science and therefore the following factors can provide no more than a working guide.

1. *The criticism of deviation and the possible implementation of sanctions*. In the experience of the author it is often the outrage of concerned parties when a rule is perceived to have been infringed that provides the most reliable clue to the existence of a rule. Outrage may be feigned, but it is not difficult to evaluate whether or not a perception of threat is authentic.[16] More often than not it is the cynical calling into question of the authenticity of a threat perception that is out of place. (Reactions in the United States to Administration outrage at Soviet behaviour in the October 1973 War and the Angola intervention are cases in point.) Conversely, the absence of any response, if only verbal, to an apparently divergent act, is a reliable indication of the absence or redundancy of a rule. Avoidance of debate in consultations between concerned parties is also a clear sign that the issue overlooked is not felt to be material to their relations and is not covered by the rules governing conduct between them.

2. *Documentary evidence*. This includes the text of treaties, agreements or understandings of various kinds setting up the rule; justifying

statements made by decision-makers referring back to the constituent agreement or claiming legitimacy for acts said to be in conformity with rules of the game; warnings and declarations intended to re-emphasize an existing rule or caution against its infringement; perhaps most indicative are internal statements found in memoranda, letters, the record of conversations, diaries and so on, not intended for publication at the time, acknowledging the presence of an agreed restraint or the expectation on the part of others of the need for conformity with a rule of the game.

3. *A consistent pattern of behaviour*. Though not, as has been pointed out, in itself proof of a rule's existence, a behavioural regularity can alert the researcher to the presence of an underlying rule, for which supplementary evidence can then be sought. In fact, as is argued below, a consistent pattern of conduct, if unopposed, is one of the ways in which rules of the game are established, whether previously formally agreed upon or not.

Chapter three

The logic of rules

Order, we learn from communications theorists, is equivalent to information. In international politics this insight has a very particular significance. Because the universe of states, unlike a pack of cards, is a dynamic system, the information required to order that system relates not to its present configuration but to the future behaviour of its constituent actors. Disorder consists in a complete uncertainty about the future conduct of others. Information about the present can be, if not always easily, acquired. Decision-makers do require knowledge of the existing state of affairs in order to make their decisions. But in a very important sense their field of action is not the present but the future. The present has been determined by past decisions and is irreparable. Benefits that have not been realized are lost and deprivations and dangers that have not been foreseen cannot be avoided. Only the future may be retrievable and reparable. Hence the task of decision-makers must be to prevent unpleasant future effects and facilitate future desired benefits.

Once this preoccupation with the future is grasped then the meaning of an otherwise obscure comment by Mr Callaghan becomes clearer. Asked about the possible subject of conversations with President Carter to be held on a prospective trip to Washington, scheduled for the spring of 1977, the British Prime Minister replied: 'I want to talk to him about 1978.'[1]

Given that decision-makers are obliged to apply themselves to the problems of a future 'they can neither demonstrate nor fully discern',[2] the peculiar quality of their predicament is self-evident. Only the past can be known; the future, by definition, can only be conjectured about and is concealed by a blanket of uncertainty.[3] States can be likened to sailing ships attempting to navigate through narrow straits in thick fog without the use of radio or radar. Both fog and future are equally opaque. The shape of the channel and the position of the ship may be known; the great danger is of collision with other ships similarly edging their way through the mist. In this sort of situation the problem of the ship's officers is twofold: to plot a safe course for their own vessel and to estimate the probable courses of other ships out there in the fog. Whether a collision is to occur or be avoided will depend on all sides correctly estimating the relative position and movement of ships with respect to each other. In navigation as in international relations, it takes two to collide. In Dr Kissinger's words: 'What endangers international peace and security is not determined by the unilateral declaration of the country going to war but also the reactions of other members of the international system.'[4]

States, unlike old-fashioned sailing ships out of sight and hearing, can communicate with each other. This is what diplomacy is all about. One can perceive the past courses of other states and attempt to plot their present positions. What cannot be known with any confidence is their future direction or the impact on them of unforeseen events. It is at this point that the limits of even the most comprehensive and perfectible communications system are reached. Information about what is happening at any given moment can, theoretically at least, be transmitted. Information about something that has not yet occurred is not available, though it is crucial to the decision-maker. Without such knowledge collision is a fateful risk and the benefits of cooperation, such as mutual support and profitable exchanges, are ruled out. All future action which is dependent on anticipations of the conduct of others is called into question.

In a world of interacting states the problem of uncertainty is reducible to one of communicating reliable information about *intended future courses of action*. Only on the basis of such anticipations, which are less than knowledge but which can substitute for it in the making of decisions, can collision be avoided and coordinated behaviour achieved. Rules function as the classic solution to this problem of communication by providing a source of justifiable expectations about the future conduct of others.

Communication about an uncertain future, as a logical problem, presents certain features shared by other areas of human behaviour. In domestic society we are often faced by the need to base our actions on anticipation of how others will act and react. David Hume, reflecting on the institution of private property and the importance of stable possession for social order, wondered how men could arrive at such a convention. It could not be by contract or promise because promises themselves arise from convention. Indeed even language, he hints, which would underlie any exchange of assurances, is based on convention. Hume's solution to the problem is worth quoting at length because of the light it sheds on the question posed here about the ways in which the uncertainties inherent in the international system can be mitigated:

I observe, that it will be for my interest to leave another in the possession of his goods, *provided* he will act in the same manner with regard to me. He is sensible of a like interest in the regulation of his conduct. When this common sense of interest is mutually expressed, and is known to both, it produces a suitable resolution and behaviour. And this may properly enough be called a convention or agreement betwixt us, though without the interposition of a promise; since the actions of each of us have a reference to those of the other, and are performed upon the supposition that something is to be performed on the other part . . . repeated experience of the inconveniences of transgressing [the convention] . . . assures us still more that the sense of interest has become common to all our fellows, and gives us a confidence of the future regularity of their conduct; and it is only on the expectation of this that our moderation and abstinence are founded.[5]

Thomas Schelling has provided a similar account of the structure of tacit restraint in wartime, when normal diplomatic channels of communication may be cut off or precluded. Mutually destructive escalation, for instance in nuclear war, may be avoided, he argues, by the *coordination of mutual expectations*. Engaged in a common, if separate, effort to contain a process which, taken to its frightful conclusion, will result in mutual annihilation, both sides will be forced to rely on a sort of 'psychic' communication. Each will wonder, like people separated in a department store, what the other may reasonably expect him to do, assuming that both seek to establish a common link or limit. The solution, according to Schelling, will lie in the choice of a *focal point*, some salient feature of the situation or landscape, to which their attention will be drawn and which, they will understand, will present itself equally prominently to both of them. Moreover no other solution has this same salience. Out of a dialectic of mutual expectations, in which each side asks himself what his partner is likely to expect him to decide, they will 'agree' at a point of convergence where their individual anticipations intersect.[6] Thus the problem of tacit communication is soluble on a basis of coordinated expectations, of arriving at common anticipations to those of other actors.

The puzzle solved by Hume and Schelling is essentially one and the same: how can separate wills, in the absence of language, coordinate their behaviour in mutually beneficial ways? Both seek the answer in the logic of mutual and reliable expectations, derived, in Hume's argument, from the lesson of previous transactions, and in Schelling's version, from a common search for some salient feature of the situation. Whatever the origin of shared expectations, however, the implication for the problem originally posed in this chapter is clear. Rules of the game can perform the role in international relations of Hume's conventions and Schelling's focal point solutions. By setting up a structure of mutually reliable expectations they permit glimmerings of certainty to be projected on to an otherwise impenetrable future so that decisions which depend on the intentions of others can be taken with at least minimal confidence.

The logic of rules, described here at a purely theoretical level, should not be thought to be of esoteric interest alone. In the following sections some of the practical applications of the theory will be considered and illustrated from statements of decision-makers. Diplomats and statesmen can be shown to be fully aware of the need to generate and maintain reliable guides to future conduct and of the central role played by the various facets of rules of the game in this effort.

The 'boundary' function of rules

As a boundary, or a set of limits on action, rules of the game guide expectations by delineating the area into which actors must not trespass. Such limits can be indicated most tangibly by geographical features: frontiers, spheres of influence, 'red lines', defensive perimeters and so on come into this category. More abstractly, limits may consist of prohibitions on certain defined activities.

At a minimal level rules in their boundary role obviate the routine friction which is inseparable from the contact between wilful sovereign entities possessing distinct interest, outlooks and ambitions. American Secretary of State Cordell Hull graphically described this role when he warned President Roosevelt in 1933 to avoid recognition of the Soviet Union before the 'rules' to govern their relations had been clearly laid out: 'Until a substantial basis for mutual understanding and common purpose has been established', he wrote, 'official intercourse with its increased contacts is bound to lead to friction.'[7]

More crucially, as Richard Falk has argued of spheres of influence, understandings, patterns of conduct and control 'contribute to the confinement of conflict and violence within tolerable limits, given the present character of international society'.[8] Although he was commenting on Soviet–American relations, Falk's justification of spheres of influence is precisely that put forward by Ribbentrop to Stalin at the time of the Nazi–Soviet Pact of 1939 which, among its various provisions, provided for the partition of Poland. By agreeing on a division of influence, Ribbentrop pointed out, German and Russian interests would be prevented from 'coming into conflict with each other'.[9]

Like the rule of the road, rules of the game can help to avoid unwanted collision by sketching out for the benefit of interested parties the area within which they can safely manoeuvre without encroaching on the interests of others. Contemplating the risks inherent in a spontaneous scramble for gain on the part of the great powers in the event of a break-up of the Ottoman Empire, Tsar Nicholas pointed out in 1853 to the British Ambassador the advantages of an informal understanding. It could establish 'less what was wanted *than what was not wanted*; what would be contrary to English interests; what would be contrary to Russian interests; so that, if the case arose, each side could avoid actions *which contradicted those of the other*'.[10]

The 'signpost' function of rules

A second way in which rules guide expectations is by functioning as a sort of sign-post pointing towards some predetermined pattern of behaviour which it is agreed will come into effect in certain defined circumstances. To return to our naval metaphor, if the rule of the road at sea prevents collision by indicating how boats travelling in opposite directions should sail in relation to each other and thus performs a boundary function, the mayday convention performs a signpost function and avoids confusion in the provision of assistance to a ship in distress by imposing on ships nearest the source of the signal the duty of offering help.

In international politics treaties of alliance, legal provisions and other kinds of agreements, implicit and explicit, can set up signposts to facilitate cooperation. Since states are sovereign no court can compel their compliance with agreements, however formally binding. But should states wish to cooperate, then existing known arrangements are available and can be the best means for them to coordinate their behaviour.

In the wake of the Soviet invasion of Afghanistan, Lord Carrington and the Sultan of Oman met to consider sharpened perceptions of a Soviet threat. On the one hand certain transactional arrangements were agreed upon including the despatch of a squadron of Jaguar fighters and a wide range of military equipment. From the point of view of rules of the game negotiations for some kind of defence agreement were important. While ruling out a formal treaty and expressing his preference for an informal arrangement, the Sultan perceptively characterized the signpost function of any contingency agreement. The important thing, he noted, was a political and strategic 'meeting of minds' so that Britain and Oman 'would always steer the same course in this storm'.[11]

The 'timetable' function of rules

The advantage of a timeable – a fixed schedule of arrivals and departures – is that it permits complex traffic arrangements to be coordinated on a routine basis. No regular transport system could be organized without its guidance. A timetable, in fact, is the ultimate elimination of uncertainty about the future; it is a map of tomorrow's events. Now in some ways relations between states can be seen as a complex network of transactions covering a broad and varied spectrum of activities of shared concern. To consider the scope of contacts between the Soviet Union and the United States, for example, there can hardly be a part of the globe or an area of international activity that does not impinge on their relations. Managing such an extensive interface of contact can be compared to the task of coordinating a transport system. Without a routine schedule of operations to be performed on an ongoing basis by the administrative apparatus concerned, neither a traffic system nor a set of political relations could be sustained on a day-to-day basis. The continual need to clear obstructions and untangle the muddle of contradictory instructions would rapidly exhaust the capacity of any administration.

In international politics the problem is compounded by the fact that key decisions are conventionally made at the top bureaucratic and political levels, but the upper echelon of government is concerned not only with foreign affairs but with the entire gamut of national life. It cannot, therefore, afford to restrict its limited attention to one field of activity alone on a sustained basis in time of peace. Except in some rare cases (Hitler's Germany, Qadaffi's Libya [?]) the focus of attention of any peacetime government is necessarily on domestic concerns – welfare, economic management, social tranquillity and the requirements of staying in power – and not on foreign policy. Even regimes sworn to exporting revolution inevitably find their concern increasingly drawn to domestic problems. In these circumstances the 'routinization' of those areas of contact which need not require a decision at the very highest level, is essential. And this, yet again, is a task of rules of the game. By placing matters of international concern on to a routine basis not requiring incessant intervention, the hands of decision-makers are freed for the resolution of those problems, mainly domestic, of a greater political priority.

The 'tripwire' function of rules

As a consequence of their boundary role rules of the game also act as a tripwire setting off an alarm if violated and as a permit, should this happen, to counteraction. It is also hoped that by virtue of the prospect of opposition signalled by the presence of a tripwire, counteraction will actually prove unnecessary because violations will be discouraged. This is the deterrent aspect of a boundary. Without a defined line of demarcation it is difficult to demonstrate or even to ascertain the performance of an act of trespass. A known boundary between the permitted and prohibited removes any doubt involved.

Friedrich Kratochwil, comparing rules of conduct with the conventions of language, makes a similar point by suggesting that rules are useful in enabling meaning to be assigned to otherwise unintelligible events and actions, just as language invests meaning in otherwise unintelligible noise. 'The crucial idea', he argues, 'is that rules serve as *inference guidance devices* by helping to define situations and by providing justifications for particular inferences.'[12]

A burglar alarm is the classic example of this kind of device. It is set off by an act of trespass; it proclaims and draws attention to the performance of such an act; it is intended to thwart the intrusion either by scaring off the intruder or by inviting the opposition of the community; finally, one hopes that its mere presence will act as a deterrent.

A contemporary illustration of this principle on the international scene has been the justification given at various times for the presence of NATO conventional forces on the West German border with the east. Too weak actually to defeat an attack by Warsaw Pact forces and certainly useless in an offensive capacity, NATO troops have been assigned by some strategists the role of a tripwire or a plateglass window: to announce the break-in, set off the alarm and justify a speedy resort to nuclear weapons in the event of a communist attack.

An historical example of the actual operation of a tripwire is provided by the Nazi occupation of the remnant of Czechoslovakia in March 1939. Until that date many leaders had believed that Hitler, in spite of everything, could be brought to terms because his foreign policy was limited by two principles which they could tacitly accept: the restoration of the right of national self-determination to German minorities and the redress of unjust aspects of the Versailles Treaty. The destruction of Czechoslovakia dispelled such illusions. Czechoslovakia had never been part of Germany and no longer contained an unwilling German minority. By violating these tacit limits Hitler broke the tripwire. In the words of the permanent head of the British Foreign Office: 'I always said that, as long as Hitler could pretend he was incorporating Germans in the Reich, we could pretend that he had a case. If he proceeded to gobble up other nationalities, that would be the time to call "Halt!"'[13]

By demonstrating infringement the crossing of a tripwire also legitimizes and frequently mobilizes counteraction. The collective guarantee of the independence of Luxembourg was interpreted by Lord Derby in 1867 as giving any of the signatories 'a perfect right to declare a *casus belli* if she thinks fit, because of the violation of the guarantee'. Taken in this sense in 1914 the Luxembourg Guarantee provided an impeccable justification for a British entry into the war against Germany already compelled for other reasons.[14]

Finally an effective tripwire is also an important component of the concept of deterrence. (Credibility, the other central element of the concept, is not treated here.) For deterrence to operate, a limit on permissible action has to be delineated. Two schools of thought are discernible. One stresses the advantages of imprecision in discouraging a potential trespasser, seeing ambiguity as a safeguard against recklessness. The other emphasizes the need for precision, preferring the certainty of clearcut restraints. Both views have their strengths and weaknesses. Imprecision has the virtue of inclusiveness, avoids commitments later found undesirable and may encourage caution on the part of an uncertain opponent. On the other hand it may encourage instability by actually tempting an aggressive opponent to see how far he can go. Received wisdom has it that the absence of an explicit British commitment to France in 1914 encouraged German aggression. Extreme precision in drawing the limit of one's *non possumus*, although avoiding misunderstanding, may be counterproductive by simultaneously defining the area within which one's opponent can enjoy freedom of action. Dr Kissinger describes with incredulity the 'warning' given by American Secretary of State Rogers to the Soviet Union in 1970, at the height of the War of Attrition between Egypt and Israel, not to introduce 'Soviet military personnel into the delicate Suez Canal combat zone [within thirty kilometres of the Canal]'. On the surface it seemed a strong warning. 'What it really did, however', Kissinger claims, 'was to give the Soviets a blank check; it acquiesced in the Soviet combat presence in Egypt except in the immediate vicinity of the Suez Canal. The Soviets were in effect told that they were free to build up substantial forces in Egypt so long as they did not move them directly into the combat zone.'[15]

The worst possible error of draftsmanship is to draw a line which has neither the inclusiveness of ambiguity nor the indubitability of precision. It may have been just such an error that encouraged North Korea in 1950 to believe that it could strike south without fear of American intervention. Six months before the invasion, on 12 January 1950, Secretary of State

Dean Acheson, in a public address, defined the 'defensive perimeter' believed to be required for the defence of Japan. He sketched a line through the islands off the Asian mainland, pointedly omitting the Korean peninsula. 'So far as the military security of other areas in the Pacific is concerned', he added, 'it must be clear that no person can guarantee the areas against military attack.'[16] This was as explicit a statement as could be made by a diplomat that the United States had no intention of fighting on the Asian mainland. Certainly this was the impression received by such an experienced hand as Gladwyn Jebb.[17] Far from preventing conflict, Acheson's misleading demarcation is thought actually to have contributed to it.

Chapter four

The language of international politics: grammar

Rules of the game, it has been established, are a way in which states can coordinate their behaviour in situations of uncertainty by setting up reliable mutual expectations. To the extent that they serve a defined community – professional participants in the diplomatic process – involve the manipulation of distinctive symbols in a more or less uniform fashion and are capable of communicating a wide and flexible range of intelligible information, they can be viewed as a sort of language of international politics. Obviously there is a sharp limit to this analogy since rules of the game actually presuppose language in its conventional sense and are not a substitute for it. However, looking at rules in this way does suggest certain questions, the answers to which can shed light on some aspects of foreign policy-making and international behaviour. One question that arises is whether a set of underlying common principles or axioms can be discerned by which rules of the game are generated. Does the symbolic mechanism by which rules of the game are communicated possess characteristics significantly different from conventional languages of discourse? What are the implications for the conduct of international affairs of the existence of a specialized language of international politics?

The syntax of a language consists of those principles which determine what can meaningfully be said in that language; it provides the scaffolding, to borrow an image from Wittgenstein, upon which propositions in the language are erected. In language as such, grasp of the grammar is inherent in speech; membership of the language community does not require special qualifications. In international politics this is not the case. Strangers to diplomacy usually do not possess the specialized skill either to understand or communicate meaningful propositions in the language of international politics and often cause damage and confusion while they are learning. A grounding in the grammar of rules of the game is a necessary qualification for participation in the making of foreign policy and diplomacy. The 'grammatical axioms' to be sketched below determine the meaningfulness of propositions about rules of the game and relate to the central structural questions of any rule system: the validity of rules, in both a prescriptive and a temporal sense; the relation of rules to each other within the rule system; the pattern of obligations inherent in a rule; the ways in which rules can be formed; and the principles of meaning of the symbolic system by which rules of the game are communicated.

Rules are to be kept

One of the abiding puzzles about rules and obligations is why states should maintain them at all. A Machiavellian outlook is frequently ascribed to diplomats, 'men sent abroad to lie for their country', in the belief that duplicity and the violation of rules can achieve benefits otherwise unobtainable. Why this is not so is partly accounted for by the very ubiquity and utility of rules. Notwithstanding individual cases of breakdown and infringement, rules as an institution are preserved because they are too useful to abandon; as long as order is desired, rules must be maintained. Other incentives to rule maintenance are as follows:

1. *Commitment to maintain a rule is like undertaking a promise.* To follow Hume's account again, rules, like promises, can be seen as assurances of future conduct. 'After these signs are instituted, whoever uses them is immediately bound by his interest to execute his engagements, and must never expect to be trusted any more if he refuses to perform what he promised.'[1] So, short-term benefit as a result of duplicity can entail a high price in the subsequent loss of all credibility. An actor who cannot be relied on to keep the rules will find it difficult in the future to persuade others of the reliability of his engagements.

2. *Deviant behaviour jeopardizes the overall benefits states derive from their relationships.* As Hume points out, conventions arise from interactions which are both mutually beneficial and mutually conditional: 'I observe, that it will be for my interest to leave another in the possession of his goods, *provided* he will act in the same manner with regard to me. He is sensible of a like interest in the regulation of his conduct.'[2] Thus to break a rule is to put at risk the reciprocal advantages derived from the cooperation or restraint of others. There is a tendency (to be discussed at greater length in the chapter on rule infringement) to perceive the blatant violation of a rule as undermining the very structure of a relationship. The consequences of selective observance may go far beyond the issues immediately affected.

3. Paradoxically, *the existence of conflict in itself contributes to the maintenance of rules.* If conflict were to take place between the same actors all the time there would be an absence of even a minimal basis for building international order. Rules to regulate conduct are only possible because conflict takes place between different opponents at different times. One may call this the *even distribution of conflict principle*.

According to Gould and Barkun, 'Enemies in one context are allies in another. What we may call cross-cutting as opposed to parallel conflicts serve to moderate, if they do not eliminate, disagreements. Since one shares common future interests with the party with whom one is currently in conflict, one hesitates to escalate to the level where a total breach becomes necessary.'³ This was the very factor permitting the Nixon–Kissinger opening to China. Embroiled in profound disagreement with each other, both communist giants were impelled to regulate their lesser quarrels with the United States. The fruit of the American insight was the Shanghai Communiqué establishing a code of good manners in US–Chinese relations and the Declaration on Basic Principles of Relations concluded with the Soviet Union. Peace was seen to depend on no state considering itself the permanent enemy of others.⁴

At its most primitive level a rule of the game may be nothing more than a convention – a convergence of mutual expectations; sufficient that it should guide conduct. Although it is most usually the product of a more or less formal verbal or written exchange, this is not a necessary condition for the establishment of a rule. But even in the absence of an offer and an acceptance (which constitutes a contract in law) it seems that actors are reluctant to disappoint others' justifiable expectations.

An instructive example of the logic underlying this reluctance can be found in a memorandum of 1860 in which Lord Palmerston advocated a public British commitment, together with France and Sardinia, against Austria and outside interference in Central Italy: It is so natural that we should side with France and Italy [he explained,]

that our holding back from doing so would be looked upon by Austria as a proof that there is some strong undercurrent which prevented us from doing so; and the Austrian Government would not unnaturally reckon that when the war had broken out, that undercurrent would drive us to side with Austria against France; and this speculation would be a great encouragement to Austria to take a course leading to war.⁵

Note that in this case Britain had no formal commitment but that Palmerston was arguing, nonetheless, that she was in some sense bound by Austria's justifiable expectations. Disappointment of those expectations could be seriously misleading. A famous similar argument can be found in Sir Edward Grey's case for British entry into the war against Germany in 1914 which was posited on his sense of the binding force of French expectations, notwithstanding the absence of a formal commitment.⁶

All agreements are of limited validity

In a world of shifting circumstances this is, paradoxically, the only realistic way in which the reliability of understandings can be maintained. This does not imply that agreements can be infringed with impunity. On the contrary, it is accepted that by recognizing that circumstances inevitably erode the application of agreements, the chances that an actor will be obliged to break the rules of the game are reduced.

Statesmen, regardless of their ideological complexion, can be found to base their policies on this sceptical assumption. The dichotomy often portrayed, between totalitarian regimes which do not maintain their obligations and elective democracies which do, is an exaggeration. The point is not that states undertake obligations intending to abandon them at the first opportunity, though this does happen, rather that states do not perceive obligations as existing independently of the circumstances in which they are contracted and in which they may have to be redeemed.

From Bismarck to de Gaulle we can find evidence of this principle. In Bismarck's memoirs he warned his contemporaries about the Triple Alliance:

> It would be unwise to regard it as affording a permanently stable guarantee against all the possible contingencies which in the future may modify the political, material and moral conditions under which it was brought into being . . . it no more constitutes a foundation capable of offering perennial resistance to time and change than did many another alliance . . . of recent centuries.[7]

Stalin made the same point during the negotiations with Finland of October 1939 in which he demanded various territorial and strategic concessions for the defence of Leningrad: 'Whoever emerged as victor in the World War', he argued, 'would inevitably attack the Soviet Union. The pact with Germany was no eternal guarantee: "Everything in this world can change".'[8] The ten-year non-aggression pact between Germany and the Soviet Union referred to by Stalin had been concluded only two months previously.

De Gaulle echoed almost these very words to Israeli diplomats in 1967, come to remind him of the French declaration of 1957 recognizing Israel's right to defend herself physically against blockade. The French President 'admitted that France's declaration of 1957 on freedom of navigation was correct juridically, but 1967 was not 1957. Picot's statement had reflected the "particular heat" of 1957.' Since then 'things had changed'.[9]

Within a given rule system, all rules are perceived discredited when one rule is flouted

The rules of the game governing a particular relationship or community are perceived to form an integrated, mutually reinforcing structure. First, selective rule-maintenance violates the balance of advantage and disadvantage which lies at the basis of the concept of rules. Second, since the blatant violation of a rule casts doubt on the overall reliability of the infractor, it forces the conclusion that he would only risk his reputation if he wished to overthrow the overall system of order. If an international actor sees fit to flout one obligation, what reason do others have to suppose that he respects the remaining rules more highly?

Both Thomas Schelling and Morton Halperin, the distinguished American strategists, have remarked on the importance of this principle.[10] Evidence of its application to diplomacy is also extensive. In 1831, for instance, Lord Palmerston felt obliged to oppose restoration of Polish independence, though he would have welcomed it as a private individual: 'One scarcely sees how that can be accomplished without breaking the Treaty of Vienna, which however objectionable in some of the details of its arrangements, is yet, with its accessories of Paris and Aix-la-Chapelle, the great security of Europe against the inveterately enervating spirit of France.'[11]

Similarly, Marshall Pilsudski, the great Polish leader, in an argument which hints at the link between territorial indivisibility and that underlying logic which views rules of the game as an integral unity, believed that the territorial settlement of Versailles had 'to be defended unflinchingly': 'Any doubts as to the value of frontiers and the solidity of the territorial division would bring us straight to chaos and war conflicts.'[12]

Reciprocity is a necessary condition of the stability of rules of the game between powers of equal status

The importance of reciprocity arises from the very nature of rules: a rule of the game differs from a plain behaviour pattern in that its preservation is contingent on the behaviour of the other party to the understanding. The moment the other party ceases 'to keep his side of the bargain' any incentive to maintain the rules is removed.

Between powers of unequal status representatives of the weaker partner may insist, for reasons of prestige, on an appearance of reciprocity. In treaties of alliance this may take the form of mutual assurances to come to each other's aid in the event of attack. In reality the commitment is only of significance for the security of the weaker partner. Similarly, where the balance of obligation between the parties derives from the dependence or the domination of the one by the other, reciprocity is not a necessary condition of stability. Again, in formal agreements this reality may be disguised by a tactful form of words. For instance Moscow's Friendship Treaties of 1948 with Bulgaria, Romania and Hungary contain clauses requiring political consultation in peacetime and automatic mutual assistance in wartime. In form reciprocal, in substance these obligations legitimize Soviet hegemony. In the case of tacit agreements or norms even this face-saving device is unnecessary. Thus informal practices that emerged between the Soviet Union and her satellites, such as the prohibition on withdrawal from the Warsaw Pact or the replacement of the unitary rule of the communist party, and the supervision by Moscow of the satellite's foreign ties – norms which were blatantly onesided – were never put into treaty form.

Between powers of equal status, however, such a bias is completely unacceptable. Where an obligation is left over as an unpleasant reminder of a past period of unusual weakness on the part of one of the powers, it is likely to be a source of friction and resented for its inequality.

Franck and Weisband, in a study of superpower relations, place great emphasis on the principle of reciprocity. They point out that between great powers (and superpowers) restraints, to be acceptable, must be, on the whole, mutually advantageous. Reciprocity, they argue, is the key to creating the mutuality of benefit essential to the building of stable relations.[13] Any absence of reciprocity between the Soviet Union and the United States has had destabilizing consequences for relations between the superpowers. In October1962, at the time of the Cuba Crisis, Khrushchev complained bitterly about the asymmetry of American and Soviet strategic situations. Why was it forbidden the Soviet Union to install missiles ninety miles away from the United States in Cuba and permitted for the United States to maintain them on the borders of the Soviet Union, in Turkey? 'Do you believe that you have the right to demand security for your own country and the removal of weapons which you describe as "offensive" while not recognizing this right for us? ... How then does recognition of our equal military possibilities tally with such unequal relations between our great states?'[14]

The same problem arose with the Carter campaign on human rights: 'I'm sure the Soviet Union has always maintained that ideological struggle was legitimate, and they never refrain from doing so', Carter explained. 'I don't feel any inclination to refrain from doing it either.'[15] Unfortunately, although Carter may have sought to do no more than to subject Soviet society to the same kind of criticism that the Soviet Union has long applied to the western system, its effect was perceived to be quite different. Soviet support of United States communists, for example, has no discernible political effect in the United States. But Carter's support for Soviet dissidents was seen as a major threat to the Soviet system.[16]

The principle of reciprocity has other interesting implications. Not only is an agreement which distributes benefit unequally likely to be a source of instability, but insistence by one side on the negotiation of such an agreement risks being seen as proof of unfriendliness or at least a lack of serious negotiating intent. (This does not preclude negotiators demanding a stiff opening price.) Unreciprocated British gestures of friendship towards Mussolini's Italy, and Italian insistence on the unconditional recognition of her annexation of Abyssinia, were viewed with increasing bitterness by Anthony Eden, Foreign Secretary from December 1935 to February 1938. Improved relations, he reiterated, 'could only be realized on a basis of reciprocity. That reciprocity was never forthcoming then or later, until Mussolini brought his reluctant nation into the second world war.'[17]

The converse of this principle is equally valid. A gesture of friendship, to be credible, must require reciprocity. Otherwise it will be viewed at the best with suspicion and at the worst as an act of weakness. (This was one of the drawbacks to the policy of appeasement; unilateral concession, far from paving the way to a general settlement, as was intended, merely created a cumulative impression of democratic feebleness if not actual soft-headedness.) General Eisenhower discovered this to his discomfiture when he was Commander of the US Occupation Zone in Germany. Against professional diplomatic advice he offered, as a gesture of goodwill, to allow Red Army personnel to visit the American zone. As predicted, the invitation was received with a mixture of incomprehension, suspicion and embarassment.[18]

Any departure from previous patterns of behaviour may be seen as a precedent for future action

Rules of the game act as guides to expectations and thereby reduce uncertainty. Conformity to an established rule ensures predictable reactions on the part of others. The consequences of an action not covered or prohibited by existing rules are unpredictable and possibly dangerous to established order. However once an innovative or deviant action has been performed and the reaction of others – favourable, unfavourable or indifferent – elicited, then the future consequences of an act falling under the same description will cease to be unpredictable. *A precedent will have been set*, or, in terms of Schelling's theory of the coordination of mutual expectations, a focal point solution will have been provided for future problems of the same type. Expectations will now focus on the historical paradigm. Among different possible courses of action and reaction the tested behaviour pattern will stand out as a *conspicuous alternative*, both for the initiating actor and for other concerned participants who wish to anticipate how the actor will behave in the future. If an act is firmly resisted, then the initiator may or may not choose to continue with that particular pattern of conduct; at least he knows what to expect. If an act turns out, for whatever reason, to be acceptable, then the safety of that course will have been demonstrated.

The implication of the principle of precedent is that actors are obliged to remain continuously alert to the possibility of changes in others' conception of existing rules. Any move may be interpreted as a potential precedent, indeed as a deliberate attempt to 'test the water'. Denials that a particular action constitutes a precedent are unlikely to overcome suspicion. Moreover, since rules of the game are perceived to form an interrelated structure, the repercussions of an initiative in one area will have repercussions throughout the system.

The Soviet invasion of Afghanistan is a case in point. The first time since the Second World War that Soviet troops had been used outside the communist bloc, immediate fears were expressed throughout the interna-

tional community of a new trend in Soviet behaviour. The departure in
Soviet policy, it was felt, was in itself partly a response to a growing
American reluctance since the Vietnam War to respond firmly to cases of
communist intervention. In the Angola crisis of 1975–6, in which communist military aid was openly provided to one side in an African domestic conflict, Dr Kissinger warned that Congress had set an 'ominous precedent' by halting American support for anti-Soviet factions fighting in
Angola: 'If the pattern is not broken now we will face harder choices and
higher costs in the future.' For the first time, he argued, the United States
had 'failed to respond to Soviet military moves outside the immediate
Soviet orbit. And it is the first time that Congress has halted national
action in the middle of a crisis.' Finally, Angola represented the first
occasion on which Moscow had moved militarily at long distance to
impose a regime of its choice. The Soviet Union and its Cuban ally,
whose troops were actively engaged in the fighting, would have to understand 'that Angola sets no precedent, that this type of action will not be
tolerated again'.[19] Unfortunately, as Dr Kissinger well knew, it was not
for him to say whether or not a precedent had been set. In every confrontation of the Cold War American policy-makers had defined the crisis in
question as a 'test case' of American will and had responded accordingly.
Now that American will had faltered they could hardly redefine the
significance of the event.

The Soviet Union has been scarcely less sensitive to the principle of
precedent. Fear of setting a precedent for the return of acquired territory
has been an important theme in negotiations between Japan and the
Soviet Union. Several rounds of talks between the two sides broke down
on the Soviet refusal to return the four southern Kurile Islands held by
Russia since the end of the Second World War, to Japanese sovereignty.
Returning the islands to Japan would, it was feared, set a dangerous precedent in territorial disputes with other states.[20]

Two principles of communication: (1) The meaning of a signal is its function in the political process; (2) No signal is redundant in the information it contains

One of the characteristic features of diplomacy and the making of foreign
policy is the preoccupation with information. Not only official statements
and material specifically intended for foreign consumption are the object
of attention. Any item of news, domestic, economic, personal, may be
eagerly received and its foreign policy implications carefully analysed, if
not always open-mindedly. Political leaders quickly learn that for public
figures there are no such things as 'private remarks'. When a diplomat
volunteers his 'personal view' this is well understood to be on the instructions of his government. From a coal strike in Poland to a demonstration
in Hebron, any event may be scanned for its significance. The international system may be described as a universal communications network.

All acts, verbal or nonverbal, intentional or unintentional, are potential signals which feed into the network and are liable to reach all listeners and be
read by them for the message which they convey. Moreover any message
may be read together with, and understood in the light of, the collective
body of evidence already communicated or later to be communicated by
the actor about his expectations. The plea, therefore, that the meaning of a
certain action has been misinterpreted is irrelevant. As in all systems of
communications the meaning of the information transmitted cannot be
arbitrarily determined by the sender alone. It means what others understand it to mean in the light of the underlying grammar. Put another way,
it is the reasonably foreseeable effect, not the announced intention, which
defines the meaning and hence perceived purpose of an action. It is not
what you intend to say that counts but what others take you to mean.
President Carter's initial declamatory policy of denouncing human rights
violations in the Soviet Union, however well-intentioned, could not be
and, indeed, was not seen as anything other than a disguised attack on the
'code of conduct of détente', in Giscard d'Estaing's phrase, between the
superpowers. After nine difficult months of vocational training Carter
finally realized 'that actions or statements that I make here do affect the
attitude of leaders in places like Malaysia, or Singapore, as well as those
countries that we think about daily, like Israel, or Great Britain and the
Soviet Union'.[21]

Two reasons can be suggested for decision-makers' preoccupation with
information. The first derives from the interrelatedness of rules and the
role played by precedent. Divergent behaviour by an actor in one area, or
his weak reaction to a provocation elsewhere, is perceived to possess
implications for the overall structure of rules. Whether he likes it or not
the conduct of the actor is therefore being continuously scanned for the
information it can provide about his ability or willingness to maintain
certain rules, about his view of the validity of rules maintained by others
or which others have attempted to introduce, whether new precedents are
being set for future action and so on.

A second possible explanation is that the fundamental uncertainty and
complexity of the international system on the one hand, and the dependence of the state for its wellbeing on the behaviour of so many actors
over whom it has no control on the other, render decision-makers acutely
sensitive and alert to the slightest scrap of evidence which may mitigate
their uncertainty. The superpowers, having the most extensive involvement in global affairs in terms of their commitments, interests, ambitions
and fears, have both erected the most massive and pervasive
information-gathering apparatuses in history. And even so they are still
subject to momentous – and frequent – errors of prediction.

In the following chapter we shall go on to examine the far-reaching
implications of these principles for communication between states.

Chapter five

The language of international politics: vocabulary

Conscious of the very close attention paid by diplomatic observers to actions and articulations of all kinds and of the paramount importance of being able to say no more and no less than is intended, the diplomatic profession has evolved, over many years, a very subtle and variegated stock of words, phrases, euphemisms, gestures and manoeuvres, each item having its own weight and shade of meaning.

That states of different culture, religion, ideology and language communicate intelligibly with each other is one of the remarkable aspects of international politics. Without this ability rules of the game facilitating international order could hardly be arrived at. Misunderstanding is of course far from rare in international affairs. It is extraordinary that comprehension is possible. Notwithstanding the problems involved states somehow mostly succeed in communicating their intentions – transmitting encouragement, warning, approval or displeasure when required, negotiating understandings of subtlety and complexity. All this is thanks to the possession of a common code or language of discourse.

One of the great diplomatic achievements of modern times was surely the opening of contact between the United States and the People's Republic of China. Here were two states, estranged for a generation and about as far apart on every dimension as could be conceived. And yet through the tenuous and intermittent medium of the good offices of the President of Pakistan an exchange of views was initiated which within three years resulted in a presidential visit to Peking and tacit Sino-American collaboration at the time of the Indo-Pakistan War of 1971. Some of the first signals were off target. When the American writer Edgar Snow stood and was photographed at the side of Chairman Mao on China's National Day, the symbolism was missed, partly because the event was not brought to the attention of American leaders.[1] (The symbolic principle behind the message should have been familiar to the United States: in 1945 Stalin had amazed everyone by inviting General Eisenhower to stand beside him on Lenin's tomb.[2]) Apart from such oversights an involved dialogue of word and gesture proceeded until the first face to face encounter took place.

In order to understand how something as improbable as the Sino-American alignment of 1971 could evolve, in other words how rules of the game are transmitted, it is necessary to provide a basic sketch of the vocabulary of international politics. In the following section we shall consider two dimensions of communication: diplomatic language in its specifically verbal sense; and the 'body language' of international politics, including the symbolism of protocol and diplomatic procedure.

Diplomatic language

The principle underlying diplomatic language is that of non-redundancy. Ideally a diplomatic communication should say neither too much nor too little because every word, nuance and omission will be meticulously studied for any possible shade of meaning. Nor is the convention of tact and politeness in the wording of diplomatic communications just an anachronistic tradition but refers back to the same principle of non-redundancy: rudeness or abruptness would in itself be assumed to carry an important aspect of the message. Fascist brutality of language was not arbitrary but a deliberate technique of pressure and expression of superiority. The Italian *tono fascista* was unconciliatory precisely because it was intended to rule out compromise.[3]

One aspect of diplomatic language is the use of legal terminology. When even a spoken promise or declaration, a letter or a communiqué, may create political and moral expectations, not to speak of the binding character of formal arrangements, contractual precision is clearly required. Thus the legal specialist plays an important role in any foreign office in the drafting and clearing of diplomatic communications. A legal training is a customary if not essential qualification for the diplomatic (and, indeed, governmental) profession. As a result many technically useful legal expressions have come into the language of diplomacy. Terms such as *ad interim* (temporary), *ad referendum* (subject to confirmation), *casus belli* (an action justifying a declaration of war), *ultra vires* (not within the law) have a particular legal/diplomatic connotation and also testify to the early European tradition of using Latin in legal and diplomatic documents. From about the eighteenth century to the beginning of the twentieth French was also extensively used in diplomacy. *Démarche* (an initiative or approach by a government), *force majeure* (unavoidable and usually unforeseen circumstances), *quiproquo* (a misunderstanding) and many other terms stem from this tradition.[4]

Procedures, functions and instruments all have their own precise appellation, something which clearly facilitates the conduct of diplomacy. For example the title of a diplomatic document may carry a conventional significance, though there is sometimes disagreement between jurists on this point. 'Declaration' suggests that the parties were not making a full-blown legal instrument; *modus vivendi* usually refers to an understanding of a provisional character; an 'exchange of notes' is a record of routine agreement, whereas 'treaty', 'convention', 'act' have a more solemn and weighty sense; *aide mémoire* is a note explaining a government's action or point of view; a *bout de papier* is a communication without heading, signature or date and is therefore less official than an *aide mémoire* and theoretically disclaimable.

Legal experts will also be on the alert for expressions intended to weaken the force of an obligation or nullify it altogether. Qualifying words such as undertakings 'to use best endeavours', 'to take all possible measures', 'such action as the signatories deem necessary', all have the effect of leaving considerable leeway for discretion and hence of diluting the obligation. On the other hand great care will be taken to ensure that where evasion or ambiguity is not required the form of words leaves no room for doubt about the obligation.

The precise drafting of a diplomatic document can be significant in several ways. Without any concession of principle future options can be left open by a formulation that carefully *avoids premature preclusion*. When the Chinese government, in the light of the American attack on Cambodia in 1970, deemed 'it no longer suitable' for a meeting of Chinese and United States ambassadors 'to be held on May 20 as originally scheduled', they were ruling out the timing but not the fact of the meeting.[5]

Constructive ambiguity has the similar role of leaving future options open, though it does this by formulating a position which can be accepted with equal satisfaction by both sides as a point of departure for negotiations or at least to avoid deadlock and a breakdown of talks. UN Resolution 242 of November 1967, called, among other things, for a 'withdrawal of Israeli armed forces from territories occupied in the recent conflict'. By withholding the definite article from the word 'territories' it was hoped to avoid prejudgement between contradictory Israeli and Arab positions – the one calling for territorial changes, the other rejecting them entirely. George Brown, who, as British Foreign Secretary at the time, was one of the architects of the resolution, points out that if there had been anything more definite, 'it would have been impossible to get the resolution through'.

Each side must be prepared to give up something: the resolution doesn't attempt to say *precisely* what, because that is what the negotiations for a peace-treaty must be about. However unpromising it may look, the fact of the matter is that Resolution 242 is the only basis on which negotiations for a peace-treaty can ever be started. It is both interesting and important that, whatever is said by anybody, the one thing on which all parties are agreed is that they still claim to accept Resolution 242.[6]

Loaded omission is a linguistic device used by diplomats permitting unpleasant and embarassing points to be made without their being articulated in so many words. At the time of the 1956 Suez crisis Britain and France both hoped that they could rely on the American nuclear umbrella in the face of Soviet threats. This illusion was shattered by the State Department message that the United States would 'respect its obligations under the North Atlantic Treaty arrangements'. The contingency feared by Britain and

France was not an attack on their homelands, which were covered by the treaty, but on their forces at Suez, which were not.[7]

Finally *periphrasis* is a form of diplomatic expression which permits controversial things to be said in a way understood by all but without needless provocation. The declaration, in a British-Romanian communiqué of March 1980 (after a visit by Lord Carrington to Bucharest) that the 'deterioration of the international situation is the result of policies based on force and violation of national independence' sounded vague, but was actually an implied condemnation of Soviet moves in Afghanistan. Anything more explicit would have upset the studied balance between independence and caution maintained by Romania in its relations with the USSR.[8]

Alongside its specialized legal terminology and turn of phrase diplomacy has evolved a whole vocabulary of expressions based on the principle of *diplomatic understatement*. By separating tone from content this stylized form of communication permits precision without enthusiasm. A 'frank exchange of views' describes a conversation in which both sides put forward their positions without reaching agreement. If acrimony did enter the discussion there is no point in complicating further negotiation or benefiting third parties by making the point obvious. When a diplomat replies to a question that he has 'no information' or 'no knowledge' this is not necessarily literally true but means that his government wishes to avoid taking a position on an issue. 'Agreement in principle' may be a tactful way of postponing, perhaps indefinitely, a firm commitment. Expressions of 'concern', 'surprise', 'disquiet', are all intended to express more or less strong disagreement at the act or policy of another government. 'Cannot remain indifferent' is a warning of intervention. 'An unfriendly act' is one which threatens war. Refusal 'to be responsible for the consequences' indicates the firmest possible warning of forcible action or opposition.[9] In this way serious and unambiguous statements of a government's position are made without complicating or clouding the situation by unnecessary emotion; in diplomacy emotion is itself assumed to have a purpose.

Misunderstandings, as always, arise when amateurs enter the picture. It is true that the division of sovereignty in the Aegean Sea between the Greek Islands and the Turkish mainland is, straightforwardly speaking, an 'unusual arrangement'. In the mouth of the American ambassador-designate to Greece, speaking at his Senate confirmation hearings, the phrase took on less neutral diplomatic overtones and released a storm of protest in Athens.[10] The appointment was withdrawn.

A final linguistic mechanism to note is the use of 'code words' or 'code phrases'. These are ostensibly innocuous terms which are used as a shorthand to express a more inclusive concept. As with other diplomatic devices the codeword permits something unpleasant or controversial to be said in an anodyne or even ingenuous way. The term itself, frequently a euphemism, acquires its wider connotation by convention. An example is the use of the term 'hegemony'. First found in the 1972 Shanghai communiqué published on the occasion of the Nixon visit to the People's Republic of China, the word was apparently a suggestion of the Americans to describe Soviet ambitions without saying so in so many words. Since then it has become a veritable slogan of Chinese diplomacy, a sort of rallying-cry against the Soviet Union, pressed for whenever possible in joint documents.[11] When the 1978 Sino-Japanese Treaty of Peace and Friendship was found to contain a clause non-specifically opposing efforts by any state to establish hegemony in Asia, the Pacific or any other region, the Soviet Union reacted with immediate anger, rightly seeing the inclusion of the word as a victory for Chinese diplomacy and a slap in the face for itself.[12] Following a period of tension in Soviet-Japanese relations (against a background of Soviet rigidity on the question of the return of the Kuriles) Japanese signature of the treaty with its anti-hegemony clause was a step taken in full awareness that it would be universally understood *and therefore signified* a tilt away from the Soviet Union and towards China.

The Soviet Union, in its turn, has its own code words. The phrase 'proletarian internationalism' has long been used by Moscow as a shorthand way of describing its continued domination of foreign communist parties. Kept out of a communiqué by representatives of West European communist parties following a meeting of European communists in Moscow in 1976, the omission was judged as an important assertion of independence, later reflected in more specific policy positions.[13]

A fruitful field in recent years for verbal disputation concealing profound issues of substance has been the Arab–Israel dispute. Debates about words have provided an arena for the clash of opposing conceptions; attempts to achieve the acceptance of contrasting formulae by various governments or in international forums have been, in effect, battles for support for competing outcomes to the Middle East conflict. Where Israel, for instance, called for 'defensible borders', meaning boundaries that would include part of the territory occupied since 1967, Arab governments emphasized the counter-concept of 'secure and recognized borders', interpreted to mean total Israeli withdrawal. When Israel called for 'true peace', meaning full diplomatic, commercial and cultural relations with the Arab states – in short, legitimacy – Arab governments offered an 'end to belligerency', suggesting a military agreement entailing something less than acceptance of the statehood of Israel.[14]

It is tempting to dismiss the use of linguistic nuances as mere verbal juggling which does not reflect matters of substance. However, this would be a mistake. To the extent that certain words and phrases are commonly understood by participants in the diplomatic process, their use, misuse and avoidance can have an important influence on expectations and hence, at one remove, on behaviour in the future. It does not matter in the least what a word or phrase means in plain English; what is important is the meaning conventionally imputed to it.

'Body language'

Recent suggestive studies of nonverbal communication between individuals, popularly known as 'body language', point to the value of an examination of signalling between states. The subject has received some attention in the past but a systematic analysis is lacking.[15] If signalling is treated here at greater length than verbal communication this is both because of its relative neglect and also because the nonverbal component of a message often carries a greater influence than the ostensible verbal element: 'acts speak louder than words'. (Note that by 'signalling' is meant the transmission of messages which both sender and receiver believe to be deliberate. I am not interested in the sort of questions posed by Robert Jervis and Erving Goffman about the way in which competitors manipulate purportedly unintended messages in order to achieve strategic advantage.[16])

Although the vocabulary of nonverbal signals might appear at first glance to be limited, a surprisingly wide range of meanings and nuances can be communicated. Where ambiguous, the burden of meaning is made clear by the sequence of events and the structure of the situation within which the act takes place. An analogy from everyday life would be the variety of messages that car drivers succeed in transmitting using only lights and horn.

It will be convenient for the purposes of this review to distinguish between the following mediums of communication.

Leadership gestures

In general national leaders perform a central signalling role because they are at the focus of both national and international attention; they are felt to represent the honour, pride and will of the state in their own person; and they are authorized to make binding pronouncements and decisions on behalf of their state. Leadership gestures are most effective in communicating what Ekman and Friesen call *affect displays*[17] – attitudes of friendship, gratitude, hostility, esteem, especial consideration, interest and so on, on the part of one state towards another.

Dulles's refusal to shake hands with Chou En-lai at the 1954 Geneva Conference was a cutting signal of rejection and contempt by the United States towards the People's Republic of China and rankled for years with the Chinese. Conversely when another American Secretary of State, James Byrnes, ostentatiously went over to the Italian delegate at the Paris Peace Conference of 1946 to pat him on the shoulder this was a small but significant sign of American encouragement for a formally defeated state, the object of bitter Soviet invective, but seen as an important member of the Western community.

Leadership gestures encompass the classic repertoire of human contact which researchers into body language have so emphasized, including hugging, kissing, patting, squeezing, 'turning a cold shoulder' and shaking hands. They can also include marks of courtesy, such as President Sadat placing his private jet at the disposal of Israel Defence Minister Weizman (in November 1979), or dramatic setpieces such as Sadat's attendance in the same month at prayers for the Muslim Feast of the Sacrifice at the great mosque in El Arish. The latter gesture integrated two powerful themes for Egypt and the Arab world on the eve of an Arab League summit: the motif of religious piety and tangible proof that the capital of the Sinai had returned to Egyptian hands.

The importance of context for leadership gestures can be illustrated by two contrasting examples. The first flight made by Neville Chamberlain to Germany in September 1938 was described in the circumstances by Sir Robert Vansittart as 'going to Canossa', in other words submitting to humiliating self-abasement.[18] (The example also points up the distinction between purpose and meaning in diplomatic signalling.) In contrast, the visit of President Sadat to Jerusalem in 1977, which could have been an act of submission, was transformed, by subtle choreography (of timing, manner of arrival, places visited and the bearing of the man himself) into a diplomatic triumph.

For a leadership gesture to acquire its full effect and symbolic resonance it must obviously be publicised, and preferably photographed or televized. This visual dimension permits the actors in the drama to play out attitudes and emotions which could not be as effectively carried by conventional diplomatic channels. One reason for this is that a simple statement of emotion – anger, fear and so on – is inherently incredible as a straightforward political announcement. The tone of the message contradicts its ostensible content. Although a Hitler could convincingly express extreme feelings, most statesmen are unable or unprepared for this kind of histrionic diplomacy. Second, affect displays, as deliberate attempts to arouse an emotional response in observers for political reasons, work best at a symbolic or ritual level. This seems to be simply a fact of human behaviour attested to by the arts, especially by oratory and drama.

Roland Barthes accounts for the force of dramatic enactment by arguing that 'myth' (by which he means a stylized performance of the kind referred to here) works by giving its meaning a 'sensory reality' – 'unlike the linguistic signifier, which is purely mental'. Second, it gives the signified theme 'a natural and eternal justification . . . a clarity which is not that of an explanation but that of a statement of fact'. Finally, 'myth acts economically: it abolishes the complexity of human acts, it gives them the simplicity of essences, it does away with all dialectics, with any going beyond what is immediately visible, it organizes a world which is without contradictions.'[19]

Barthes's insight is certainly exemplified by such political gestures as Willy Brandt's act of contrition when he knelt before the Warsaw Ghetto Memorial in 1970 on the occasion of his state visit to Poland; or the remarkable ceremony of reconciliation performed by de Gaulle and Adenauer when they knelt together before the high altar of Reims

Cathedral in 1962. Moving, dramatic, essential, these tableaux symbolized with unmatched power and economy before national audiences the reality of great turning-points in European history.

Protocol

Strictly speaking protocol is the body of customs and regulations governing the ceremony and etiquette of diplomatic intercourse. The term will be used here in the more inclusive sense of diplomatic procedure and choreography during the course of negotiations and contacts. Protocol is a convenient medium for signalling because a diplomatic slight, for instance, signifies in a graphic way political disapproval; diplomats are 'only human' and are deeply sensitive to the nuances of honour and esteem; it is easily regulated and can be reversed; and it is a conveniently accessible instrument of signalling during negotiations.

Although protocol is a less flexible medium than the leadership gesture, it can also be used for affect displays. Esteem, or lack of it, of one state for another can be symbolized by various stylized devices such as the rank of the welcoming or farewell delegation for a visiting dignitary, the length of time allotted to him (if any) by the head of state or, in communist regimes, by the first secretary of the party, the luxury or prestige associated with the residence placed at his disposal and so on. Convention lays down a certain minimal framework of ceremony. Improvements on the norm signify varying degrees of added esteem; detractions from the norm are unusual and so especially insulting as to risk far-reaching consequences.

Protocol is also effective in communicating nuances of approval or disapproval and can therefore be useful in conveying the attitude of one government towards the policy of another and can be more easily disavowed that a verbal message. 'Atmospherics' can be rapidly orchestrated and the diplomatic climate changed from warm to frigid as tactics dictate. Especially in an authoritarian society treatment of the ambassador is a reliable gauge of official policy. In Moscow before the Second World War the United States Ambassador was almost alone in his range of contacts and freedom from petty harassment. Other envoys found themselves neglected and subject to niggling marks of official disapproval; the personal effects of retiring diplomats were examined and taxed in violation of traditional rights. When Joseph E. Davis left his Moscow posting in June 1938 he and the diplomatic corps were amazed at his reception by Stalin, a unique occurrence in the diplomatic relations of the Soviet capital. The Soviet Union, seriously disturbed by the possibility of war against both Germany and Japan, and gravely mistrustful of Anglo-French policy, was clearly very interested indeed in a closer relationship with Washington.[20]

Time plays a significant role in calibrating the modalities of approval or esteem. Keeping an envoy waiting on some pretext is not a breach of protocol and therefore not irreparable, but its meaning is clear. Similar devices are the postponement of a meeting or delay in replying to a communication or invitation.

The key role of diplomatic choreography is in the transmission of *intrinsic signals*. There are two primary differences between affect displays and intrinsic signals. First, intrinsic signals are largely instrumental whereas affect displays are, by definition, largely demonstrative. A second difference lies in their contrasting principles of coding – the conventions governing the correspondence between the signal and its meaning. This relationship may be either extrinsic or intrinsic. 'An extrinsic code is one in which the act signifies or stands for something else, and the coding may be arbitrary or iconic.' Display signals are arbitrarily coded in that the relevant acts bear no visual resemblance to that which they are supposed to signify, they are rituals or signals which conventionally or because of the immediate context acquire an understood significance.[21] (Iconic codes, in which the act looks in some way like its meaning, are found in nonverbal communications based on the principle of analogy. For instance deliberate insults to the person of an envoy are intended to imply contempt for the state which he represents.)

Intrinsic signals, like iconically coded behaviour, visually relate to that which they signify. But their distinguishing feature is not that they resemble their significant; they *are* their significant.[22] This category of messages is the reverse of what J. L. Austin has called 'performative utterances', cases in which 'in saying what I do I actually perform that action'.[23] (For instance, saying, 'I do' in a marriage ceremony.) The actions to be considered below could be described, analogously, as 'expressive performances', cases in which 'in doing what I say, I actually express my message'. A warning shot by one ship across the bows of another carries the warning of a repetition of the very same act, this time with the intention of sinking the target vessel. Thus the intrinsic message is a peculiarly graphic and expressive enactment of the encoded significant.

Almost any detail of negotiating procedure can come to reflect or symbolize some central theme of the negotiations, so that procedural disagreement has in effect substantive implications. The symbolism may commence with the venue of the negotiations. Hans Morgenthau points out that the choice of meeting place bestows prestige and that 'the shift from one favorite meeting place to another symbolizes a shift in the preponderance of power'.[24] One of the areas of disagreement between the appeasers and their domestic critics in the 1930s was over the importance of diplomatic modalities in negotiations with the dictators. Mussolini, for instance, well understanding the significance of venue, insisted that any negotiations between Britain and Italy be held in Rome. Neville Chamberlain was prepared to concede the point since he was eager to commence talks and took the commonsense – but unprofessional – view that substance was more important than form. Anthony Eden and the Foreign Office strongly disagreed, arguing that to announce discussions in the circumstances would 'be regarded as running after the Italian Government'. To hold negotiations in Rome rather than London 'would be regarded as another surrender to the dictators'. In the end Chamberlain won and Eden was forced to resign. Looking back Eden concluded that 'the more critical the negotiating position of a democracy, the more important it is to hold to the tested forms of diplomacy'.[25] The impression made on the Italian Government was precisely that predicted by Eden. Foreign Minister Ciano noted in his diary in March 1938: 'Chamberlain is more interested than we are in achieving agreement.'[26]

A second modality conveying information about the interest and intention of the negotiator is the level of delegation. In June 1939, with the position of the Soviet Union one of the keys to the European situation, the British Government (together with France) decided to despatch a special envoy to Moscow. Its choice was William Strang, a Foreign Office official without political standing. Not only was this choice mistaken in Churchill's view but 'the sending of so subordinate a figure gave actual offence'. Then in August a military mission was sent by sea, arriving in Moscow after a long delay. Its members possessed no written authority to negotiate.[27] Here was eloquent testimony to the Soviet Government that Britain (and France) had no serious intention to reach an agreement. The episode is a sharp reminder of the attention that a skilled foreign policy must pay to diplomatic 'body language'.

The discouraging behaviour of the British mission in 1939 can be contrasted with the businesslike manner displayed by the Soviet Union in 1955 at the time of the breakthrough in Austro-Soviet negotiations for the Austrian State Treaty. When the Soviet Government was ready to conclude the agreement an invitation was despatched to Vienna for the Austrian Chancellor to come to Moscow, accompanied by representatives of his own choosing, for the purpose of bilateral negotiations. The purport of this gesture was immediately understood and created a sensation in the Austrian Government.[28]

Even the shape of the table, as was discovered during the course of negotiations to end the Vietnam War, can be a major political symbol. In Dr Kissinger's account:

This was not a trivial issue; it was of great symbolic significance to our South Vietnamese allies, who, considering themselves the legitimate government, were not ready to accord equal status to Hanoi's arm in the South, the National Liberation Front. For three months, therefore, Saigon had resisted Hanoi's proposal for a four-sided table at which Hanoi, the NLF, Saigon, and the United States were each accorded equal status. By this proposal Hanoi sought to use the beginnings of negotiations to establish the NLF as an alternative government.[29]

Among other resonant modalities of negotiation have been their auspices, name, presence or absence of press and photographers, whether one room or several rooms, whom consulted before and after, printed layout of final agreement and, perhaps the ultimate in minutiae, the position of an ashtray. (The Iraqi delegate at the United Nations objected to sharing an ashtray with the representative of Israel.)

The movement of armed forces

As ultimate symbols, of the most dramatic and even awesome kind, of national sovereignty and the authoritative possession of the means of external and internal coercion, armed forces of all kinds are a particularly apt and evocative medium for the expression of attitudes and policies related to the position and security of the state in the international community and the modalities of its relations with other states.

In the following sections I shall concentrate on the role of naval power. At different times other arms of the services have performed an identical function: the despatch of air squadrons, troop movements, convoys and concentrations, military parades, armed alerts, nuclear tests and so on have signalled important messages. However naval power has been the most ubiquitous and fine-tuned instrument of communication in the postwar period. A sketch of the repertoire of meanings, principles of coding and functions of various kinds of naval display is the best way to illustrate the role of armed force as an instrument of political communication.

As affect displays naval movements can paint a broad palette of national emotions. Consider the following examples:

Triumph. On 22 March 1939, one week after the dismemberment of the rump of Czechoslovakia, the Lithuanian Government was obliged by a virtual ultimatum to cede the Baltic port of Memel to Nazi Germany. To dramatize the occasion and to emphasize that what had taken place was a triumph of arms, achieved by the threatening use of overwhelming force, Hitler arrived in Memel harbour on the following day on the bridge of the pocket battleship *Deutschland* accompanied by the whole German battle-fleet.[30] Internally the ceremony stressed German invincibility, mobilised support and aroused national pride. Externally it carried the message of German might and predominance in the Baltic. One may also guess at the personal symbolism of the occasion: the *Führer* carried ashore by a ship bearing the name of the German nation in order to reincorporate a former German territory.

Resolution. In the dark days of January 1941, after the fall of France and evacuation of Dunkirk, when Britain stood alone and faced by a seemingly hopeless situation, British Prime Minister Churchill transformed a routine diplomatic appointment into a dramatic gesture of national resolution. In his own words: 'In order to clothe the arrival of our new Ambassador, Lord Halifax, in the United States with every circumstance of importance, I arranged that our newest and strongest battleship, the *King George V*, with a proper escort of destroyers, should carry him and his wife across the ocean.'[31] With the Lend-Lease Bill still before Congress the political message to the American people contained in this determined act of pride was clear: Britain was still a going concern, willing and able to fight on!

Defiance. In December 1936 President Roosevelt arrived at Buenos Aires for the opening session of an Inter-American conference on board the cruiser *Indianapolis* escorted by the USS *Chester*. An intimidating display of naval power, intended to signal the United States' ability to ensure compliance with its wishes on the American continent, the gesture underlined Roosevelt's reluctance to accept Argentina's affirmation of the principle of non-intervention in others' internal affairs. Two years later Argentina broadcast her defiance of United States policy and an increasingly independent line by sending her foreign minister to attend the Pan-American conference in Lima on board the cruiser *La Argentina*.[32] (Note again the symbolism of the name.) By echoing the American gesture Argentina signalled that she was not to be intimidated. Defiance by repetition of an aggressive display finds a parallel in the animal world. Aggression between certain species is announced by the aggressor putting on a ritual display for his victim. In cranes this function is performed by the display of a red patch on the head of the bird. A counterdisplay of the aggressive emblem signifies that the challenge has been taken up.[33]

Displeasure. Following the Anglo-French invasion of Egypt in November 1956 in collaboration with Israel the two European governments were condemned by the United States, both in private, and in public at the United Nations, and subjected to severe pressure to withdraw. In addition to diplomatic expressions of disapproval the American position was also put across with brutal clarity by means of harassing tactics employed by the Sixth Fleet against British and French warships. These measures obviously stopped well short of open hostilities; nor did they make any difference to the conduct of the operation. They did provide, however, a sobering and disheartening demonstration of displeasure from a former wartime and present NATO ally.[34]

Displays of naval power can also serve to let off steam in a situation following a blow to national pride. In this sort of case the demonstration of force can act as a surrogate for its exercise. Finally, as is often the case in the animal and human world, the most potent symbol of hostility can also be transformed into a gesture of friendship. Hence the courtesy visit which is by far the most frequent form of naval display.

As intrinsic signals, armed forces can act as a medium of communication creating expectations of the permitted bounds of future action. In this they perform a central role in the definition and maintenance of rules of the game. By actually enacting the message which is to be sent, the possibility of misunderstanding is reduced to the minimum and the credibility of future action enhanced.

Threat of bombardment. On the evening of 29 May 1937 the German battleship *Deutschland*, at anchor off Ibiza on the Spanish coast, was bombed by Spanish republican aircraft. After due deliberation the German Government took their revenge. A cruiser and four destroyers bombarded Almeria, causing nineteen deaths. At the same time the German

Foreign Minister demanded guarantees against any repetition of the original incident.[35] Hence the bombardment performed two functions: it was
an act of retaliation and it was also a warning of further punishment if a
German ship were again attacked. No German warships seem to have
been subsequently bombarded. In contrast, attacks on British ships,
which were never responded to by anything but diplomatic protests, continued throughout the Spanish Civil War. In this example the opposing
effectiveness of intrinsic as opposed to explicit diplomatic communication
is especially marked.

Right of passage. Since the Second World War the right of innocent
passage through international waterways, challenged by local claims in a
long series of cases, has been asserted by the warships of different states.
The straits of Corfu, the Dardanelles, Mahassai, Malacca, Taiwan and
Tiran have all been under contention in this way. A non-Western example
of action to assert the right of passage occurred in 1969 when Iranian
warships escorted an Iranian merchant ship from Khorramshahr through
the Shatt al Arab to the Persian Gulf in successful defiance of an Iraqi
threat to stop any ship flying the Iranian flag from sailing through these
waters.[36] At stake in this confrontation, of course, was not the issue of
the single merchant ship but the principle of free passage itself. Compelled to give way to similar threat in 1961, Iran now signalled to Iraq that
she possessed the naval strength to overcome any attempt at obstruction
in the future.

Threat of interception. Naval blockade involves the use of naval patrols
to prevent seaborne supplies from reaching an enemy. Conventionally,
such action is taken in wartime and preceded by an appropriate declaration of intent. The message in this case is transmitted on two channels: by
the verbal announcement and by the visible presence of warships in position at sea. It should be noted that although an undeclared blockade is
perfectly feasible, if illegal, an unenforced declaration is a contradiction
in terms. Under international law, indeed, a blockade is recognized only
if sufficient naval forces are available to make it effective. Because of the
various conditions hedging round the imposition of a blockade under
international law, there have been various examples in recent years of
undeclared 'blockade-type' action. The United States has used the expedient on various occasions off Central America.

For example in May 1954 the United States Navy established what
amounted to a blockade of the Guatemalan coast to prevent the government of that country from importing arms to resist a revolution organized
by the CIA. The principal Western seafaring nations were asked permission by the State Department for their merchant vessels to be stopped and
searched on the high seas for arms shipments en route to Guatemala – in
breach of international law in peacetime. In individual cases the government involved would be informed 'if there was time'. In the face of a
universal refusal to comply with this request Secretary of State Dulles

nevertheless continued with the blockade, arguing that in cold war conditions past rules were no longer applicable.[37]

In the circumstances there was nothing that governments and merchant ships involved in trade with Guatemala could do but take account of the fact of the naval patrols by submitting to search or turning back. It is in this that the effectiveness of the expedient can be seen. Rules of the game, as has been pointed out, like 'no trespassing' notices, can be overlooked or, if read, ignored. A fence – a physical obstacle – can be neither overlooked nor ignored (though it can be forcibly broken through). Blockades, like fences, transmit information about the limits of permitted action in a way that simply must be taken into account.

The final role of displays of armed force is to transmit reinforcement signals – messages whose meaning extends beyond either the immediate content of the action or the affective impulse behind it, but is intended to establish, illustrate or emphasize a wider foreign policy stance of the actor. (To the extent that this distinction is partly arbitrary and ideal there is some overlapping with the two previous categories.) In the following section I shall concentrate on two reinforcement functions of this kind: the expression of support and the articulation of coercive threats. In the management and especially preservation of rules of the game these tasks are of the essence.

Reinforcement signals can be intrinsically coded, as in the case of a threat of naval action of some kind intended to produce a foreign policy effect; arbitrary, as with a naval ceremony which is endowed by convention with a particular significance; or iconic, as when the provision of naval support is understood as an analogy for a general political commitment.

Enhancement of credibility.   In general, reinforcement signals are intended to enhance the credibility of a given policy. Some of the advantages they possess over diplomatic communications in this respect are as follows: first, nonverbal signals are thought to be inherently more powerful and eloquent than words which, since they must be considered and weighed, possess no necessary link with action. Indeed they are sometimes a substitute for it.[38] Warships, which are instruments of action, necessarily possess a link with action. As Robert Jervis points out, 'capability indices', such as military or naval manoeuvres, arming or alert 'lend credence to an image because the actor is now seen as being in a better position to undertake certain policies'.[39] Second, nonverbal signals constitute a warranty of commitment in a way in which words do not. Not only warships, but also troops, missiles and aircraft are felt to possess communicatory credibility because their emplacement entails a relinquishment on the part of the initiator of future freedom of action: he has given hostages to fortune.[40] Third, there are certain circumstances in which it is desirable to transmit a message which is at once unambiguous and yet without the explicitness of a verbal statement. In case of embarrassment, again to follow Jervis, one can disclaim the overture.[41] Moreover a nonverbal communication, carrying the true message, can be transmitted together with a verbal signal claiming something quite different. In February 1977 Idi Amin menacingly ordered all United States citizens in Uganda to meet him in Kampala. In response an American naval task force, headed by the nuclear-powered aircraft carrier *Enterprise* put out from the Kenyan port of Mombasa. With its complement of warplanes and marines the force was 'regarded as a threat to Uganda' by Amin. The White House, however, in line with a deliberate policy of avoiding any comment that might provoke the Ugandan tyrant and endanger American lives, denied any threatening intent. Thus the benefit of the warning was obtained without dangerously humiliating the unpredictable Amin.[42] A final consideration has been noted by Alfred Vagts: the flexibility of naval signalling. A naval demonstration 'can . . . readily be changed from a peaceful to a hostile character – by diverse announcements – and back again. . . . Their movements can be stopped on short notice and their meanings can thus be quickly reinterpreted. Their actions can be easily disavowed as due to the initiative of local or subordinate commanders.'[43]

Political support.   Political 'support' is clearly a very inclusive concept which can range from simple moral encouragement to full-scale military commitment. Now the best way of unambiguously specifying the precise parameters of that support is by formal agreement. The disadvantages of this procedure are that many situations arise in which (*a*) precision and unambiguity are just the qualities of the message not desired; (*b*) it is necessary to signal support where a formal diplomatic announcement may be politically or bureaucratically unfeasible; (*c*) a diplomatic message might not carry through surrounding 'noise' or possess sufficient credibility; (*d*) no contractual obligation may exist and negotiations would take months. In these circumstances (and the same arguments hold for coercive threats) naval moves of various kinds can convey a surprisingly broad spectrum of meanings and nuances. In the language of communications theory, warships possess a relatively high *sending capacity* measured by three indices: transmission time, number of discriminable stimulus patterns which can be emitted, and visibility. (Compare with other devices such as economic sanctions or aid, trade agreements, the supply of arms, official visits and other expressions of support or its absence.)

Along the spectrum of political support a wide range of nuances can be detected. Circumstances and timing; the make-up of the naval force taking part in the demonstration (including age, size, capability, even name); and the power relations between the initiating actor and the object of his attention, can all effect the precise meaning of the signal. The following two examples are contrasting points on the spectrum of support:

Qualified support.   On 11 November 1965 the white minority government of Rhodesia unilaterally declared its independence from Britain. Despite strong Commonwealth and Zambian pressure to take action, the

Wilson government decided against the use of force to reassert British authority. The last thing British opinion would stomach was an open-ended military commitment against white settlers in Africa. On the other hand Zambia, which was acutely vulnerable, was very much afraid of a pre-emptive Rhodesian strike against Lusaka and its copper mines. In so far, therefore, as the British Government wished to express support for Zambia, it also had to make quite clear the qualifications on that support. One solution was the publicized presence of the aircraft carrier *Eagle* in the Mozambique Channel. At one and the same time this provided Zambia with reassurance that possible Rhodesian air strikes would be countered without committing British forces in an offensive role. Among the various options available to Britain at this time, when direct military intervention to quell the revolt was called for and even expected, HMS *Eagle* was in fact an expressively qualified response.[44]

Unqualified support.   Contrast the ambiguity or qualified nature of the commitment signalled in the previous example with the massive demonstration of unqualified support put on by the United States Sixth Fleet for the benefit of King Hussein of Jordan in April 1957. Hussein was faced by a major political crisis, in which the hand of Nasserist subversion, backed by the Soviet Union, was seen to threaten the continued independence and integrity of the Hashemite Kingdom. Units of the Sixth Fleet, including the aircraft carrier *Forrestal* and the heavy cruisers *Salem* and *Des Moines*, sailed for the Eastern Mediterranean at three hours notice. They were joined by the battleship *Wisconsin* and twelve smaller vessels. Six naval transports with 1,800 marines on board anchored off Beirut, while fifty ships carried out 'air defence manoeuvres' in the open sea. Fully confident of the unrivalled support of his powerful patron, the United States, King Hussein soon succeeded in re-establishing his authority. The Soviet Union was also left in no doubt about the determination of the American commitment and complained bitterly about the United States' 'open military demonstration'.[45]

In most policies of support there is also an element of coercion because the support is invariably provided for an actor under some kind of threat. Whether a naval demonstration is considered an act of support or an act of coercion is partly a semantic question but does have some meaning in terms of the defined objective of the signal at the time. An act of support is aimed primarily at encouraging one's ally; coercion is primarily intended to dissuade an opponent from an undesirable course of action (deterrence) or to persuade him to undertake a desired step (compellence).[46] Thus in July 1967 a Soviet naval squadron visited Egypt with the declared purpose of cooperating 'with Egyptian armed forces to repel any aggression'.[47] In the circumstances this should be seen rather as a demonstrative gesture of support to retrieve sagging Soviet prestige in Egypt than to deter a demobilized Israel.

Against a weak and vulnerable opponent the threat of intervention by a naval task force is indeed a potent and effective sanction. The Royal Navy and the United States Navy have a long record of successful gun-boat diplomacy, in the latter case, often against small Central American republics. A classic example of a coercive demonstration of naval force occurred in the 1961 Dominican crisis. In order to discourage the restoration of the family of the murdered former dictator Rafael Trujillo a powerful show of force was put on just beyond the three-mile limit which included two aircraft carriers, the *Franklin D. Roosevelt* and *Valley Forge* with 1,800 marines on board. Faced by this kind of threat the Trujillos had no alternative but to concede power to a government more acceptable to the United States.[48]

It should emerge from this sketch just how varied are the messages that can be communicated nonverbally. Moreover since nonverbal signalling is largely context-dependent for its meaning the scope for improvization and differentiation is large. Limitations of space have also necessitated only passing reference or exclusion of complete categories of nonverbal communication. Besides movements of ground and air forces, acts of government including decisions on trade, credit, the treatment of foreign citizens, tourism, sport and culture – in short, all of the non-diplomatic areas of international contact – can contribute to the international dialogue, as they did indeed in the opening stages of the remarkable rapprochements between Nazi Germany and the Soviet Union, and the United States and the People's Republic of China.

If it is true that nonverbal signalling is a form of communication in its own right, capable of imparting a varied repertoire of messages, it should follow that more elaborate exchanges of signals – nonverbal 'conversations' – can be carried on between states. That this is indeed so is borne out by the 1968 *Pueblo* affair which arose after the North Korean seizure of an American surveillance ship. At stage 1 the United States assembled a colossal task force (including three aircraft carriers) in the Sea of Japan. Its message was a compellent threat: that the *Pueblo* be released or coercive action would be taken. At stage 2 the Soviet Union manoeuvred a much weaker force between the American fleet and the North Korean coast. In military terms its potential was negligible but its political message was far-reaching; American coercive action would draw the Soviet Union in on the side of its ally. At stage 3, after believed Hungarian mediation, the aircraft carrier *Enterprise* withdrew from her position off the North Korean coast. An obviously conciliatory gesture, the signal indicated American willingness to divert the dialogue from military to diplomatic channels.[49]

A final word of caution is in order. The very expressiveness and flexibility of nonverbal communication, one's ability to say one thing while simultaneously broadcasting a contradictory nonverbal message, imposes on its user the responsibility of absolute control and complete awareness of the consequences of its employment. The meaning of a nonverbal signal is what observing actors understand it to mean. Denials and retractions cannot retroactively cancel out the understood message. A commitment nonverbally signalled may be as politically binding as any solemn oath and a failure to honour it as consequential. This is surely one of the overlooked lessons of the Bay of Pigs debacle. On 12 April 1961, several days before the ill-fated landing of CIA-trained Cuban exiles on the beaches of Castro's Cuba, President Kennedy pledged at a press conference that United States armed forces would not 'under any conditions' intervene in Cuba. When no action was taken to salvage the bungled invasion this was proclaimed as a victory for straight talking and consistency. Unfortunately quite a different message was signalled via nonverbal channels. Throughout the landing ships of the United States Navy, including the aircraft carrier *Essex*, lay visible offshore.[50] Their nonverbal message, transmitted repeatedly in previous Caribbean crises, was one of support for the rebels and threatened intervention in the conflict. To deny this was futile and to fail, in the event, to honour this broadcast commitment must seriously have damaged the credibility of the new administration.

Part two

Rules of the game: a classification

Chapter six

Tacit rules

If rules of the game are considered as a sort of language or code of communication between states with a discernible 'grammar' and 'vocabulary' then the propositions of that language can be thought of as the permissions, restraints and obligations which make up the rules themselves. In the following chapters I shall suggest a typology of those rules and present a selection of concrete examples.

Rules of the game vary on a broad range of characteristics including their degree of specificity or generality, permanence or variability, universality or restricted application, abstraction or geographical concreteness, and application to wartime or peacetime. The method of classification adopted here distinguishes rules in terms of the explicitness and formality with which they are communicated. Thus at one end of the spectrum are found rules arrived at by tacit agreement and which are not directly negotiated either in writing or by word of mouth. At the other end of the spectrum are rules deriving from formal negotiations and expressed in formal, binding agreement. In between are rules of the game contained in the 'spirit' of formal agreements, verbal 'gentlemen's' agreements, and 'nonbinding', though written, understandings. This typology is certainly not the only scheme possible but it does have the advantage of simplicity and clarity and emphasizes the common features of rules located in the different categories over and above other cross-cutting distinctions.

Rules of the game based on tacit understanding are, properly speaking, neither written down nor spoken. (Sometimes the term 'tacit' is used in the misleading sense of verbal or secret.) Tacit arrangements are not arrived at by any formal process of negotiations but via a variety of expedients, including spontaneous mutual abstention, by the dropping of discreet hints, through the mediation of a third party or by a process of nonverbal signalling involving the publicized or visible manoeuvring of one's forces. Several groups of circumstances can be discerned in which a tacit understanding is preferred to some more explicit arrangement. First there is the situation in which no direct contact exists or is possible between the parties. This applies in wartime, in the absence of diplomatic relations or in the event of an unwillingness or inability to rely on normal channels of communication. Second is the sort of situation in which admission or explicit articulation of the understanding is ruled out for reasons of self-esteem, internal politics or external (including alliance) obligations. Similar considerations apply in varying degrees to all kinds of nonwritten agreements, but tacit understandings seem to cover arrangements felt to be so discreditable and publicly indefensible as to be inarticulable even in a purely verbal form. This may occur when the infringement of some taboo is involved or on an issue about which one is simply not 'supposed' to reach an understanding at all. Since the understanding is tacit it need not be acknowledged and, on the contrary, can be safely denied without fear of contradiction. Finally tacit rules may be conveniently applied to activities which are in themselves seen as illegitimate or discreditable, for instance espionage, subversion, conspiracy, the maintenance of spheres of influence or intervention in others' internal affairs.

Wartime might be thought to provide classic conditions for the appearance of tacit rules of the game based on a common need for the combatants to contain violence within limits maintaining some kind of proportion between the political objectives of the conflict and the cost of its prosecution. Minimally it seems evident that combatants can hardly be interested in indulging in an orgy of uncontrolled mutual destruction in which losses outweigh all possible gains. In the inevitable absence, or at least neglect, of diplomacy in wartime, tacit understanding would appear to provide a natural expedient for communicating restraint.

At a tactical level this assumption is indeed borne out. Between local combatants, left to their own devices, tacit rules do emerge, deriving from the most fundamental principle of human tolerance which is 'to live and let live'. In the First World War, for example, many cases have been found of tacit restraints governing the behaviour of British and German soldiers towards each other. In the absence of commissioned officers both sides would deliberately avoid shelling, sniping or clashes between patrols in no-man's-land likely to lead to pointless loss of life.[1] Such mutual restraint exemplified three characteristic features of tacit rules: the absence of direct communication between the parties, the inadmissibility of the arrangement, and its illegitimacy – in this case its contradiction of the official doctrine of the 'offensive spirit', the duty to harass and kill the enemy whenever possible. In the Vietnam War similar sorts of local arrangements have been noted between South Vietnamese troops and officials and those of the Vietcong. A frequent arrangement of this kind involved the tacit agreement not to enter each other's areas.[2]

At a strategic level tacit rules of the game turn out to be relatively uncommon. (Unilateral restraints for whatever reason, domestic, moral, fear of drawing in third parties, or constraints deriving from an absence of capability, are quite another matter, but are not considered here.) The sort of limiting circumstances in which they do achieve any degree of permanence appear in the case of the preservation of 'sanctuaries' (targets immune from attack) in the 1969–70 Israel–Egypt War of Attrition. During the whole course of the war the Israelis continued to work without hindrance the former Egyptian oilfields at Abu Rodeis on the Gulf of Suez, while the Egyptians operated the El Morgan fields a few miles away on the other side of the Gulf.[3] One assumes that the success of this 'arrangement' arose from the negligible military significance of the oilfields combined with their almost complete vulnerability. Both sides were in hostage to the other: a strike by either would have invited retaliation by the opponent with the result of a net loss all round. There was no need for the restraint to be communicated since it was inherent in the structure of the situation.

Otherwise, tacit limits on violence based on mutual abstention tend to be invariably precarious in anything but the short term. Rules of the game rest on an intersection of common interests. The Suez oilfields in the example above remained intact because of a symmetry of Egyptian and Israeli interests. Neither side could benefit without suffering an equivalent loss. A similar symmetry is seen in the abstention from the use of poison gas in the Second World War and the contemporary nuclear 'balance of terror' between the superpowers. But by definition states at war are engaged in a struggle for contradictory objectives. Common interests are not inconceivable, but are likely to be infrequent or transitory. It is this inevitable asymmetry of opposing objectives which inserts an inherent instability into any attempt to arrive at a stable structure of behaviour. Put another way, the moment one of the combatants achieves an advantage within a given framework of rules his opponent will be strongly tempted to reject at least some of the rules in order to restore his position. Complete rule stability – let us say accepted codes of chivalry or fair play – may only be possible when the belligerents are indifferent to the outcome or attach a high regard to losing with grace. Theoretically, sport constitutes a contest of this type but the deterioration of sporting behaviour in international competitions indicates that even this may no longer be true.

The fragility of rules of the game in wartime is illustrated by the attempt to maintain limits on aerial bombardment at the outset of the Second World War. Faced with a Chiefs of Staff estimate of appalling damage to British cities in the event of air warfare, the British Government decided that, for fear of reprisals, attacks should not be made on industrial targets in Germany. Only 'strictly military objectives in the narrowest sense of the word' were to be bombed. Not until June 1940 was Bomber Command authorized to attack east of the Rhine and then to concentrate on oil installations. 'In no circumstances should bombing be allowed to degenerate into mere indiscriminate action, which is contrary to the policy of His Majesty's Government'.[4]

British and French restraints on bombing were closely paralleled, for about the first year of the war, on the German side. At the outset of hostilities Hitler issued a strict directive forbidding air attacks on either France or Britain: 'The guiding principle must be not to provoke the initiation of aerial warfare by any action on the part of Germany.' Indeed a German promise to adhere to such restraints was among the last messages passed on by the Swedish intermediary Dahlerus before the outbreak of war. He had Göering's assurance that if England did 'not bomb open cities they will not do so. They will limit aerial attacks to aerodromes and fortifications. Will make no attacks on civil population.' Such restraint had a strategic rather than a humanitarian motive. Hitler's directive made it clear that the strength of the German Air Force was to be preserved for decisive action against the Western Powers after the defeat of Poland.

After the occupation of Poland and the fall of France, Germany turned its attention to Britain. With the launching of the Battle of Britain in July 1940 Germany's primary objective became that of depriving the RAF of air superiority and establishing that of the Luftwaffe as a necessary prelude to invasion. In the relevant directive Hitler therefore instructed his air force to act primarily against military targets. After air superiority had been achieved, ports and food stores were to be attacked. Terror attacks would be held back as 'measures of reprisal'.[5]

On 13 August 1940 Germany began to send fleets of bombers against fighter bases in south-east England. But then on 24 August a flight of German aircraft strayed over London and, against orders, dropped its bombs. Nine civilians were killed. Churchill's reaction was immediate and enraged. On 25 August he ordered the night bombing of German towns, including Berlin. Within a ten-day period five RAF attacks were launched at the German capital. This was precisely what Hitler had hoped to avoid. On 7 September, obliged for reasons of prestige and morale to retaliate in kind, the Luftwaffe turned from its original counterforce offensive to bomb London. This decision probably saved Britain from invasion.

British and German abstinence from terror bombing in the period September 1939 to August 1940 provides perhaps the best example of the working of a tacit wartime rule of the game based on the logic of mutual deterrence. Moreover the constraint, although it was not set down in any joint document, was spelled out in parallel directives given to the air forces of both sides. For all this, the breakdown of the rule was surely sooner or later inevitable. First, the proximity of military, industrial and civilian targets made it impossible to demarcate the 'sanctuary' without risk of error, and within only eleven days of the launching of the full-scale German air offensive on Kent the error occurred. Second, the motive for maintaining the constraint was inherently frail. Neither Hitler nor Churchill were either personally opposed in principle to terror bombing or unduly alarmed by the prospect of reprisal. If Hitler restricted German bombing to military targets for a time this was essentially to maintain concentration of effort. If Churchill launched an offensive on civilian targets this was clearly because he believed the benefit outweighed the cost of retaliation.

This example suggests that rules of the game which are based on mutual (and therefore contingent, rather than unilateral and unconditional) abstention from some weapon or target, are unlikely, in the heat of hostilities, to hold up. Miscalculation, the wish to achieve a decisive advantage or the differential effect of the prohibition on the two sides have overturned formal rules of war in the past (such as the prohibitions on poison gas and submarine warfare in the First World War[6]) and there is no reason why tacit restraints should be more secure. Restrictions placed on the bombing of civilian targets in 1939–40 (and in the 1969–70 War of Attrition) looked less like reliable restraints on action than mere pauses in the escalatory spiral. At best rules may be only temporarily effective or permanently effective in marginal cases and under special conditions.

The limited utility of tacit rules in wartime is not, however, reflected in time of peace. On the contrary, tacit rules of the game are one of the crucial mechanisms for maintaining international order.

Clandestine activity is one area which naturally lends itself to tacit rather than formal regulation. Espionage, which comes into this category, possesses two features which explain why this should be so: on the one hand considerable risk of friction and embarrassment, and on the other hand a common interest in maintaining discreet mutual surveillance. Unspoken accommodation has the advantage of preventing 'incidents' where possible and avoiding unwanted repercussions on wider relations without openly admitting the existence of practices which are, on the whole, illegal.

One example of a tacit arrangement in the field of clandestine surveillance is the Nazi–Soviet tacit understanding of 1940–1.[7] Since neither side was officially supposed to suspect the good intentions of the other, and since the permissibility of overflights by military aircraft of each other's territory could hardly be given formal sanction, an understanding could not be openly stated in written or even verbal form. Nevertheless its advantages in removing suspicions and thereby avoiding pre-emptive and untimely attack could not be denied. (That Nazi Germany saw it as a temporary and cynical expedient did not obviate its utility in the short term.)

The seeds of the tacit understanding were planted in a discreet hint dropped by the Soviet assistant military attaché in Berlin to Reichsmarschall Göering on 28 March 1940. Soviet border troops, the attaché remarked, were under standing orders 'not to fire on the German planes flying over Soviet territory so long as such flights do not occur frequently'. For a year, it appears, the Luftwaffe exercised this grant of surveillance within the stated bounds of moderation. But in both April and June 1941, on the eve of the German attack on Russia, the Soviet Government complained of the excessive frequency of German overflights, thereby admitting both the norm and its infringement.[8]

For its part, the Soviet Government was equally engaged, with tacit German consent, in aerial surveillance of the German lines. Confirmation of this is provided in a directive from the High Command of the German Armed Forces to Army Group B of 19 March 1941 in which orders were given to begin the construction of defensive works and fortifications on a large scale along the Soviet border as a concealment of Germany's offensive preparations. The directive continued that special attention was required to give 'the enemy's air reconnaissance the opportunity to recognize the positions being built and to photograph [them]'.[9] One month later the German High Command noted almost daily border violations by Soviet planes but confirmed that *standing orders* 'for the exercise of the utmost restraint nevertheless continue in force'.[10]

What can happen when an espionage incident gets out of hand can be seen from a recent episode in Soviet–American relations. The incident was precipitated in June 1978 when the United States FBI, amid a blaze of publicity, arrested two Soviet citizens employed by the United Nations and charged them with trying to buy secret US naval warfare documents. A decision by the Justice Department to prosecute the two on espionage charges was strongly opposed by the State Department which argued that the Russians should have been quietly expelled, rather than arrested and prosecuted, even though they did not possess diplomatic status and immunity. President Carter, it is said, was warned that prosecution would be interpreted by the Soviet Union as a breach of the 'unwritten rules' of espionage and would 'disturb the larger framework of . . . détente with the Soviets'.

Retaliation for infringement of the rules soon followed. Soviet police, in an act seriously affecting US–Soviet relations, dragged an American businessman from his car on a Moscow street and charged him with currency violations. In the end the inevitable exchange of the American for the two Russians followed. Although domestic American legal procedures had been satisfied, in foreign policy terms nothing was accomplished. As a State Department official reportedly summed up: 'All it did was trigger an incident that unnecessarily tied up much of the US government, including the President and the Secretary of State, in a wasteful and enervating effort to try and undo the damage.'[11] It is precisely this kind of internal and external disruption that rules of the game are intended to avoid.

Superpower relations in general have provided ample scope for tacit regulation. Poised between bitter worldwide rivalry and the exigencies of at least minimal coexistence in the thermonuclear age, the Soviet Union and the United States have had extensive recourse to tacit rules of accommodation covering, first, regional involvement – the exercise of power – beyond their own borders and, second, the restraint of competition should regional curbs prove ineffective.

The basic tacit rule of superpower relations is what Richard Falk calls the exclusive 'exercise of supervisory intervention' by the hegemonial power in its own sphere of influence. At one time, particularly in the period before the First World War, states felt no inhibitions about reaching formal agreements on the division of influence. Contemporary norms of international law enshrined in the United Nations Charter, including absolute respect for the national sovereignty and self-determination of all states, regardless of size and location, together with the formal prohibition on the nondefensive use of military force, have precluded any explicit acknowledgement of the rule and dictated its tacit form.[12] President Ford indiscreetly expressed what is usually left unspoken when he actually admitted that although American intervention in South America exceeded the bounds of legality, it could nonetheless be considered as falling within the realm of the permissible. Reacting to allegations of US involvement in the overthrow of the Allende regime in Chile Ford declined 'to pass judgement on whether it is permitted or authorized under international law. It is a recognized fact that historically as well as presently such actions are taken in the best interest of the countries involved.'[13]

In a recent analysis Edy Kaufman has demonstrated the ways in which each superpower tacitly acknowledges the supremacy of the other in its own sphere of influence. First there is 'the relative ease with which military intervention is carried out within the spheres of influence'. Active help to anti-government invasions, as in Guatemala in 1954 and Cuba in 1961, and even the participation of United States troops, as in the 1965 invasion of Santo Domingo, produced, at the most, a verbal reaction from the Soviet Union. Similarly, Soviet intervention in East Germany in 1953, Hungary in 1956 and Czechoslovakia in 1968, produced deep humanitarian distress in Washington but an abstention from any practical reaction and the studied avoidance of any behaviour that might be considered provocative. Only three weeks after the Czech invasion President Johnson declared in a speech his hope that the 'setback' would only be 'very temporary'.

A second way in which each superpower tacitly acknowledges the other's sphere of influence is by restricting its overt intervention in that area to the realm of the verbal and rhetorical. (At the level of covert operations, different rules of the game apply.) Ideological declarations about the 'victims of communist aggression/imperialist exploitation' are balanced by the reservation that active intervention is simply not a practical proposition. Thus Dean Rusk admitted that 'our capacity to influence events and trends within the Communist world is very limited. But it is our policy to do what we can to encourage evolution in the Communist world towards national independence and open societies.' On the whole the Soviet Union has also been abstemious in its interference in Central and South America. Its conduct towards Allende's Chile was cautiously circumspect. The gravity of the Cuban crisis was, of course, a direct result of Soviet infringement of the rule. Several analysts have tried to account for this aberration by arguing that errors of American signalling may have projected the impression that the United States would not resist incursion, and hence unintentionally precipitated the ultimate crisis. Soviet intervention in Cuba emphasizes that the infringement of a rule is far from inconceivable. But if it is infringed the delinquent should be fully aware of the potential risks involved.

Finally, mutual recognition by the superpowers of the preponderance of the other in its own sphere of influence finds subtle expression in the low priority given to discussion of these areas on the agenda of Soviet-American summit conferences. As Kaufman argues:

> While other problems are regarded by the superpowers as being crucial and are discussed, the lot of the 'satellites' and periphery countries is left untouched. This legitimation by omission, by tacit acceptance, or by indirect compliance with the rigid doctrines of the superpowers' right to protect their spheres of direct influence, is a primary requirement for the maintenance of quasi-absolute rule and also discourages many secondary powers from adopting a challenging attitude.[14]

Spheres of influence have contributed to international stability because they regulate behaviour in areas of competition outside the bounds of formal jurisdiction where the possibility of misunderstanding is correspondingly greater. It is no accident that some of the gravest threats to international peace have arisen in areas where a clear definition of great power influence was lacking. Before the First World War the Ottoman Empire and the Balkan Peninsula were two such regions. In the Ottoman Empire the absence of any agreed scheme of partition was compensated for by a collective acceptance of the *status quo*. Towards the end this tolerance was beginning to fray at the edges and the situation was widely perceived to contain the seeds of a great conflict. The test never came because Austro-Russian competition in the Balkans went out of control and dragged the rest of Europe over the abyss. In the Middle East, frequently called the 'Balkans of the contemporary period', superpower competition has threatened the same kind of disaster although so far diplomacy has succeeded in imposing restraints where any permanent system of demarcation has not. This reminds us that no single dimension of rule behaviour can ever, by itself, ensure stability. Ideally, peaceful relations between states should be supported by a network of interlocking rules each one of which combines with and strengthens the others.

Supplementing the 'exercise of supervisory intervention', therefore, has arisen a tacit code of conflict regulation between the superpowers. Writing in 1964, Edward McWhinney described three 'groundrules' of what he called 'nuclear age due process'. These were: (1) 'the duty to avoid "surprise" or sudden change in the inter-Bloc balance of power relationship'; (2) 'the principle of Economy in the use of power'; and (3) 'the principle of Mutual Self-Restraint'.

For its part the United States has been careful to maintain these principles. The avoidance of surprise (which may be something of a general norm in great power relations, even in earlier periods) is intended to preclude the sort of situation in which one superpower, faced by a sudden unexpected shock, might resort, through panic and miscalculation, to some action threatening a plunge into nuclear confrontation. For example, before the 1972 mining of Haiphong harbour the United States gave early notice of its impending move. The less surprising Washington's decisions were, Dr Kissinger writes, 'the less likely that Moscow would react by a spasm'.[15] Evidence can also be adduced of at least Soviet awareness of the rule. As we shall see below, the USSR was careful to warn the United States of possible Soviet intervention at the end of both the 1967 and 1973 Middle East wars. After the invasion of Afghanistan a senior Communist Party official was quoted as claiming that 'Carter was warned about the situation and knew of its possible outcome'.[16] Whether true or not, this suggests Soviet acknowledgement of the need to avoid surprises.

McWhinney sees the resolution of the 1962 Cuba crisis as an instance of the working of principles (2) and (3). While American restraint in crisis situations has surely been a prominent feature of its policy since the first Berlin crisis of 1948–9, Soviet adherence to McWhinney's ground-rules has been more problematic. On the whole it has been the Soviet Union that has initiated superpower confrontation; it is hard to see the Afghanistan invasion as anything other than a brutal infringement of all three principles of 'nuclear age due reason'. During periods of relaxation and American vigilance, Soviet policy has recognized the need to avoid a continual probing for advantage. Indeed the 1972 Joint Declaration on Basic Principles signed by Nixon and Brezhnev more or less paraphrased McWhinney's groundrules of a decade before and, according to Dr Kissinger, was actually a Soviet initiative. Since then Soviet self-denial has not been a notable feature of its global policy. Apparently, internal American disarray and loss of purpose provide conditions too tempting for the Soviet Union to desist from exploiting.

Although McWhinney's rules tend often to have been more honoured in the breach than in the observance by the Soviet Union, Phil Williams makes a stronger case for two more minimal and less ambitious tacit rules of crisis conduct.[17] The first of these is the superpowers' unwillingness to initiate the use of deliberate violence against one another. Williams argues, that from the time of the Berlin crisis onwards, each side has been 'immensely careful to avoid any action that might invite a violent response from the opponent'. The instruments of the Berlin crisis – blockade and airlift – involved a studied abstention from moves likely to risk hostilities. All subsequent Soviet pressure over Berlin has been equally circumspect. The United States has also been meticulous in observance of this rule, most obviously in the Cuba crisis when the options of an invasion or air strike were ruled out as risking the lives of Russian troops. Thus, since the onset of the Cold War, and despite confrontation in a series of crises, both superpowers have maintained the pattern of prudence in the use of force and successfully avoided even low-level trials of arms.

Williams's second tacit rule of crisis behaviour is that of non-intervention in local disputes between client states.

During these latter conflicts the superpowers have generally stood on the sidelines and, although prepared to make bellicose statements and vigorous gestures of support for their clients, have been equally if less obviously active in urging caution and restraint upon them. Most important, they have been unwilling to run on the field and join the mêlée – particularly where it was felt that the opposing superpower might do the same. Attempts to influence events indirectly have not been without their dangers or their frustrations, but the superpowers have regarded this as eminently preferable to being sucked into a violent clash with each other.

As Williams correctly notes, the Middle East crisis between, on the one hand, Moscow's clients Syria and (until 1973) Egypt and, on the other hand, Washington's client Israel, has held out the greatest danger of drawing the superpowers into direct confrontation and possible conflict. Neither in 1967 nor in 1973 did this occur. However, on both occasions the termination of fighting was accompanied by Soviet threats of intervention. On 10 June 1967, the day Israel captured the key Syrian town of Kuneitra and completed all its operational objectives, the United States was warned over the hot line that the USSR would take 'necessary actions, including military' unless Israel unconditionally halted operations within the next few hours. Later that evening both Israel and Syria accepted the Security Council's cease-fire call. To deter Soviet intervention President Johnson ordered the movement of the Sixth Fleet towards the Syrian coast. In 1973 the pattern was essentially repeated: on 24 October, several hours *after* a second cease-fire had come into effect (the first cease-fire of 22 October had not held) the Soviet Union menacingly called for intervention 'by both Powers, and if this were not possible, by the Soviet Union alone'. Four divisions of Soviet airborne troops were on the alert and Soviet naval concentrations in the Mediterranean were on the increase. In deterrence of this threat US forces, including units with nuclear weapons, were put on alert throughout most of the world.[18]

In both 1967 and 1973 Soviet warnings of intervention were carefully timed to coincide with the final stages of hostilities when a military resolution had already appeared and threats were perceived to the home base of the client: in 1967 the road to Damascus lay open; in 1973 Cairo was vulnerable and the Egyptian Third Army surrounded. Thus Soviet warnings were as much deterrent moves as active preparations for intervention and were calculated to achieve, or at least appear to achieve, maximum impact on Israeli decisions to cease hostilities. Considerable credit could be expected to redound to Moscow's benefit in the Arab world. (It is worth noting that the same strategem of the 'threat that could not fail' was used by the Soviet Union at the time of the Anglo-French Suez operation of 1956 and during the ill-fated Bay of Pigs episode of 1961.) At the same time Soviet passivity, especially if Israeli threats had eventuated, would have seriously damaged her reputation as an ally. Firm American responses underlined the prohibition on unilateral intervention, created the necessary balance for a political accommodation between the superpowers and provided the Soviet Union with ample justification for holding back on its threatened action. Both crises, in short, appear as classic instances of the demonstrative manipulation of military force for political ends and do exemplify Williams's tacit norm.

A counter-example to the rule of non-intervention (in the Middle East dispute) which Williams overlooks is Soviet behaviour in the War of

Attrition. From the end of February 1970 Moscow began delivering SA-3 (anti-aircraft) missile systems to Egypt, installed and manned by Soviet crews. By the beginning of May Soviet pilots were participating operationally in the defence of Egypt. On 30 July 1970 five Soviet planes were downed in a clash with the Israel Air Force.[19] This intervention was undertaken in the full knowledge of its escalatory significance. Mohamed Heikal reports that when President Nasser of Egypt made his request in Moscow for Soviet assistance (in January 1970) Brezhnev did not conceal 'that this would be a step with serious international implications. It would provide all the making of a crisis between the Soviet Union and the United States.'[20]

Why, then, was the step taken? The answer is that the Nasser visit had brought home to the Soviet leadership that Israeli air raids deep inside Egypt (beginning on 7 January 1970) had swung the war in Israel's favour, that Egypt was facing military defeat and that an unpleasant choice had to be made between the dictates of superpower accommodation and support for an important client. Diplomatic efforts made by the Kremlin to persuade the United States to put a stop to Israeli bombing were unproductive. A Kosygin letter of 31 January warned that if Israel continued to bomb Egyptian territory, 'means' would be put at the disposal of the Arab states to 'rebuff the arrogant aggressor'.[21] This vague warning had no effect on President Nixon and deliveries of Phantom aircraft continued to Israel. Intervention then, to protect Egyptian civilian and military targets, was seen as the only way to prevent a further débâcle which would have ruined Soviet prestige. The fact that the Soviet umbrella shifted the strategic balance to Egypt's offensive advantage does not alter its defensive motive.

According to the Kissinger account, he, as National Security Adviser, was deeply disturbed at what he saw as 'a unique turn of Soviet policy – never before have the Soviets put their own forces in combat jeopardy for the sake of a non-Communist government'. Other United States Government agencies blamed the development on Israeli intransigence and were not inclined to confront Moscow over it. An American decision to freeze aircraft deliveries to Israel, announced only a few days after the Administration had learned of the despatch of Soviet combat personnel to Egypt, signalled acquiescence in the move. Other statements legitimized the Soviet presence.[22]

The lessons of the 1970 episode in terms of Williams's thesis are threefold. First, there is evidence that a tacit rule of non-intervention was known by both sides to exist. Second, the rule was infringed by Moscow in full awareness of the possible consequences only as a final resort to save a client from defeat after other expedients had failed. Third, the infringement was effectively complied with by Washington and thereby legitimized. The episode, therefore, should not be seen as a refutation of the non-intervention rule, but as a demonstration of the limits of its application.

In general the Middle East conflict has provided fertile ground for the local contestants to evolve their own tacit rules of the game. Formal principles of good-neighbourliness have been ruled out by Arab reluctance to acknowledge the legitimacy of the State of Israel. On the other hand, except in the short periods of open warfare, the necessities of living side by side have impelled the emergence of minimal norms of mutual sufferance.

After the Six-Day War of 1967, in which Jordan's West Bank was captured by Israel, an unprecedented arrangement evolved between the two states, based on the organic economic and social link between the Arab populations on the two banks of the Jordan river. At a formal level no diplomatic relations existed, as they never had existed, between Israel and Jordan. Informally, goods, tourists, students and family visitors passed over the 'open bridges'. King Hussein was permitted to maintain links with Arab notables and local government officials to the extent of even continuing to pay towards their salaries. On the tragic death of the King's wife in a plane crash in February 1977, delegations from the West Bank were warmly received in Amman. Such a relaxed *modus vivendi*, accompanied by 'good manners in political statements' and a peaceful border, almost completely free of terrorist incursions, was long preferred by the Israeli Government to a negotiated interim settlement of the kind reached with Egypt and Syria. 'If we change the current situation for diplomatic haggling for another arrangement', Israeli Defence Minister Peres commented in 1976, 'we might lose what we already have in hand.'[23] In a formal agreement Jordan, conscious of a critical pan-Arab opinion, could never have agreed to such far-reaching contacts. The informal understanding avoided the need to even solicit approval and bypassed official Arab taboos against relations with the Jewish State. Had both sides attempted to formalize their understanding much wider issues of principle would necessarily have come under review. As long as there was no possibility of resolving these wider issues it was better to leave them alone. Hypocrisy is not just the compliment paid by vice to virtue: it may also be the price paid by vice to preserve virtue.

Even Syria and Israel, the bitterest enemies in the Middle East conflict, have developed tacit groundrules to regulate their relations. During and after the Lebanese Civil War of 1975–6, for example, both parties successfully steered clear of war, in a situation fraught with danger, by a tacit process of mutual accommodation based on a temporary convergence of interests.

Syria, on the one side, had become involved in the civil war because of anxiety at its domestic and strategic implications. Israel, on the other side, wished to prevent a Palestinian victory in the civil war which would have brought the Lebanon into the ranks of the confrontation states. During 1975 Syria became involved in energetic diplomatic efforts to bring about a ceasefire as a first step to a settlement of the dispute between the warring factions which included a so-called left wing supported by the Palestine Liberation Organization and a so-called right wing supported by Christian groups. Israel's strategy was to issue veiled warnings to Syria not to intervene directly since this would lead, it was believed, to a Palestinian-controlled Lebanon allied to Syria against Israel.[24] The fear of the American State Department was that the intervention of either Syria or Israel would draw in the other party and set off an overall Middle East war.[25]

Throughout 1975 Syrian understanding of Israeli sensibilities permitted the preservation of an uneasy *modus vivendi*.[26] As ceasefire after ceasefire broke down this became increasingly difficult to maintain and Syria began to express open fears of a partition of the Lebanon which might create a Christian enclave possibly allied to Israel. In January 1976 Syria sent units of the Syrian-controlled Palestine Liberation Army into Lebanon, thus avoiding a direct confrontation with the Israeli prohibition, in order to impose a ceasefire and permit the implementation of a political settlement negotiated with the opposing factions. With the United States apparently acting as a go-between, Israel was assured that the PLA would be withdrawn once stability was re-established. Israel decided on a policy of restraint while continuing to stress that overt and direct Syrian intervention would be unacceptable.[27] She had, in effect, accepted, albeit nervously, a modification of the existing rules of the game, reassured that Syria – which could not be certain of the support of an unfriendly Egypt – still wished to avoid a military confrontation.

At this point in the civil war an extraordinary shift took place in the Lebanese political constellation. With the breakdown of the January 1976 ceasefire the Syrian Government was driven to the conclusion that it was the PLO which constituted the greatest obstacle to the achievement of a political settlement. The Syrian-backed Palestine Liberation Army was therefore sent against its nominal comrades-in-arms, the Palestine Liberation Organization, creating a tacit confluence of Syrian–Israeli interests. Now committed beyond the point of recall, the Syrian Government, again using the good offices of the State Department, decided to send its own troops into the civil war. Israel gave her consent to this innovation, in the face of domestic criticism, defining a 'red line', beyond which Syria was warned not to advance, made up of geographical and quantitative elements which were left publicly vague.[28] By now it was clear that both Syria and Israel, with American help, had successfully worked out a pattern of rules to regulate their interests in the civil war, which could be adjusted to the changing situation. In June Syrian troop levels were reported to have reached a strength of 5,000 to 6,000. Israel continued to exercise restraint, government ministers refusing to be drawn about the 'red line' of Israeli tolerance except to say that it was apt to shift with the changing circumstances; it depended on the motive for Syrian intervention, the size of Syrian forces, the duration of their stay and their location.[29] Speaking to the Foreign Relations Committee of the House of Representatives, Dr Kissinger gave a revealing account of the tacit accommodation between the two enemies. He confirmed that there existed 'an understanding in both Syria and Israel of the limits beyond which the dangers of escalation may become unmanageable'. No *agree-*

ment existed, there was 'no communication as such' between the two countries, nor were messages being passed on. The United States, however, was giving its judgement 'as to what various parties are likely to do, and to try to suggest directions within which they might find common positions'.[30]

And so the situation and the rules governing it continued to develop. Throughout the latter half of 1976 and up to the final ceasefire in Lebanon, Israel continued to avoid direct intervention in the civil war though assistance to Christian forces in the south and the opening of the Lebanese–Israeli border for humanitarian purposes stressed a commitment to maintaining a buffer zone free of Syrian and, as far as possible, Palestinian influence. For the most part Syria tacitly recognized this zone and avoided any configuration of forces which Israel might interpret as threatening. Publicly, the existence of any kind of understanding was denied; scorn was poured on the very suggestion.[31] Had Israel climbed down from her policy of threatening to use force to bar the south to the Syrian army, Syria would doubtless have extended her area of control; there was no question of the tacit understanding possessing cooperative overtones. It was simply that as long as it was in the mutual interest of both sides to maintain their truce, the Israeli 'red line' constituted an available focus for the coordination of restraint.

Chapter seven

The spirit of agreements

The concept of the spirit of an agreement is a familiar one to the student of diplomacy. Surprisingly, there has been scant treatment of the subject though, as we shall see, its operative significance may be considerable as a guide to expectations. The spirit of an agreement can be considered as the tacit dimension of a formal written accord. As such it is located on our continuum at the point at which negotiated (written and verbal) agreements overlap with tacit understandings arrived at without formal negotiation.

One can distinguish two related meanings of the concept. The first is the understood interpretation placed on the written text. To this aspect of the problem the literature on international law has directed adequate attention. The Vienna Convention on the Law of Treaties in Articles 31 and 32 identifies certain general rules for treaty interpretation. Its key provision is that 'a treaty shall be interpreted in good faith in accordance with the ordinary meaning to be given to the terms of the treaty in their context and in the light of its object and purpose'. According to commentators this entails, *inter alia*, that the meaning of a clause must emerge in the context of the treaty as a whole, its language must be understood in the light of contemporary usage, obvious errors of drafting are to be disregarded and so on. 'Context' includes instruments drawn up in connection with the treaty. Subsequent agreements, practices and provisions of international law relating to the treaty are also to be taken into account.[1]

Adequate as guidelines for the narrow interpretation of a text, the Vienna Convention does not deal with that broader, tacit dimension which goes beyond the 'ordinary meaning' of the words themselves. Nor does most of the specialist literature. This second sense of the spirit of an agreement refers to the general meaning or intent of the document derived from the constituent convergence of interests or purposes underlying its creation. From this point of view the plain text is simply the outward expression of a more fundamental meeting of minds. The 'textualist' approach denies that there is any added dimension beyond the 'plain meaning' of the document itself. Certainly to admit its existence raises countless difficulties for the jurist. However, the textualist view, whatever its academic merits, does not reflect the political reality which is most definitely that there is such a thing as the spirit of an agreement in a wider sense.

As a concept of law, it should be remarked, the textualist view has not gone completely unchallenged. An original and controversial critique has been put forward by McDougal, Lasswell and Miller. Arguing that the overall context in which it was concluded, rather than the text alone, provides the key to the meaning of an agreement, a radical approach is proposed to treaty interpretation: 'interpret the focal agreement according to the expectations shared by the parties during the course of their interaction, including the making and performance of the agreement, as indicated by the context considered as a whole'.[2] The authors' stress on the 'genuine shared expectations' of the signatories opens the way to giving due weight to the spirit of an agreement in its wider sense.

As a point of departure it will be useful to distinguish between treaties which embody transactions of various kinds such as commercial contracts and exchanges of territory, the terms of which are put into effect by the performance of certain actions within a defined period; and treaties laying down open-ended principles of conduct which do not simply entail the implementation of set tasks ('executed' as opposed to 'executory' agreements). In the first case the problem is one of strict interpretation. Only in the second case does the question of the wider spirit of the agreement arise.

A number of considerations emphasize the salience of the concept of the spirit of an agreement. First, a rigid attitude to the letter of the written text fails to take into account the needs of applying an agreement in circumstances which are either different from those existing at the time of its conclusion, or could not have been foreseen. It is true that changing circumstances may invalidate an agreement altogether. But if the political confluence which underlay the agreement in the first place has not altered, then the problem is not one of abrogating the accord but of adjusting it to fit shifting requirements. Without the political will to breathe life into the text, it will inevitably become a dead letter. And the moment we talk about a political will reflecting a congruence of interests we must acknowledge the validity of the spirit of an agreement.

A second reason for flexibility is that a written text, however carefully drafted, is still, inevitably, a general statement of intentions. It can only be 'fleshed out' and given specific reference when its application becomes relevant. There may also be cases where the written terms are left deliberately vague for political reasons, for instance to avoid the embarrassment associated with a commitment directed against a third party.

Finally there may be an aspect of an agreement not written into the text in so many words because it seemed self-evident at the time or was in fact one of the assumptions underlying the conclusion of the agreement. If an accord was concluded out of mutual fear of a third party, even though it is neither explicitly nor even tacitly directed against that party, this can hardly be articulated. It is still part of the political fabric of the accord.

Before the First World War, Anglo-Russian relations were regulated by the convention of 1907. Not all its provisions were contained in the written text. Underlying the entire agreement was the assumption that a regularization of Anglo-Russian affairs in the limited areas of Persia (Iran), Afghanistan and Tibet would lay the groundwork for a wider understanding between the two powers with respect to European security and the German problem. Although opposition to Germany constituted the philosophical basis of the treaty, this is nowhere mentioned. In fact the word 'Germany' does not appear at all. The wider significance – the spirit – of the treaty is implicit not so much in the bare text as in the mere fact of the agreement and its historical timing.

At a detailed level, Article 1 of the Convention committed Britain to desist from seeking or supporting third parties from seeking commercial, including railway, concessions in a defined Russian sphere of influence in northern Persia. (Article 2 dealt with a British sphere of interest in the south.) What was not stated, though it was implied, was that Russian predominance in its own sphere was an exclusive one and was not to be shared with others, especially not the joint rival Germany. Futhermore the Anglo-Russian division of Persia naturally entailed that the signatories had a claim to be consulted on general issues affecting the arrangement, such as negotiations with a third party on matters concerning Persia. These two assumptions were contained in the spirit and not the letter of the treaty.

Any doubt that there might have been about the detailed application of the agreement should have been removed by a conversation of 17 October 1910 on the eve of a summit meeting of the Russian and German Emperors in Potsdam. The Russian Acting Minister for Foreign Affairs had confirmed to the British Ambassador that the Baghdad Railway (the German project to build a railway down from Turkey to the Persian Gulf) would be on the agenda at Potsdam; more specifically, the question of the junction of a branch line running from Baghdad to Khanikin (on the Persian–Mesopotamian border) with the future Persian railways. Buchanan had then pointed out that His Majesty's Government of course hoped that he would keep them fully informed of anything that passed regarding the Baghdad Railway and Persia, and that he would conclude nothing without consulting them. The Russian Minister had concurred, stating that his Government 'would insist that Germany should seek no concessions of a territorial character, including railways, in the Russian sphere'. Any railway to Teheran would be built by Russia.[3]

It came as an unpleasant surprise, therefore, when the British Government were informed at the turn of 1911 that, in contradiction to explicit recent assurances, Russia was about to conclude an agreement with Germany consenting to (1) a railway from Baghdad to Khanikin to be built by Germany; and (2) a line to be built by Russia *with German assistance* from Khanikin to Teheran. As the British Ambassador stated, Sazanov, the Russian Foreign Minister, had 'made proposals respecting Persia and the Baghdad Railway without consulting our views or wishes. He was, it is true, not bound to do so by the terms of the Anglo-Russian Agreement, but he has, none the less, laid himself open to the reproach of not having observed the spirit of the tacit understanding according to which no arrangement was to be concluded with Germany respecting the Baghdad Railway by any one of the parties to the Triple Entente, until the other two had also come to terms with her.'[4]

It can be seen from this evaluation, fully shared by the Foreign Secretary, that the tacit dimension of the 1907 Convention had a far-reaching influence on the formation of British expectations. Basing their case 'less on the letter than on the spirit' of the accord, the British Government pressed their opposition to German participation in the Teheran line with righteous determination. Eventually, albeit grudgingly, the Russians were obliged to concede the British right to be consulted before any agreement on the Baghdad Railway and the branch-line to Teheran was concluded. They were in no doubt that, whatever the formal legal position, the political implications of a refusal to accept British claims would be critical. The Russian Ambassador in London, for one, acknowledged that although the Anglo-Russian Convention did not afford any basis for the British protest, German involvement would call its 'political effect' (i.e. Russian hopes for wider cooperation) into question:

According to the whole spirit of the Convention of 1907, Russian influence in Northern Persia is intended to be exclusive, just as English influence in the South. A railway line, under German control, would give this power first-class political influence in Persia. Therefore, England would also have to reckon with Germany at Teheran. ... Such a renunciation would ... give the *coup de grâce* to the Anglo-Russian policy in Persia.[5]

In the end, the Russo-German Agreement of 19 August 1911 took full account of the British position. True, negotiations had been drawn out and coordination not always complete. The 1907 Convention had nevertheless provided Britain with justifiable grounds for insisting that the rules of the game in Persia be maintained by Russia. Russia could hardly ignore this appeal without undermining the entire basis of its relationship with Britain. The British appeal and the Russian response fully demonstrates the very real existence of the tacit element, the spirit, of the more formal treaty.

A second example, in this case of the infringement of the spirit of an agreement, relates to Anglo-Italian relations at the time of the Spanish Civil War. In November 1936, after a period of tension between the two states, both sides concluded that the time had arrived to reach a *modus vivendi* in their relations. At the beginning of December, negotiations were set in train which finally resulted in a 'declaration' published on 2 January 1937, known as the Gentleman's Agreement. According to the terms of this understanding, which was not intended to possess the binding legal status of a treaty, both Governments recognized and undertook to respect each other's 'vital interest' in the Mediterranean and disclaimed any desire to modify the territorial *status quo* in the area. Finally in a cloudy and generalized clause it was 'agreed to discourage any activities liable to impair the good relations which it is the object of the present declaration to consolidate'.[6]

By this latter clause the British Government hoped, at the very least, to encourage Mussolini to desist from those activities, ranging from anti-British propaganda to active intervention in the Spanish Civil War, which were a cause of such embarrassment. Clearly no formal agreement to this effect could ever be published because Italy would never admit that she was engaged in 'unfriendly activities'. Nor could an explicit verbal assurance be given, for Italy was still officially a member of the Non-Intervention Committee set up in September 1936 to monitor and discourage intervention in Spain. Nevertheless, though the agreement was ambiguous, it was obvious what Britain had in mind. After all, it was the uninterrupted flow of mostly Italian arms and 'volunteers' to the rebels which had been the main cause of the deterioration in Anglo-Italian relations and had particularly incensed sectors of British public opinion. To underline the point the British Government, in separate notes of 26 December 1936 – that is, towards the end of the negotiations with Italy – urged the Governments of Germany, Portugal, Russia and Italy to ban the movement of volunteers to Spain.[7] Further evidence that the British Government considered a restriction by Italy on her intervention in Spain to be written between the lines of the Gentleman's Agreement is provided by a report from the United States Ambassador in Rome of 29 December 1936. In it he quoted the opinion of the British Embassy

that the conclusion of this accord will create a favourable atmosphere in which it may be possible to work out a more satisfactory agreement as regards Spain. While it was not actually said, the impression was gained that with the improvement of the relations between the two countries Great Britain anticipates that Italy will be willing to play a more active role in the Non-Intervention Committee.[8]

Almost immediately the Italian Government violated what Eden describes in his memoirs as 'the spirit of the agreement'. On 4 January 1937, two days after the publication of the declaration, the British Foreign Office learned of the arrival of further large consignments of Italian volunteers in Spain. It seemed to Eden 'only too likely that Mussolini had used our negotiations as a cover plan for his further intervention'. He 'knew perfectly well that this action must impair the good relations which it is the object of the present declaration to consolidate'.[9] It was possible, Eden informed the French Ambassador on 5 January, 'that these men had left Italy before the signature of the agreement. But the organization of these reinforcements did not appear any the less like a most singular way of conforming to the spirit of the talks then under way.'[10] The result of this perceived demonstration of Italian bad faith was to put an end, for the time being, to attempts to restore Anglo-Italian relations. The Gentleman's Agreement remained stillborn.

It could be argued that the collapse of the agreement was due to an honest misunderstanding. But it seems highly unlikely that Rome was not well aware of British expectations and the fact that there could be no

détente without a solution to the problem of intervention. Perhaps Mussolini believed that he could have his cake and eat it, since Eden would be
too embarrassed to admit that he had been deceived. A *Times* report from
Berlin of 7 January 1937, which may have been inspired by Italy, noted
that some circles had taken the declaration to mean that England would
be more apt to condone intervention in Spain as a result of Italy's renunciation of territorial demands.

Whatever Italian motives, the following conclusion clearly emerges. It
is one thing to recognise that the philosophical premises and the detailed
application of an accord in future unknown circumstances must of necessity be confined to the tacit spirit of an agreement. It is quite another
thing to leave an essential provision of the understanding unstated, however tempting the prospect of an improvement in the atmosphere of relations. In dealing with such an unreliable character as Mussolini, Eden
should never have left so much on trust. By doing so he left himself open
to being at the best misunderstood and at the worst doublecrossed.

A far more successful example of the working of the spirit of an
agreement can be found in postwar Finnish–Soviet relations. The decisive juridical documents governing this relationship are the 1947 Treaty
of Peace and particularly the 1948 Treaty of Friendship, Cooperation and
Mutual Assistance. So much has changed, however, since these treaties
were concluded that their contemporary significance and application go
well beyond the minimal and often outdated details of the text. Hence the
operational rules of the game guiding the conduct of the parties have
grown up in the tacit dimension of the spirit of the two agreements.
'Besides treaties', former Finnish President Paasikivi pointed out, 'among
individuals as well as among nations, there are unwritten laws of neigh-
bourliness and good will which also guide relations between neighbours.'[11] Why and how these 'unwritten laws' have grown up and their
connection with the basic texts will be seen below.

Article 20 of the Treaty of Peace commits Finland to cooperate fully
'with the Allied and Associated Powers with a view to ensuring that
Germany may not be able to take steps outside German territory towards
rearmament'. Within a very short time of the conclusion of the 1947
treaty the terms 'Allied and Associated Powers' and 'Germany' ceased to
have the original meaning assigned to them. Both wartime allies and
defeated Germany split up into two opposing camps. Given Finland's
geographical location and the circumstances of her surrender in 1944 it
was only to be expected that the Finnish Government, interpreting Article
20 within the spirit of the agreement, would largely identify the 'Allied
Powers' with the Soviet Union and 'Germany' with Western Germany.
The operative conclusion has been that Finnish foreign policy has steered
well clear of any conduct that might conceivably be viewed as a contribution to West German rearmament or even a strengthening of the latter's
political position. At the same time the sensitivities, real or imagined, of
the Soviet Union towards Western Germany, have had to be scrupulously
taken into account.

Such 'weighted' interpretation comes out even more clearly in the Finnish exegesis of Article 3 of the Peace Treaty which prohibited the signatories from entering into alliances directed against the other party. In practice this has simply meant that Finland has not felt able to join any international organization towards which the Soviet Union holds a negative attitude. Not surprisingly this has ruled out, above all, membership of NATO. But the principle has also been extended to cover abstention from economic projects of which Moscow disapproved, such as the European Recovery Programme (the Marshall Plan) and the Organization of European Economic Cooperation. Clearly such interpretation of Article 3 goes far beyond the 'ordinary meaning' of the clause conventionally required by international law.

For many years it was understood that EEC membership for Finland was also unacceptable to the USSR. With the enlargement of the Community in 1972 and a softening of Soviet hostility towards that body Finland was able to negotiate a free trade agreement strictly limited to the lowering of trade barriers but excluding either membership or association. In the parliamentary debate on ratification it was carefully stressed that the agreement did not affect Finland politically and would not alter 'earlier international obligations'. Were Finnish–Soviet relations damaged, Finland would cancel the agreement. A balancing accord was simultaneously negotiated with the Communist Council for Mutual Economic Assistance.[12]

The central component of Finland's foreign policy since the war has been the maintenance of friendly relations with the USSR. Article 5 of the 1948 Friendship Treaty affirms the 'determination' of the signatories 'to act in the spirit of cooperation and friendship with the object of further promoting and consolidating economic and cultural ties'. In itself this clause could mean everything or nothing; it is precisely the kind of generalized affirmation that can only acquire its operative meaning within the context of ongoing relations. In practice Article 5 has been interpreted by Presidents Paasikivi and Kekkonen in a very broad and active way. Mutual trade and other links have been maintained at a high level. Propaganda and literature hostile to the Soviet Union or even communist ideology have been kept within strict bounds. A continuous effort has been made to avoid any kind of action which could be interpreted as a sign of hostility to Moscow.

Article 2 of the Friendship Treaty has given rise to some of the most interesting problems. According to its terms: 'The High Contracting Parties will consult each other in the event of a threat of military attack . . . being ascertained.' It is to be read together with Article 1, which calls for Soviet assistance to Finland in the event of German aggression on Finland or on the USSR through Finnish territory. Under one interpretation this might mean that an arbitrary Soviet announcement of the existence of a German threat would oblige Finland to enter into consultations with a view to the provision of Soviet military assistance – in effect, occupation on the lines of Moscow's East European satellites.

For obvious reasons this version was rejected by President Paasikivi who argued that both parties had to recognize the existence of a threat of aggression before consultations could take place. This reading was neither accepted nor challenged by the Soviet Union for many years.[13]

The decisive test came in the 'Note crisis' of October–November 1961. In an atmosphere of European tension over Berlin and Soviet anxiety over the possible results of the forthcoming Finnish presidential elections, a Soviet note was delivered on 30 October asking for joint military consultations 'in view of the threat from Western Germany'. No one was aware of the existence of any such 'threat'. Had Helsinki conceded the assumption underlying this note it would have had far-reaching implications for its independent and neutral position. President Kekkonen, therefore, in a tough meeting with Khrushchev, reiterated his Government's traditional interpretation of Article 2 and pointed out the destabilising implications of military consultations on Scandinavian opinion. In a joint communiqué following their talks (the Novosibirsk statement of 24 November 1961) the Finnish view 'that the USSR should not insist on its proposals for consultations' was set out, followed by Khrushchev's declaration 'that the Soviet Government found it possible to postpone for the time being the military consultations it had suggested'.[14] In the opinion of former Finnish Ambassador at the UN Max Jakobson, this statement effectively conceded the Finnish position: a Soviet claim that a threat existed had failed to trigger consultations. Even more positive from the Finnish point of view was the implied suggestion that it was up to Finland to take the initiative for further consultations. 'This amounted to a reinterpretation of the Finnish–Soviet Treaty in a direction that further strengthened Finland's neutrality.'[15]

In recent years Article 2 has come under renewed contention with the publication in 1976 of a controversial book on Finnish–Soviet relations, obviously inspired by the Soviet Government. Greater emphasis is placed on the military aspects of the 1948 treaty, implying that it has the characteristics of a military cooperation agreement.[16] Were this to be accepted by Finland it would seriously compromise her neutral aspirations. And so the debate on the spirit of the treaty continues; an argument over the very substance of Finland's place in the world.

Chapter eight

Rules established by nonbinding agreements

'Nonbinding agreement' sounds like a contradiction in terms. What is in fact referred to are understandings not intended by the parties involved to possess legal force. These include oral promises, agreed records of conversations containing assurances and various kinds of documents. Not referred to here, it should be stressed, are agreements such as those of Yalta and Potsdam which functioned as binding treaties to all intents and purposes but which are controversial from a juridical point of view, or so-called treaties in 'simplified form' which are legally binding agreements with the difference that they are negotiated and ratified by an abbreviated procedure intended to facilitate their rapid entry into force.[1]

International lawyers tend to feel uncomfortable with nonbinding agreements. If an understanding creates obligations, they argue, it must, *ipso facto*, be a treaty. If it is not a treaty then it cannot create obligations.[2] However, as we found with the spirit of agreements, political reality flies in the face of legal purism. Nonbinding instruments, from the gentlemen's agreement to the final communiqué, are expedients central to the conduct of diplomacy which observably do form expectations and guide conduct; in short, create rules of the game.

Oscar Schachter, one of the editors of the *American Journal of International Law*, in an effort to rescue nonbinding agreements from their 'twilight' legal position, stresses that the absence of a legal obligation does not vitiate their political and moral force. He quotes Dr Kissinger's testimony that certain of the Sinai Disengagement Agreements of 1975 were 'not binding commitments of the United States' but that did 'not mean, of course, that the United States is morally or politically free to act as if they did not exist. On the contrary, they are important statements of diplomatic policy and engage the good faith of the United States as long as the circumstances that gave rise to them continue.'[3]

J.E.S. Fawcett is also of the view that such agreements create effective obligations and emphasizes their importance for 'the maintenance of international order'. He compares the relation between political and legal obligations to that between the moral obligations of individuals and private law contracts. 'International community life can be carried on only if common declarations of policy and agreements for the solution of common administrative and technical problems are adhered to and carried out. To the extent that they are broken or disregarded, international order breaks down. Their fulfilment is what international order means.'[4]

The difference between binding and nonbinding agreements, Schachter and Fawcett agree, is not in their working, since both accept the significance accorded to them in international relations. Two factors constitute the distinction: the first is that noncompliance with a nonbinding agreement would not be a ground for a claim for reparation or for judicial remedies. The second is that nonbinding agreements are not governed by international law.

Recourse to nonbinding agreement can be accounted for in various ways. Oral promises of greater or less significance are simply an inherent part of all human contact to which diplomacy is no exception. In the first instance they arise from the basic need to harmonize conduct and coordinate expectations in the short term over ongoing issues where written agreement is thought either to be superfluous or to indicate an insulting measure of mistrust. A request 'to put that in writing' is often meant and understood to imply doubt and unease.

Between friendly powers it is quite normal for preliminary or transitional agreements to take a purely oral form. Sometimes such understandings are incorporated in a written communiqué. Frequently they are not. If friends cannot rely on each other's word in their current transactions, all diplomacy might as well cease. Meeting General de Gaulle in Paris in November 1944, Churchill and his Foreign Secretary Eden discussed the postwar occupation of Germany. The British ministers accepted de Gaulle's wish that France be allotted a specific zone of occupation – a preliminary understanding later given more formal content at the Yalta Conference the following February.[5] Similarly, in discussions between the British and West German Governments in 1954 on the question of West Germany's entry into NATO, we find Adenauer anticipating the later formal arrangement, informing the British High Commissioner that his Government would be prepared voluntarily to undertake to limit its armed forces.[6] Such examples are common.

Short-term understandings of this kind can also be useful in fluid situations of potential conflict. At times like this actors need more than ever to know the limits of permissible behaviour in order to avoid unwitting and potentially disastrous violations of the vital interests of other parties. Efforts to arrive at more formal understanding in the midst of a swiftly unfolding situation would be counterproductively time-consuming and very likely fruitless. Events would overtake painstaking drafting. Sometimes short-term expediency requires rapid improvisation.

In the the last days of the Ogaden war between Somalia and Ethiopia in February–March 1978, with the Somali army on the verge of disintegration, the United States was able to avoid a dangerous confrontation with the USSR which was heavily backing the Ethiopian forces. As the Ethiopian army pushed towards the international frontier the United States Secretary of State declared that he had received assurances from Moscow that Somali territory would be respected. The understanding was quickly confirmed by the Ethiopian Government. In return, it appears, Mogadishu agreed to withdraw its forces from areas of Ethiopia occupied the previous year. Thus crisis diplomacy succeeded in putting together a formula limiting the scope of the conflict; the simple and clear guidelines contained in the understanding proved quite adequate for defusing the immediate situation.[7]

Another reason for expressing agreement in purely verbal form is the need, especially of Western democratic governments, to avoid the possible complications and embarrassments of domestic debate. Written documents, however informal, have the unfortunate habit of leaking out to a hostile opposition. Totalitarian societies are better able to rely on secrecy and discretion. Assuring the German Ambassador in 1892 that Italy could feel reassured that any British Government 'was bound to help Italy in the event of an attack', Lord Roseberry, the newly appointed British Foreign Secretary, explained his wish to avoid a written assurance:

Failing the certainty of discretion in Rome, a written assurance was too dangerous, first because he was not yet sure of the consent of some of his colleagues, which for such a step he could not dispense with, and also because he personally must be prepared during the next session for questions by Labouchere and the rest of the Radicals on whatever engagements he might have with Italy. But if the state of things here were understood in Italy, there would be no need for anxiety on her part, even without a written assurance.[8]

According to Paul Reuter, gentlemen's agreements, which in their original meaning are verbal exchanges of promises, are neither legally nor even politically binding. They are simply 'concluded by governmental representatives in their own name without the intention of committing their respective states'.[9] This view cannot be left unchallenged. Clearly understandings reached by word of mouth between low-level officials are likely to be of doubtful validity. Yet verbal accords between leaders of states hardly come into the same category. A statesman conducting negotiations of international significance is not acting as a private individual. The only reason for him to arrive at a political understanding is to engage the state on whose behalf he is negotiating; his word is accepted as binding precisely because of the prerogatives of his political status and not by virtue of his private qualities. And if the promise of a statesman leads to modification of his country's policy, then he was self-evidently not acting as a private individual. It is true that there are examples of personal agreements (such as the abortive alliance agreed upon by Kaiser William and Tsar Nicholas at Björkö in 1905) which were later repudiated by their respective Governments. However the repudiation derived from political rather than procedural difficulties.

One of the more far-reaching gentlemen's agreements of contemporary history was the Churchill–Stalin 'percentages agreement' of October 1944 by which the Balkans were divided into British and Russian spheres of influence. The example counts against Reuter's view and also illustrates another reason for preferring an oral promise to a written accord: to minimize its apparent significance and evade the disapproval of third parties. As Churchill recalled, having jotted down on 'a half-sheet of paper' the respective degree of predominance which the parties were to have in the various countries, the British Prime Minister pushed the note across to Stalin. After a slight pause the latter ticked it with his blue pencil. A long silence followed. 'The pencilled paper lay in the centre of the table. At length I said, ''Might it not be thought rather cynical if it seemed we have disposed of these issues, so fateful to millions of people, in such an offhand manner? Let us burn the paper.'' ''No, you keep it,'' said Stalin'.[10]

The paper, of course, was in no sense a written document but was merely a 'visual aid' for Churchill to get his point across. Despite the casual appearance of the understanding, it was no improvisation. The British Government had been concerned for some months about the possibility of Soviet-British conflict in the Balkans in the postwar period but were inhibited by American distaste for 'old-style' spheres of influence agreements.[11] Thus the Churchill–Stalin verbal agreement would serve its essential purpose by mapping out the limits of each side's predominance and at the same time could be tactfully – and vaguely – presented to Roosevelt as something less than a fullblown accord. Moreover, Churchill probably believed that Stalin's verbal assurance was as likely to be as reliable as any formal document. The latter's record of treaty observance hardly inspired optimism. Whatever the form of the agreement enforcement would depend on Britain's determination to uphold her rights and interests.

Understandings possessing political rather than legal force may also take the form of a written document. Into this category come memoranda of understanding and joint communiqués or statements. Exchanges of letters, agreed minutes and declarations may or may not be legally binding, depending on whether the parties had the intention to create legal obligations.[12]

The joint communiqué or statement is an announcement published at the conclusion of diplomatic talks or following the official visit of the representative of one state to another. Its significance is considerable in the conduct of diplomacy. Contrary to appearances the communiqué may well be the outcome of lengthy deliberation, for every word and nuance is of the essence and will be meticulously evaluated by observers. Nevertheless, as a diplomatic expedient it is valuable, not so much for setting the seal on an arrangement – for this the formal treaty is better suited – but as a sort of benchmark, the definition of the 'state of the game' at a given point in time in a continuing process. To trace the development of a series of bilateral communiqués is very much to decipher the changing pattern of norms governing the relations between the parties over time.

The communiqué, then, is a primary instrument expressing the rules of the game between states at any given period. Broadly speaking, it may confirm the validity of the existing state of affairs, put them in a different light or even set out some new understanding. It may also reflect the current state of formal agreements. It need not confine itself to bilateral issues but may express the position of the parties on a wider international question.

Without the solemnity or sense of permanence associated with the formal treaty the communiqué may still constitute, in special cases, a decisively formative document. The Belgrade Communiqué of 1955 issued on the occasion of Khrushchev's visit to Yugoslavia, the terms of which have been periodically reaffirmed, has been considered almost sacrosanct by the Yugoslavs and really takes the place of a formal treaty. Indeed it is clear that Belgrade has preferred such a document in order not to renew the treaty relationship with Moscow established in 1945 and abrogated in 1949 following Tito's assertion of independence.

Another classic example of an innovative understanding which took the form of a joint statement is the Sino-American Shanghai Communiqué of February 1972. 'In no position', as both sides realized, 'to make formal agreements', the document was a remarkable attempt to set up, after years of hostility, a framework of rules or good manners within which further dialogue could take place between the People's Republic of China and the United States towards a solution of outstanding problems and an eventual opening of diplomatic relations. Dr Kissinger described it in 1972, as

an attempt by two countries that had been out of contact for a long time to find a basis to convey first some immediate understandings, but beyond that, to start a process by which they could bring about a closer relationship over a period of time and by which they could, where interests converged, act in a more nearly parallel fashion and where interests differed, to mitigate the consequences of those disagreements.[13]

Until the opening of diplomatic relations in 1979 – that is, for seven years – the Shanghai Communiqué successfully guided relations between the two states and 'provided the foundation for a common if informal strategy by which different – even clashing – purposes produced an extraordinary parallelism in action'.[14]

There are several reasons why treaties lack the flexibility of the joint communiqué or statement. First, international politics is too fluid, complex and inherently unpredictable to permit prior legislation on all possible contingencies and developments. International treaties can only constitute broad frameworks of relations rather than precise and exhaustive blueprints. There is a limit to the degree of foresight which can be inserted into a written document. Exactly the same limitations on the scope of formal contracts exist in our everyday life. While defining the major obligations of our social existence – marriage, employment, house purchase – the warp and weft of personal and community relations are left to the regulation of norm and informal arrangement.

Second, in a fluid situation, where the future alignment of forces and interests remains inherently obscure, formal agreement might be both dangerous and unrealistic in imposing invariant commitments on a still developing situation. International treaties, while they create reality, are also a product of a given constellation of factors which have reached a stage at which they are sufficiently stable to be given formal expression. They do not lend themselves to the fine-tuning required of an evolving situation. If every step in the diplomatic process had to be regulated by a binding legal document, accommodation between states, far from being facilitated, would be hopelessly handicapped. Imagine, analogously, that all our social relationships and interpersonal transactions had to be regulated by formal contract. To raise the suggestion is immediately to demonstrate its absurdity. Neither an orderly social life nor the law would be feasible under these conditions.

A third consideration which effectively reduces the scope of treaties is that in many cases the actors are insufficiently confident of the permanence or stability of an agreement to put it in the form of a solemnly concluded legal agreement. Treaty revision entails inherent technical difficulties. It may also prove politically awkward, because of the tendency of interested parties to insist on the written word precisely because it reflects a more favourable state of affairs which has ceased to exist. A communiqué, on the other hand, simply lapses as circumstances and interests change and can be replaced if necessary without damage to one's reputation.

In contrast to the communiqué, other documents detailing nonbinding agreement may or may not be published. In examples considered, this kind of informal understanding tended to arise from the reluctance of the parties to go through the complicated, possibly controversial and drawn-out procedures associated with a fullblown international treaty.

The Nesselrode memorandum of 1853, whose perceived infringement was one of the causes of the Crimean War, was actually the Russian summary of a verbal understanding arrived at between England and Russia about the future of the Ottoman Empire. A more formal document was ruled out on several grounds. First, London was simply not prepared to discuss in detail the partition of the Ottoman Empire behind the backs of the other great powers. An agreement limited to Britain and Russia, it was argued, was more likely to cause a general war in the Near East than to prevent one. Second, there was a traditional reluctance to treat hypothetical contingencies which might never eventuate, particularly when this concerned the fate of an 'old friend and ally'. Third, an agreement could not be given legal form without being laid before Parliament and thereby acquiring a significance which would have gone far beyond the intentions of the British Government, even supposing that the other powers would have reconciled themselves (which was unlikely) to such a momentous measure.

At the conclusion of talks it was agreed that the Russian Government would do their best to maintain the *status quo* in Turkey in return for which Britain gave the assurance that no initiative would be taken in the Eastern Question without previous concert. The utility of this understanding was carefully explained by Russian Foreign Minister Nesselrode. It was not, he argued, to be considered 'a formal transaction'. Rather it was 'a simple exchange of opinions' to prevent the two states acting at cross-purposes.[15]

Regrettably, the atmosphere of goodwill heralded by the understanding proved to be shortlived. In July 1853 Russia occupied the Christian principalities of Turkey, to the shock and indignation of the British Government, setting into motion the train of events which led to war. G.B. Henderson, in his definitive study of the Seymour conversations (as the Anglo-Russian talks of January–March 1853 are known), argues that at the root of this diplomatic breakdown lay a classic misunderstanding of the meaning of the agreement rather, than as was popularly held, a deliberate attempt to deceive the British Government. (The deception theory entered into British historiography as a result of the feeling aroused by the Crimean War.) In Henderson's view Tsar Nicholas did indeed desire to maintain the *status quo* in Turkey and was later very upset that his word was questioned. The origins of the misunderstanding lay in opposing interpretations attached by the two sides to the concept of the *status quo* in Turkey. By *status quo* Britain understood the state of affairs in Turkey as it existed in March 1853. On this interpretation the Russian occupation of the Christian principalities was not only a blatant infringement of the agreement but also made the conclusion of the agreement in the first place quite incomprehensible. But in the Russian version, according to Henderson, Nicholas all along envisaged a *status quo* in which Turkey was dominated by Russia, basing his interpretation of the term on those clauses of the Treaty of Kuchuk-Kainarji of 1774 in which Turkey had formally acknowledged Russia's right to champion Orthodox and Slav interests.

This still leaves unanswered the puzzle as to why Nicholas could possibly believe that he had British consent to this somewhat unusual, to say the least, exegesis. The answer lies, Henderson suggests, in a reference in a British despatch at the time of the negotiations in February to 'that exceptional protection [over the Christians in Turkey] which His Imperial Majesty has found so burdensome and inconvenient, though no doubt prescribed by duty and sanctioned by Treaty'. Lord John Russell, the British Foreign Secretary who had just entered office, probably never envisaged that his careless phrase might be taken by the Tsar as a signal of British consent to Russian claims in the Ottoman Empire. However it was precisely on the validity of these claims that Russia based her demands to Turkey, rejection of which led to the Russian invasion. On the brink of war with England Nicholas admitted to his Chancellor, Orlov, that he had been deceived as to Russian rights over the Christians in Turkey. Had he not been misled, he declared, his policy would have been a different one.[16]

The unfortunate consequences of the Nesselrode Memorandum are reminiscent of the equally abortive outcome of the 1937 Anglo-Italian Gentleman's Agreement discussed in the previous chapter. Both exemplify the dangers of ambiguity and a reliance on 'atmospherics' in diplomacy. In both cases one can say with hindsight that no agreement would have been better than the agreement reached. Does this then vitiate the utility of informal understanding? Probably not, since the substantive considerations underlying informal understanding explored so far still stand. Moreover both in 1853 and 1937 errors of diplomatic judgement arose from particular rather than universal causes. What it does is to demonstrate that the informality of an accord does not release diplomacy from the need for a very careful evaluation of the relative benefits in any one case of precision versus ambiguity. Finally, the very gravity of the consequences of the perceived violation of the two informal understandings emphasizes that they were indeed politically binding, even if they possessed no legal force.

Not all nonbinding agreements lead to misunderstanding. The Taft–Katsura Memorandum of 1905 proved effective in demarcating American–Japanese interests in Asia. The document itself was in the form of a summary of a conversation between the American Secretary of War and the Japanese Prime Minister, drawn up later and agreed to by both sides. According to its terms Japan disclaimed 'any aggressive designs whatever in the Philippines' in exchange for the 'personal view' of Taft 'that Japan should establish a suzerainty over Korea'.

For many years, Jongsuk Chay has argued, historians somewhat missed the point by asserting that the agreed memorandum was a 'secret pact' and thus an effective international treaty.[17] Raymond Esthus then overcompensated for this misreading of the document by relegating it to a mere exchange of views. Neither view is correct. For one thing Taft and Katsura were careful to avoid any form of words that might imply the creation of legal rights and obligations. Qualifying terms such as 'personal view' and 'observation' stressed the nonbinding intentions of the parties. Furthermore Taft explicitly denied the possibility 'for the President of the United States to enter even an informal understanding without the consent of the Senate'. (By 'informal understanding' here Taft presumably refers to the American practice of the legally binding executive agreement rather than nonbinding agreement in the sense used in this chapter.)

Although devoid of legal form, the propositions of the 'understanding' (as it was known to the Japanese themselves) fulfilled the conditions I have attributed to rules of the game. It served the purpose of setting minds at rest on both sides by removing the fear that either party had designs on the vital interests of the other. In the words of President Roosevelt, the statement 'was merely to clear up Japan's attitude which had been purposely misrepresented by pro-Russian sympathizers'. It demonstrated that Japan and the United States had 'the same interests' (with Great Britain) 'in preserving the peace of the Orient'.[18] Finally, the understanding did serve as a guide to conduct. When Japan announced, the following November, that she was taking full charge of Korea's foreign relations, the United States gave immediate approval and promptly closed its legation in Korea. Nor did Washington protest when, five years later, Japan transformed her protectorate over Korea into complete sovereignty.[19]

Chapter nine

International treaties and norms

At one end of the rules of the game spectrum have been placed tacit rules – guides to conduct which are neither written down nor spoken. Moving along, rules of varying degrees of explicitness have been discussed. Now, at the opposite end of the spectrum, are found rules of the game expressed in the explicit and legally binding form of international treaties and norms.

Sir Gerald Fitzmaurice has comprehensively defined a treaty as 'an international agreement embodied in a single formal instrument (whatever its name, title or designation) made between entities both or all of which are subjects of international law possessed of an international personality and treaty-making capacity, and intended to create rights and obligations, or establish relationships, governed by international law.'[1] This definition draws attention to the following points: first, that an international treaty, as distinct from the various kinds of implicit understandings discussed above, is set out in a formal document which is available in an authentic and ratified version. Second, the term 'treaty', alongside its particular meaning, as in the title 'Treaty of Versailles', is also used in a general sense to embrace a wide variety of instruments, serving an identical purpose, but which go by names other than that of 'treaty'. The terms charter, covenant, pact, protocol, convention, act, declaration, agreement, accord and so on, are among the numerous designations applied to the treaty form. Some of these names are reserved for particular tasks. For instance 'charter' would probably designate an agreement setting up an international organization, but there are no rigid rules about this.[2] Third, treaties are contracts between states or organizations of states creating legal ties between them. Private individuals or companies and non-state bodies cannot be parties to an international treaty. Finally, the rights and obligations created by treaties are governed by international law, which means that the established forms, criteria of interpretation, conventions and practices of international law provide the framework within which the agreement derives its significance and problems arising are supposed to be resolved.

Treaties are the major single instrument by which states regulate their relations. It is estimated that more than 20,000 treaties have been concluded since 1914. Whether it be to provide assistance, encourage trade, establish a consulate, promote cultural ties, facilitate a joint venture, define a boundary, settle a dispute, cement an alliance or attain any of a hundred other objectives of foreign policy, the international treaty is resorted to as the appropriate device. Treaties, as we have seen, are not the only form in which states coordinate their conduct. It is a common fallacy to think otherwise. J.A.S. Grenville, for one, goes so far as to claim that 'only those treaties which are formally drawn up and concluded and which create legal rights and obligations concern the student of international affairs'.[3] Partly this is a tautology. (A treaty is by definition an agreement creating legal rights and obligations.) More seriously it overlooks large areas of diplomacy and international history. Nevertheless, emphasis on the treaty instrument, as long as it is not to the exclusion of the other forms of understanding described above, is justified by the central role treaties perform. Indeed in many instances any other form for expressing agreement would be largely inconceivable. What, then, are the reasons why agreements are so frequently framed as binding accords rather than one of the other devices I have considered?

Reasons for the use of treaty

Convention

In a sense the real question is exactly the opposite of the one posed here. In the absence of any one of the various unusual reasons for preferring a tacit, verbal or nonbinding agreement, in other words, in normal circumstances, the treaty is simply the conventional form for an honourable and permanent agreement between states to take. Arrangements that are not temporary, discreditable, embarrassing or provocative are naturally and traditionally drafted as treaties. For an international agreement not to be formalized in this way requires special justification, not the reverse. The treaty has been used to record agreement for as long as there have been separate, literate, political entities, as can be seen from the ancient archives of Egypt, Ebla, Mari, Uruk and so on. By the time Solomon concluded his treaty with Hiram to exchange corn for cedar wood to build the Temple in Jerusalem the instrument was already thousands of years old.[4] It is not surprising, therefore, that there is a universal assumption that the treaty is a fitting and expected way for states to express agreement between themselves. Since the treaty far predates international law it is clear that the legal qualities of the instrument need not be the decisive factors in its choice.

The 1963 Franco-German Treaty of Cooperation is a case in point. No other expedient could have set the seal in quite the same way on the relationship. In essence the treaty, which provided for regular consultations between the two Governments, did not contain any major substantive innovations. Had it been framed as a declaration rather than a contract it would have made little practical difference. Partly the treaty, with its surrounding ceremonial, was a great symbolic event. But it was Adenauer's personal wish, more than anything, that the accord be given

the most solemn form possible. He certainly meant by this to underline its fundamental character. Above all he wished to bind his successors by a juridical act which would assure in any case the permanence of Franco-German cooperation. It would also be the last important deed of his active political life and he was determined to mark it. Thus it was finally decided to transform the initial memorandum into a treaty of due and proper form to be submitted to the parliaments of both states.[5]

The reinforcing effect of the law

As we have seen, a treaty is an agreement which is governed by international law and, theoretically at least, enforceable by judicial process. When states enter into a treaty relationship, therefore, they are buttressing their agreement with the full weight of the law. In practice, recourse to litigation is probably the least benefit derived from the reinforcement of the law. Nevertheless there are certain inherent advantages. First, infringement of a contract cast overall doubt on the law-abiding reputation of the defaulting actor. The consequences are more far-reaching than those involved in breaking a promise, since the latter affects only the immediate parties to the pledge, whereas the former concerns the international community as a whole. Harold Macmillan justified Britain's signature of a Test Ban Treaty with the Soviet Union in 1963 on the grounds that cheating would put Moscow 'at great risk'. 'Although they might have no moral inhibitions in breaking their word, I think they would be abashed at being publicly shown up before the world.'[6] The modern practice of registering treaties with the United Nations (as before that, with the League) serves to emphasize the interest of the world community in the maintenance of agreements falling under international law. Hence the element of publicity accruing to the international treaty is believed to improve the likelihood of its being honoured, or at least to raise the cost of its infringement.

A second reason for providing the reinforcement of international law is that states prefer, where possible, to ground action in legitimacy. In the event of an infringement of a treaty the law provides a sound and defensible basis for counteraction against the delinquent. Simultaneously, the offender himself is deprived of the benefit of legal support. Without overstating the reliance on legal considerations alone, there is no doubt that states much prefer to go with, rather than against, the grain of the law, if only to provide internal and external justification for their actions.[7]

Treaties are felt to minimize misunderstanding

One of the reasons for conforming to legal procedures is to reduce the possibility of textual confusion to a minimum. Established practices and forms of drafting were developed out of accumulated experience of the dangers of inaccuracy. Should disagreement arise about the import of an agreement, as is very likely, the official document in its authentic and ratified version is available for reference. International law, most recently under the Vienna Convention, defines recognized principles of interpretation should reference to the original text prove insufficient to settle disagreement. It is true that not even an apparently watertight text can absolutely preclude dispute where important interests are at stake; it is a dull lawyer who cannot find some kind of legal basis for his client's point of view. Nevertheless the existence of a formal document, drawn up, signed and ratified by due process has a reassuring quality not necessarily possessed by less formal understandings. Dr Meir Rosenne, the Legal Counsel of the Israel Foreign Ministry, explained why the Israel–Egypt peace agreement of 1979 took the form of a binding legal document rather than a verbal deal settled by a handshake: 'The purpose of the written agreement is to prevent future misunderstandings. It has to be clear later on that, if there was an infringement, this was indisputably so. Formulations must be clear and unambiguous.'[8]

The symbolic factor

States have always been faced by the insoluble problem of ensuring others' compliance with their undertakings. In the final analysis international society provides no foolproof method of preventing infringement. Self-help often replaces judicial recourse as the only effective expedient. One way of reinforcing agreements between states, in all periods of history, has been to surround the written contract with its accompanying procedures of signature and ratification with such solemnity and ritual as to transform the treaty from a secular deal into a quasi-sacred compact. The early Near Eastern treaties, indeed, call on the deities as witness to the covenant and hold out the prospect of dire divine wrath as a punishment to the transgressor. Renaissance treaties similarily invoke the Holy Church or Christendom as a warranty for the good faith of the signatories.[9] Even the 1879 treaty of peace between Christian Russia and Muslim Turkey was concluded 'in the Name of Almighty God'. However in the twentieth century the absence of shared religious assumptions has ruled out this kind of invocation. Its place has been taken by the solemnity of traditional forms and ceremonies. In either case the intention is clear: to make breach of the treaty tantamount to a sort of sacrilegious act flying in the face of piety and honour.

There is another rather different way in which the symbolism of the treaty substantially adds to its straightforward regulatory function. Anthropologists have observed that the passage of individuals or groups across social boundaries is always associated with ritual. The major transitions of personal life, such as birth, marriage and death are marked, even in 'advanced' societies, by ceremonial rites of passage[10] (and, it should be noted, closely governed by law and documentation). In the

Arab world the reconciliation of rival families or clans can only take place in consequence of the ceremony of the *sulkha*, which is a joint feast preceded by the fulfilment of certain agreed acts of compensation for past wrongs.

Analogously, the solemn treaty can be thought of as part of the ritual intuitively felt to be required when states enter into new relationships – from peace to war, from estrangement or simply disjunction to friendship or alliance, from dispute to reconciliation. Seen in this light, clearly the form of the understanding is of the essence. Only the appropriate formal document possesses the symbolic weight necessary for the rite of passage. When states move from peace to war it is not simply the terms of the contract that count but the very fact of the transition. For the reconciliation to be symbolized by anything other than a solemn peace treaty would deprive the act of a central component. Understanding of the symbolic resonance of the formal document impelled Israel's insistence on a contractual peace, departing in no way from the practices of international law, as part of a final settlement with its Arab neighbours. Peace without *sulkha*, it was argued, would not be peace. This symbolic element cannot be provided by an alternative instrument of understanding. On the contrary, where a substantive change of relationship is concerned, as opposed to the regulation of some aspect of an ongoing relationship, reluctance to frame agreement in the form of a treaty would raise serious doubts as to intention.

As a guide for the bureaucracy

A final task of the treaty is to provide an authoritative guide for the bureaucracies of the respective signatories. In the final analysis relations between states are conducted at the day-to-day level not by the leaderships but by the bureaucracies. A failure to convert high-level agreement into routine administrative procedure will abort the best of political intentions. Dr Kissinger, for one, warned that principles of conduct negotiated with the Kremlin might remain 'a sort of palliative while the bureaucracies on both sides . . . continue on traditional courses'.[11] However the very inertia of bureaucracy and its proclivity for standard operating procedures can provide the decision-maker with a helpful point of leverage: once an agreement has been internalized by the bureaucracy it is likely to be tenaciously applied. Obedience to international law should not be underrated as a key to the conduct of foreign ministries.[12] By grounding the agreement with another state in international law and, in most cases, publishing the official text, the bureaucracies are provided with strong incentives for compliance. They have before them an explicit and authoritative guide to action, legitimized by all recognised procedures and to which their masters have unambiguously and publicly set their seal. In the circumstances evasion is likely to be seen as wilful insubordination and the claim to ignorance deprived of credibility.

What the treaty can do, then, is to provide a mechanism for translating official policy into bureaucratic practice. This was, in French Foreign Minister Couve de Murville's view, the virtue of providing a contractual framework for Franco-German relations in the shape of the 1963 treaty. It would facilitate the organization of the common work of the two countries. Contacts in a whole range of fields and at all levels of government would be permanently coordinated.[13]

What, then, is the particular contribution of treaties to efforts by states to achieve political accommodation in the form of rules of conduct? In a sense all treaties concluded by sovereign actors affect their political relations: they are the outcome of policy decisions and where relations are hostile even minor technical accords are likely to be ruled out. American ostracism until the Nixon presidency of the People's Republic of China precluded any kind of legal tie for whatever purpose between the two states. In such, albeit unusual circumstances, agreement to open a consulate, regulate air traffic or to exchange scientific information, acquires great political significance.

Classes of treaty

Given this note of caution, many writers and also governments do conventionally classify treaties into those of a political character involving international peace and stability (with which I am concerned here) and those of a welfare or technical character. Japanese practice, for example, distinguishes between political treaties and those dealing with culture, economics and communications. Political treaties cover agreements arising out of crisis or conflict situations or the resolution of basic questions of foreign relations. In this category are found peace, defence and security treaties and the settlement of territorial questions. Under this classification only about one-fifth of Japan's bilateral treaties are political in scope.[14]

Soviet practice makes a similar distinction. The Foreign Affairs Commissariat classifies its treaties into political treaties and those dealing with problems of law, economics, communications, transport, culture, repatriation of citizens, health, and humanitarian issues. Incongruously from a western perspective Soviet political treaties exclude military assistance agreements, armistices and the suspension of hostilities or territorial questions. Treaties coming under the political classification include those of alliance, mutual assistance, nonaggression, neutrality and peace. About one-quarter of the 2,500 or so treaties concluded by the USSR in the period 1917–57 were considered political.[15]

Of the large number of treaties concluded by the world community, therefore, only a fraction are directly relevant to international order. In the following sections I shall follow a classification of political treaties in terms of their broad functions, and suggest some of their implications for the concept of rules of the game.

Peace treaties

Peace treaties crucially affect rules of the game in the international system in two ways: they define the cartographic limits on international conduct and they determine the rights and duties of states in their bilateral and multilateral relations. The map of Europe is largely a product of the great peace settlements of modern history, Utrecht, Westphalia, Vienna, Berlin, Versailles and Paris; the delineation of frontiers, exchange of territory, creation of·new states, dismantling of empires have all fallen under their purview.

In comparison with other aspects of peace treaties, and indeed of political treaties altogether, their cartographic provisions have, on the whole, displayed a relatively long-term stability. Partly this can be accounted for by the fact that they actually modify the shape of the political environment. Any subsequent attempt to alter a boundary delineated by international treaty and demarcated on the ground must inevitably run up against considerable forces of inertia and resistance to change. Geographical studies have also demonstrated that a convergence of geographical and political factors can modify both the feasibility and wish for boundary modifications. First, political boundaries may be naturally reinforced by such physical features of the landscape as rivers and mountains. Second, long-lasting borders can aquire a greater degree of permanence as a result of such human activities as land clearance, afforestation, settlement and the construction and integration of transport networks.[16]

Another reason for the durability of the territorial provisions of the great peace treaties has been the stake possessed by the international community in their preservation. The shape of the map is a central element in the overall structure of international order. In the logic of rules of the game the violation of a constituent part is perceived as an offence against the total structure (see chapter four). Lord Castlereagh made the point in 1814 during negotiations to redraw the map of Europe after the Napoleonic Wars as a rejoinder to excessive Swiss preoccupation with the defensibility of their borders. Claims to strategic boundaries, he argued, could be pushed too far. 'Real defence and security come from the guarantee which is given by the fact that they cannot touch you without declaring war on all those interested in maintaining things as they are.'[17]

It is clear that in the absence of a formal peace treaty to recognize the territorial changes brought about in Europe by the Second World War, the Soviet Union has seen the force of the Final Act of the 1975 European Conference on Security and Cooperation (which referred to the 'inviolability' of all European frontiers) not so much in its legal status, which is denied by other signatories, as in the willingness of the European states 'in concert' to associate, within a single document, the permanence of the post-1945 *status quo* with the concept of peace and security in Europe. Any violation of those boundaries, they were saying in effect, would be considered as an offence against the very structure of European order.

Besides their cartographic aspect, peace treaties have been a primary instrument defining the permissions and restraints placed upon the foreign relations and armament of defeated states. The Japanese Peace Treaty, which was not concluded until 1951 because of an intractable territorial dispute between Japan and the Soviet Union, confirmed the provisions of the 1946 Japanese Constitution in which Japan renounced the threat or use of force as a means of policy. However, the prohibition on the maintenance of armed forces of 1946 was not reflected in the later peace treaty. The withdrawal of all occupation forces symbolized the restoration of Japan to full sovereign status within the international community. In lieu of a formal peace treaty, relations between Japan and the USSR were set on a normal basis by a Joint Declaration of 19 October 1956. Its provisions were similar to those of the earlier peace treaty. Like the latter it marked a pivotal point in Japanese foreign relations. Following the Declaration the way was clear for the development of normal ties between Japan and, in effect, the entire Soviet bloc. With the USSR agreements were concluded on fishing, rescue on the high seas, trade, air transport and so on; normal relations then followed with other communist countries, starting with Poland and Czechoslovakia. Thus the Japanese peace settlement was not simply a catalogue of deprivations and restrictions but also a green light for Japan to resume the normal activities of a sovereign state.

The Austrian State Treaty of 1955 can be looked at in a similar light. On the one hand there were prohibitions on an *Anschluss* with Germany, on the possession of various types of weapons and, in a juridically separate but politically connected Resolution of the Austrian Parliament, a commitment to abstain from joining military alliances or permitting the establishment of military bases by foreign states on her territory. On the other hand there was a withdrawal of occupying forces and the re-establishment of Austria as a free and independent state. Within the limits of the State Treaty and its accompanying Resolution Austria has, since 1955, taken on an active and highly individual role within the international community.

Earlier in this chapter it was suggested that the treaty could be viewed as part of the ritual by which societies mark the transition from one relationship to another. In this respect the peace treaty can be seen not only as directly defining rules of the game between the signatories but also as creating the conditions in which the inhibitions and convergencies of peaceful relations replace previous belligerency. Alongside the peace treaty mention should also be made of treaties of friendship and normalization. Postwar Japanese diplomacy has used the friendship treaty in a number of variations to bridge the gap between belligerency and cooperation. The Treaty of Amity and Friendship of 1955 with Cambodia was used in this way and was followed by economic, technical and assistance agreements. Similarily the 'normalization' agreements negotiated by the West German Government within the framework of *Ostpolitik* turned a new leaf between West Germany and her eastern neighbours, the Soviet Union, Poland, East Germany and Czechoslovakia. Taking as their point of departure an affirmation of the 'inviolability' of the post-1945 frontiers – in effect West German acceptance of the European *status quo* – they cleared the way for the development of cooperative ties in a broad range of fields.

Treaties for the contingency of war

The classic example of a contingency agreement of this kind is the treaty of defensive alliance by which the signatories undertake to render assistance, 'including the use of armed force' (as the treaties establishing both NATO and the Warsaw Pact put it) 'in the event of armed attack' on one or more of the signatories. Additional obligations may include consultation in the event of an impending threat, the exchange of information and the establishment of consultative or military bodies to facilitate preparation for the eventuality envisaged under the terms of the alliance.

Treaties of alliance obviously do become the basis for joint involvement in war, as was the case with the pre-1914 Triple Alliance or the pre-Second World War Anglo-Polish Alliance. This should not obscure the equally fundamental point that treaties of this kind exercise a crucially formative impact on the expectations of actors in situations short of war. Diplomacy is concerned with future contingencies, in planning for their occurrence and working for their prevention, and no contingency is more fateful and of greater concern than the event of war. Treaties of alliance, which envisage the distribution of forces in defined circumstances and align partners in preparation for the contingency, are therefore crucial in sketching out the political map of permissions and prohibitions which constitute rules of the game.

An initial motive behind the conclusion of a treaty of alliance is to limit the freedom of action of the treaty partner so as to ensure the predictability of his future behaviour in the decisive area of concern. In 1879 Bismarck wanted to ensure armed British support in the event of trouble with Russia in the Balkans because in its absence he would have to tread very much more carefully. When he failed to extract a firm British commitment, Bismarck opted for as friendly a policy as possible towards Russia.[18] In contrast, Britain's 1902 treaty with Japan, by ruling out the latter as a potential Far Eastern foe, enabled Britain to keep only a modest fleet in Chinese waters. If the treaty were abrogated both partners would then have to plan for the contingency of the other's enmity.[19] In both these examples one can clearly see the influence on policy of the absence or presence of the commitments created by treaty. Rules of the game cannot determine the future course of events, but they do frequently create the framework of expectations within which decisions moulding events are made.

Not the least important advantage of a treaty of alliance is that it removes uncertainty about one's own likely course of action. This may seem paradoxical, but only confidence in the future conduct of others can resolve ambiguities about one's own position. The guarantee to Poland of

March 1939, announced by Neville Chamberlain (which grew into the Anglo-Polish alliance) could not, in the judgement of a senior official, actually protect Poland against attack. 'But it set up a signpost for the prime minister. He was committed and in the event of a German attack on Poland he would be spared the agonizing doubts and indecisions.'[20]

A further level at which alliances influence expectations is in their deterrent effect on potential opponents. In our own time this is widely seen to be NATO's major task. But deterrence should not be thought to be a modern idea. It is simply an inherent part of the reflexive logic of expectations which characterizes strategic analysis. Bismarck, in the nineteenth century, was a past master of the art of deterrence. Proposing an Anglo-German alliance in 1889, he argued that war would be avoided by the mere publication of the treaty. Britain's potential enemies at the time, France, Russia and the United States, would not dare to break the peace knowing that an attack on either ally would face them with the armed might of the other party.[21]

How reliable are treaties of alliance? Like other political engagements they are subject to the principles of redundancy described in chapter four. Many have been honoured; some were never put to the test (but were effective as deterrents); others failed to live up to expectations. Treaties, it needs emphasizing, are the point of departure for a relationship. Should that relationship fail to prosper then the formal contents of the treaty inevitably lose their significance. There is nothing cynical or discreditable about this; it is just a fact of political life which, if appreciated, need not give rise to disappointment. The Munich crisis is often held up as a demonstration of the worthlessness of international treaties, since under their 1924 Treaty of Alliance France was committed to maintaining the integrity of Czechoslovakia. However it had long been clear to the international community that Czechoslovakia would be foolish to count on French assistance. That Czechoslovak President Beneš chose to do so in the face of warnings to the contrary was a matter of self-deception as much as French duplicity.[22] Poland, which was equally allied to France under a treaty of 1925, was more realistic about the applicability of an agreement concluded under completely different circumstances from those existing in the late 1930s.[23]

Neutrality and nonaggression treaties, by which the signatories commit themselves to maintaining neutrality in the event of the other's involvement in war, or pledge themselves to resolve any dispute by peaceful means and renounce war as an instrument in their relations, play an equivalent role in forming expectations. Former Soviet Defence Minister Marshal Malinovski is reported to have claimed that thanks to Finnish neutrality only one Soviet division had to be maintained in the Murmansk region. 'If Finnish policy were different', he argued, 'much greater forces would have to be kept there.'[24]

The heyday of the nonaggression treaty came in the interwar period when it was a principal instrument of Nazi and Soviet policy. Since many of the signatories of such treaties were later occupied by Russia, Germany or both, this device has come into bad odour. However, as late as 1963 Soviet Foreign Minister Gromyko proposed a nonaggression pact to British and American diplomats. Contemporary examples of this kind of accord are China's 1960 treaties with Afghanistan and Cambodia.

Even in those cases from the 1930s in which nonaggression treaties were eventually violated it can be shown that they still had a political effect by influencing expectations and conduct during their period of working. For instance when the idea of a nonaggression agreement between Germany and Poland arose in 1934 a German analysis acknowledged that it would restrict German 'freedom of action' even if 'at the proper time it would be possible to bring on a military showdown with Poland'. The main significance of such an agreement, it was argued, lay in its political rather than legal effect. 'Two states which solemnly renounce any aggressive military action in their mutual relations show thereby that there are no really vital conflicts of interest between them or that their policy is in any case no longer seriously directed toward the settlement of such conflicts.' In Germany's case, the writer continued, this would be seen as a substantial weakening of the claim, vigorously maintained until then, for the revision of Germany's eastern borders with Poland. It is true that the 1934 agreement was denounced by Hitler after the final dismemberment of Czechoslovakia in March 1939; but for as long as it remained valid it did constitute the basis of the rules of the game between Poland and Germany. The momentous consequences which followed its denunciation amply justify the judgement of the writer of the 1934 memorandum that the pact 'could not be simply ignored'.[25]

Treaties for the prevention and settlement of disputes endangering international peace and security

Although important for the maintenance of international order, treaties settling disagreement do not in themselves contribute to the definition of rules of conduct. They may pave the way for political cooperation by removing obstacles to progress, but they need not specifically contain provision for this. In international law the distinction is drawn between an executed treaty and an executory treaty. The former, for instance an agreement settling a boundary dispute, concerns issues which, once dealt with, are disposed of. Executory treaties, in contrast, of which treaties of alliance are an example, formulate rights and duties which continue to apply through time. Only the latter concern us from the point of view of rules of the game.[26]

Bilateral or multilateral treaties for the peaceful settlement of international disputes, from the League Covenant, via treaties of arbitration, to the United Nations Charter, equally fall beyond the scope of this present work. Again their purpose is not to regulate ongoing relations but to envisage machinery of conciliation which is available in case of need (and choice). They are procedural rather than substantive.

Treaties regulating the exercise of exclusive influence

Treaties of this kind seek to regulate those 'overlapping pretensions of authority' in Richard Falk's phrase, that are such a potent source of conflict. Just as national boundaries obviate dispute between neighbours as to the extent of their jurisdiction, agreements apportioning the exercise of influence by hegemonial powers beyond national boundaries serve to obviate misunderstanding and contain competitive ambitions by setting limits on the scope of permitted action.

Agreements on spheres of influence express the mutual recognition of the signatories of areas in which each has his own exclusive interests and in which the other abstains from interference. At stake may be the partition of a former (or prospective) zone of overlapping and hence antagonistic mutual involvement or simply the allocation of an entire region to the control of a single party. The basis of the exclusive interest may be strategic, economic or ethnic, or some combination of these factors.

The most prolific era for spheres of influence agreements was the period of imperialist competition preceding the First World War when the powers sought to extend their trade and presence throughout the globe. A long series of treaties partitioned their influence in Africa, the Near East, Central Asia and the Far East. Some of them, such as the Anglo-Russian Convention of 1907, regularized an existing situation on the ground. Others, like the 1912 Serbo-Bulgarian Treaty, sought to parcel out in advance the territory of a prospective victim.

Treaties can also provide an instrument by which the hegemonial power establishes or formalizes its hold over the weaker partner. In the scramble for colonies that followed the Berlin Conference of 1884–5, West Africa became the target of many European treaty-making expeditions. The aim of each mission was to reach a particular territory before the others and to conclude a treaty with the indigenous ruler bestowing exclusive rights on the colonizing power.[27] In the twentieth century the substance if not the form of a protectorate has often been conferred by the treaty of friendship. Between partners of unequal strength this device has been used to legitimize the domination of the weaker party by the stronger. British treaties of the interwar period with her Middle East clients Saudi Arabia (then called Hejaz and Nejd), Transjordan, Iraq and Egypt provided legal sanction for the predominance of British power in the area. India's treaties of peace and friendship with her small northern neighbours Bhutan and Nepal, concluded after independence, have very much the same purpose. In contrast, Chinese friendship treaties with neighbouring states did not establish or legitimize exclusive Chinese influence.

Friendship treaties of the USSR fall into two quite distinct categories. The first, the treaty of Friendship, Mutual Assistance and Cooperation, approximates, in substance, to the conventional treaty of alliance and contains a precise definition of the conditions under which help to repel an attack will be supplied. Treaties of this kind have been signed with all the Soviet Union's East European satellites, North Korea and China. The constitutive treaty of the Warsaw Pact, signed in 1955, goes under the same heading. Given the overwhelming disparity of power between the Soviet Union and her treaty partners such treaties have implied more than a defensive commitment on the part of the senior ally but have also legitimized Soviet predominance over the weaker party and its inclusion in the Soviet sphere of influence.

Since 1971 a second kind of friendship treaty, the treaty of Friendship and Cooperation, has been introduced to formalize Soviet ties with its newer allies in Africa and Asia. It does not contain explicit provision for military assistance in the event of attack but, with local variations, calls for regular consultation between the signatories and prohibits membership of groupings directed against the other partner. Such treaties have been concluded with Egypt, India, Iraq, Somalia, Angola, Mozambique Afghanistan and Syria. (A slightly different hybrid has also been signed with Vietnam.)

At the bilateral level the treaty of Friendship and Cooperation entails a high degree of subservience by the client in return for Soviet assistance. Egypt, which denounced its treaty in 1976, when it was already a dead letter, was not prepared to subordinate its policy to Soviet interests and bitterly complained about Soviet domineering. Somalia, for her part, overstepped the bounds by her wilful invasion of the Ogaden. At the superpower level this sort of treaty is intended to signal and legitimize the inclusion of the client in the Soviet orbit. Among other things the Angola and Afghanistan episodes demonstrate that the Soviet Union considers a treaty relationship of this kind to permit it the right of proxy or direct intervention in order to protect its interests.

Arms limitation and disarmament agreements

Like treaties settling international disputes, arms limitation and disarmament agreements do not in themselves lay down rules of the game in the sense of this book (though they set limits on or prohibit entirely defined categories of armament). They can, however, create conditions within which political restraint becomes more feasible. It is certainly not by chance that the Strategic Arms Limitation Agreements (SALT) between the United States and the USSR were seen to lie at the core of the policy of détente. Bitter experience, for instance of the Anglo-German naval race which preceded the First World War, has demonstrated the dangerously destabilizing effects of arms races. In the resultant atmosphere of mutual suspicion and fear of falling behind, the scope for constructive diplomacy is severely reduced. Absolute disarmament – the agreed abolition of weapons – has proved difficult to attain. But even arms control – the replacement of unbridled competition in armaments by permitted levels or defined rates of growth of weapons – can have a beneficial effect on political relations. By removing uncertainty mistrust can be alleviated and a climate more conducive to political accommodation created.

It was with the pre-1914 naval race in mind that the British and German Governments signed their 1935 Naval Agreement (fixing the relative strengths of the two navies). In German eyes the treaty was seen as reflecting Hitler's wish 'to exclude any possibility of antagonism between Germany and Britain for the future and thus also finally to rule out any naval rivalry between the two countries. . . . A political understanding with Great Britain has been initiated by the naval settlement.'[28]

A similar wish for political accommodation has been one of the American interests in arms control talks with the USSR. John F. Kennedy saw the political gains from the 1963 Test Ban Treaty as uppermost. 'The treaty was a symbolic "first step", a forerunner of further agreements. It facilitated a pause in the cold war in which other, more difficult problem areas cŏuld be stabilized.'[29]

International norms

A norm is a general principle of right conduct to which a community expects all its members to conform. In the world community it is possible to discern a number of universal precepts of this kind which shape the very structure of international relations. Indeed they are so fundamental that in their absence it is hard to imagine the conduct of international relations, as we now know it, at all. The best known enunciation of such constituent norms is the 'Five Principles' of peaceful coexistence, or *Panch Sila*, derived from a Buddhist concept, first enumerated in an agreement over Tibet concluded between India and the People's Republic of China in 1954. The Five Principles were: mutual nonaggression; mutual non-interference in each other's internal affairs; equality and mutual benefit; peaceful coexistence. Since 1954 this formulation has been widely drawn upon to express international communion, especially between states of differing ideological outlooks. It was included in the text of the 1972 Shanghai Communiqué released by the United States and China.

Alongside the Five Principles various other codes of a similar nature can be found in the constituent charters of such bodies as the United Nations, the Nonaligned Movement, the Organization of African Unity and so on. The right of self-defence and the prohibition on the threat or use of force are additional norms enunciated in this way. To the list so far one might add the older principle of freedom of the seas. Willy Brandt, in a personal formulation, but one which well reflects Western views, wishes to include national self-determination and human rights.[30] Soviet scholarship is also emphatic in its view of norms as a basis of world order, though its interpretation of concepts such as noninterference in internal affairs would be unfamiliar to the Western observer.[31]

Clearly the principles mentioned here are far from iron laws. Too frequently they are aspirations on the part of the deprived rather than operative rules of conduct on the part of the mighty. Problems arise when principles come into conflict – the right of self-determination with territorial integrity, for example. Nonetheless deviation from most of these norms would be generally considered to be illegitimate and grounds for communal deprecation. As with other legal provisions, conformity is the safer course.

Together with international norms of coexistence the growth of regional and ideological communities has brought with it the concomitant appearance of regional norms of conduct. Groupings such as the Organization of African·Unity, the Arab League and even the European Economic Community function as mutual protection societies against outsiders, increase the power of otherwise weak actors and provide a sense of identity, purpose and self-importance. Pressures for conformity with group norms are considerable and the sanction of group disapproval probably more potent than the condemnation of wider but looser bodies like the United Nations.

The cardinal norm of these communities is invariably that of regional solidarity against outsiders, of 'keeping it in the family' and 'looking after one's own'. At the United Nations, as such former ambassadors as William Buckley and Abba Eban testify, group loyalty is the unbreakable ethic. Voting in unison outweighs all substantive considerations. Embarrassing issues are, if possible, suppressed, to prevent disruption of group unity.[32]

A second principle is that of the right of consultation on matters of common interest. Failure to do so causes deep offence and suspicion. Both NATO and the Commonwealth have been troubled over the years by lapses from this norm.

Each community will develop its own particular group norms. In the Soviet bloc, observation of Soviet policy towards its associates suggests, a reasonable degree of autonomy may be tolerated as long as two unbreakable precepts are respected: the unitary rule of the Communist Party and continued membership of the Warsaw Pact. In 1956 Polish leaders made clear their adherence to these norms and internal developments were left to take their own course by the USSR. Hungary tried to challenge the rules and was invaded. A secondary norm of foreign policy behaviour in the Soviet bloc is that major initiatives must be approved by or handled through Moscow. West Germany made no progress in its *Ostpolitik* until it recognized this principle. Even United States diplomacy has been sensitive to its existence. In 1969 President Nixon went ahead with a trip to Romania in the face of State Department objections that the cultivation of a bilateral relationship would be viewed as 'dangerously provocative' by the USSR.[33] In the event both Nixon and Ceausescu correctly evaluated Romania's freedom of action. Sometimes professional diplomats are more constrained by other's group norms than are group members themselves. A constructive foreign policy requires awareness not only of the limits imposed by normative constraints but also of the scope for innovation within the system. In the following chapters I shall turn from consideration of rules of the game as static givens to analysis of their dynamic aspects.

Part three

The dynamics of rules of the game

Chapter ten
Making rules

It is elementary that the international community can best be considered as a dynamic system. By this is meant that the assumption of constant relations between the constituent parts of the system – the states – can have only limited application. A static approach runs the risk not only of oversimplification but of leaving out a defining characteristic of the field. To investigate the problem of stability in the international system requires an acknowledgement at the outset that any equilibrium must be dynamic, continuously adjusting to changing circumstances. Shifts in the distribution of power, autonomous changes in key parameters such as the state of technology, economic development, national leadership, popular and national expectations and so on, constantly pose new problems that must be accommodated.

Rules of the game, which define the quality of relations between states, cannot be understood as immutable laws but must be viewed in the light of the surrounding organic processes they reflect and calibrate. In this respect rules in the international community are more like the customs and norms of a primitive society, which are integrated with and adjust to the changing texture of day-to-day life rather than to laws legislated from above. Once codified the latter may begin to diverge from organic practice and cease to correspond to the needs of society, though retaining formal validity. Rules of the game, which are above all operative principles, change as the 'game' changes.

Rules of the game, therefore, can first of all provide a useful focus around which to organize the observation and analysis of the relations between states over time. In addition, however, it becomes essential to investigate the processes by which rules of the game are made, how they are maintained and the conditions under which they break down and are altered. To the extent that actors concerned to contain disruptive problems and aspirations succeed in managing these processes, an order favourable to their interests is preserved. But there is no 'invisible hand' – no self-regulating, beneficent mechanism – to ensure that all normative changes are constructive ones; the operative expectations guiding conduct at any given time can just as easily point in the direction of hegemony by a single power as tolerance for others' rights to independence. Soviet prerogatives in the Warsaw Pact are normatively grounded, though they are overwhelmingly slanted to Moscow's benefit. Worst of all is the situation of normative disintegration in which the hegemonic power gratefully accepts its new freedom of action only to be confronted by opponents desperately seeking to regain a control which has already been lost. Something like this preceded the outbreak of the Second World War.

Jurists cite two areas of activity as sources of international law: custom and treaty, or, in other words, practice and negotiated agreement. Rules of the game, which subsume law, can be thought of analogously as being made by the broader parallel categories of actions and words. Actions create precedents which become the focus of future expectations. Words are directed to achieving compliance and warning of the consequences of noncompliance with principles of future conduct.

Actions

Within the category of actions three modes of conduct will be suggested as generating rules: (1) the outcome of everyday contact; (2) the outcome of setpiece test cases; (3) acts intended to stake a claim to a particular prerogative.

The outcome of everyday contact

At the most basic level expectations about what can and cannot be done are formed spontaneously by the give and take of everyday relations. D.H.N. Johnston describes this bluntly as 'rude practice' – simply that which is done.[1] In a novel situation and in the absence of precedents and obvious constraints, actors will behave in a way which is convenient, self-serving and consonant with the means at their disposal and the requirements of the situation. Out of the immediate logic of the situation a pattern of relations will emerge which, without the sanction or need for contractual agreement, will form expectations and ascribe roles.

Of the British decision to enter the First World War Lillian Penson has concluded that 'trends of policy' as much as 'treaty obligations' can create obligations: 'Actions speak louder than words; the building of Rosyth was an action of first importance.'[2] (Rosyth being a naval base in the Firth of Forth whose construction reflected a disposition of naval forces based upon coordination with France). Indeed the evolution of the British commitment to France is an instructive episode in the formative effects of ongoing relations – 'trends of policy' – on expectations.

The basic document regulating relations between Britain and France was the Convention of 8 April 1904. Yet this agreement, in both its public and secret articles, dealt at no point with any aspect of Anglo-French interests in Europe but merely settled points of dispute between the two states in Morocco and Egypt. Far from constituting in any sense a defensive, let alone offensive alliance, the convention was a narrowly defined technical agreement. Its significance, however, went much further. By removing points of contention between the two countries it set the scene for wider cooperation and friendship. Challenged by Germany in the 1905 Moroccan Crisis, the entente, instead of being weakened, was cemented together more strongly.

One of the lessons of the crisis drawn by the General Staffs of both partners was the need to concert military plans in the event of France being drawn into war. That Britain would also become involved was beginning to be taken for granted. These first military talks were undertaken without Britain incurring any further formal obligation beyond the promise of diplomatic support contained in the published agreement of 1904. Nevertheless the British Government did believe that if Germany forced a quarrel on France over the issue of Morocco there would be a strong feeling in favour of British intervention against Germany.

Whatever was said at the time and afterwards, either to France or within the British Government, the whole trend of Anglo-French relations, including the joint planning of supposedly nonbinding naval and military technical arrangements, was to create expectations of British intervention on the side of France in a war against Germany. Entente came to mean 'tacit alliance'. As early as February 1906 Foreign Secretary Grey realized that 'the entente and still more the constant and emphatic demonstrations of affection (official, naval, political, commercial, Municipal and in the Press), have created in France a belief that we should support her in war'. To keep out of a war would lose Britain her good name and wreck her 'policy and position in the world'.[3]

Increasingly, British strategic planning came to be based on the assumption that France was an ally in all but name. In a report of July 1909 the Committee of Imperial Defence stated firmly that

a military entente between Great Britain and France can only be of value so long as it rests on the understanding that, in the event of war in which both are involved alike on land and sea, the whole of the available naval and military strength of the two countries will be brought to bear at the decisive point.[4]

Accordingly the training, equipment and logistical planning of the British Army went ahead on the assumption that in any war a British Expeditionary Force would take its place on the left flank of the French armies.

So far as the Navy was concerned Winston Churchill, as First Lord of the Admiralty, gave effect to the principle of coordination and concentration contained in the 1909 report by withdrawing the Mediterranean Fleet from Malta to Gibraltar whence it could support the Home Fleet. British interests in the Mediterranean were to be protected by cruiser squadrons remaining at Malta and, it was generally assumed, by the French Fleet.[5] By 1912 British Ministers had come to recognize and dislike 'the moral effect of our evacuating the Mediterranean, and the conclusions that would be drawn therefrom, [which] would in fact compromise us too deeply with France'.

French planning equally assumed that if France was to take on the burden of covering the Mediterranean flank of the entente, the British

Home Fleet would play its part in covering France's Atlantic coasts. Naval discussion in late 1912 and early 1913 resulted in three separate naval conventions defining British and French cooperation in the English Channel and the Mediterranean. Although these arrangements were prefaced by the proviso that they would only come into effect 'In the event of [Britain] being allied with the French Government in a war with Germany', there could be little doubt in the two Admiralties that a virtual Anglo-French Naval Alliance had been forged.[6]

Despite the growing synchronization of French and British strategic planning the British Government still insisted that no actual commitment had been made or implied. In November 1912 Grey was obliged to put the reservations of the Cabinet (especially its radical members) into a formal document for the French Government. Military conversations, which had been held 'from time to time in recent years', were not to be understood as restricting

the freedom of either Government to decide at any future time whether or not to assist the other by armed force. We have agreed that consultations between experts is not, and ought not to be, regarded as an engagement that commits either Government to action in a contingency that has not arisen and may never arise. The disposition, for instance, of the French and British Fleets respectively at the present moment is not based upon an engagement to cooperate in war.[7]

As an attempt to pacify Government opponents of a prior British commitment this document made sense. As a description of the state of Anglo-French relations and of the rules of the game governing them, it was quite meaningless. No verbal declaration could change the plain fact that policy-makers and strategic planners on both sides had formed their expectations on the basis of military and especially naval coordination which found concrete expression in the disposition and structure of forces on the ground. The building of the Rosyth naval base was one aspect of this.

To Lord Esher it was obvious that 'the mere fact of the War Office plan having been worked out in detail with the French General Staff has certainly committed us to fight, whether the Cabinet likes it or not': 'Of course there is no treaty or convention, but how we can get out of the commitments of the General Staff with honour, I cannot understand.' This was the view of many other public figures.[8] It was even the view of German observers. Describing the dispositions of the British and French Navies, the businesslike and unceremonious cooperation between them and the conversations known to have taken place, the German naval attaché in London concluded that it did not matter whether a Convention actually existed.

The fact that the Chiefs of the land and sea forces of the two Powers have come to an understanding from time to time, that, as a result of this understanding, a radical transference of the naval centres of gravity of both Powers has been effected, and that further steps, as evidenced by the use of French harbours by portions of the British Navy, have been taken in the direction of intimate cooperation – these facts are sufficient evidence that there are Anglo-French arrangements whether with or without an engagement is for the moment a matter of indifference – and that we have to reckon with them. [9]

The acid test of whether or not Britain had a political obligation ('moral' obligation was the contemporary term) came in 1914. On 1 August France mobilized in response to a German ultimatum to her ally, Russia. The British Cabinet, which had been agonizing over its interests and duties in the situation, now found itself forced to decide whether or not to stand by France. Without entering the complex debate of why war was declared, there is no doubt that the reality of a British obligation to France proved inescapable. The French Fleet, Grey was reminded by the French Ambassador, had been sent to the Mediterranean 'on the understanding' that the British Fleet, which was held in home waters, would protect France's northern and western coasts. [10] Reporting this view to the Cabinet, Grey was adamant: 'We have led France to rely upon us, and unless we support her in her agony, I cannot continue at the Foreign Office.' Thus it was decided to guarantee France's western and northern coasts – a decisive step on the way to Britain's entry into the war. The decision was to be explained by allusion to British interests and the 'moral obligation to support France conditionally at sea'. [11] Whether or not the decision was the right one is historically meaningless. What is clear is that failure, in certain circles, to appreciate that actions as much as treaties create obligations, permitted serious misconceptions to flourish about the real freedom of action of British foreign policy in the decade preceding the outbreak of war.

The outcome of setpiece test cases

As a system of communications upon which good order in the international system depends, rules of the game are under constant scrutiny by participating actors who must keep up to date about and also ensure that others are currently informed of the limits of the permissible. The cost of inattention or misjudgement can be heavy indeed.

Within the overall learning process the function of actions is bound to be central; for they demonstrate, by the very fact of their performance, what can and cannot be done at any given point in time. As the focus of attention – the conspicuous alternative – a tried and successful course of action thus becomes the standing precedent for conduct in similar situations in the future.

'Test cases' are setpiece occasions, occurring at moments of challenge, novelty or change in international relations. Just as 'the first time' is often considered a constitutive experience in human relations, setting the pattern for future encounters, the actions and reactions of states in test cases are formative for rules of the game. International crisis is a situation of this kind. Hence the assumption of participants and observers that the outcome of any contest of wills will have crucial implications for the future course of relations between the rivals. Hence also the significance attached by American political mythology to a new President's first real (or imagined) confrontation with the Soviet Union. (Instances are Kennedy's 1961 meeting with Khrushchev and Ford's 1975 *Mayaguez* rescue.)

A good example of a test case is the so-called 'baby blockade' of April 1948 out of which emerged the rules of the game for the later full Soviet blockade of Berlin and the Western airlift by which it was eventually broken. The immediate background to the blockade itself was the growing breakdown of cooperation between the wartime allies and the division of Germany. Steps taken by the Western powers from 1947 on to establish a West German state, which included plans to solve the area's grave economic problems on an independent basis, threatened Russia's ambition to set up a united and eventually communist Germany.

Determined to exert pressure on the Western Allies, the Soviet Union chose Berlin, surrounded on all sides by the Soviet zone, as the weak point in its opponents' armour. On 1 April 1948 certain restrictive procedures on highway and railway travel for Western personnel and cargo crossing the Soviet zone of occupation en route to Berlin were introduced by the Soviet Union. Lasting only ten days the episode was nevertheless to act as a crucially formative influence on the behaviour of the two sides in the main crisis later in the year.

Faced by Soviet violations of established practice, Britain and the United States determined to maintain that access to Berlin on which their position depended. First, guards on US military passenger trains were ordered to prevent Soviet troops from entering but were 'not to shoot unless first fired upon'.[12] One such train 'progressed some distance into the Soviet Zone but was finally shunted off the main line by electrical switching to a siding, where it remained for a few days until it withdrew rather ignominiously'.[13] The train crew could have attempted forcibly to turn the switch, but this might have led to a direct clash between Soviet and American troops. Thus the first rule of the crisis was established: although defensive means were permissible, on no account should the use of force be initiated.

The second prong of the Anglo-American response was to increase substantially the passenger airlift into Berlin in order to compensate for delays on the ground. Then on 5 April 1948 a British civil passenger aircraft approaching Gatow airfield in the British sector of Berlin collided with a Soviet fighter aircraft and crashed with the death of all passengers on board. In a meeting between the Soviet and British military governors the Russian representative indicated that the incident was not intentional and assurances were given that British aircraft would not be molested in the Berlin air corridor. As a result of these assurances both the British and the Americans revoked previous orders under which their planes were to have been accompanied by fighter escorts. The British political adviser for Germany went so far as to suggest – correctly, as it turned out – that the effect of the incident might even be salutary in 'discouraging further Soviet aggressive acts because . . . the public reaction in England and

[the] US would be violent enough to shock even [the] Russians'.[14]

Thus a second rule of the game was established for the forthcoming blockade: the immunity of air traffic in the Berlin air corridor. As Alexander George and Richard Smoke observe: 'The Western response to the event served to establish for the Russians how far they could safely go in their efforts to isolate the city. They recognized the possibility that serious interference with the air corridors might become a *casus belli*.' At the same time the Western allies also learnt that as long as the Soviet Union wished to avoid war it would be unlikely to interfere with an airlift.[15] When the full blockade was imposed by the USSR on 24 June, the airlift was the conspicuous expedient for ensuring access into Berlin without risking military confrontation. The April episode had acted as a test case for the real trial of strength, a learning experience in which both sides were able to explore the limits within which they could safely manoeuvre.

Staking a claim

To stake a claim is to perform an act which is conventionally recognized to assert possession to a given area. By analogy I apply the expression to political acts which are intended to establish general principles of conduct; they are, in other words, symbolic performances understood to acquire for the actor wider categories of prerogative such as access, exclusive influence, possession, involvement, the right to be consulted and so on.

Claims to an exclusive sphere of influence are staked either by the unhindered use of force, by a monopoly over certain privileges (such as representation, trade or military bases) or by the regular, visible and again exclusive despatch of means of transport such as railways, ships or planes. (All these could be used, in the event of a challenge by another power, to transfer troops to the area in question: however, the vehicle itself is understood to be sufficient to establish the presence.)

In the age of imperialism and national consolidation the great railway projects such as the Baghdad, Manchurian, Cape to Cairo and Trans-Siberian railways were intended to open up the areas they traversed to trade, development and not least influence or control. Fierce competition for railway concessions derived from full awareness of the direct or indirect political consequences of their construction rather than as a result of commercial rivalry alone.

'Showing the flag' remains, to the present day, the traditional symbol of great power presence. For four centuries it was used by the European world. Before the First World War the visit of the German gunboat *Panther* to the port of Agadir signalled that France could not ignore German interests in Morocco. In 1946, when the United States sought to extend its peacetime involvement in world affairs to the Mediterranean, it was natural for it to turn to the Navy to perform this task. Secretary of the Navy James Forrestal suggested 'sending casual cruisers unannounced –

not as a fleet or a task force, but in small units – into the Mediterranean so that we may establish the custom of the American flag being flown in those waters'.[16]

In recent years the Soviet Union has adopted this classic expedient of imperialism to stake its claim to global influence. The political significance of a naval presence is universally recognized. Colonel Qadaffi of Libya (who has since changed his position towards the USSR) at one time declined even friendship visits in order to stress his neutrality vis-à-vis the superpowers: 'I do not want to be aligned with either East or West,' he stated in 1973. 'Therefore, I refuse to allow the fleets of the big powers to anchor in the ports of my country.'[17]

The acquisition of base rights of various kinds is one of the common methods of establishing political predominance, or at least exclusive influence. Soviet requests for military base rights at the Dardanelles were vigorously opposed by the United States in 1945–6 on the grounds that they would inevitably lead to Soviet control over Turkey. (Over thirty years before the then Tsarist Government of Russia had reacted equally vigorously to the appointment of the German General Liman von Sanders and his staff to command Turkish forces in Constantinople. This was also seen as the thin end of a wedge to assert exclusive political influence.)[18] Even states that have placed naval support facilities at the disposal of the USSR, such as Egypt and Yugoslavia, have been careful to avoid the impression that permanent base rights were being conceded and have hedged the use of facilities round with restrictions intended to make clear the conditional and limited nature of the concession.[19]

Words

Rule-making by words can be divided into (1) negotiation and (2) declaration.

Negotiation

Creating a situation on the ground only partly accomplishes the task of the international actor. After all, what has been effected can also, in many cases, be reversed. It is true that an innovation in the environment must necessarily be taken into account as part of reality, however transient. But there is nothing to guarantee the perpetuation of any but the most literally irreversible physical reality. If it is agreed that states act in conformity with their expectations of the future conduct of others, then some present state of the environment, believed to be temporary, will not provide a sufficient guide to action. It exists today, but by tomorrow it may have gone. The *status quo*, in this sense, is as much a psychological as a physical condition.

Should the new state of affairs be rejected by the opponent, then there is the risk that instead of becoming part of a new structure of expectations it will become at worst a cause of collision and at best a source of uncertainty and instability. A situation which others are dedicated to reversing and the principal is unsure of retaining fails to become a full part of the psychological 'reality'. Its permanence cannot be relied on; third parties may refuse to take account of it. The territories occupied by Israel after the 1967 War are a case in point. Israel's Arab neighbours failed to accept the acquisition; United States governments were always careful to limit their commitment to Israel's security to the state existing within the pre-1967 borders. This meant that Israel could not rely on support against, nor her Arab neighbours count on opposition to, hostile acts committed against Israel in the territories occupied.[20]

A new arrangement is completed only when it becomes anchored in expectations by acquiring the acceptance of other states involved and their renunciation of attempts to reverse it. Anything less will withhold from the perpetrator of the innovation the psychological predictability which is one of the conditions of stability. Having created a certain situation on the ground, therefore, states will be concerned to acquire the stamp of formal recognition precisely in order to remove any doubt whatsoever about its permanence and validity.

Sometimes this *post facto* legitimization is effective in cementing innovation into the structure of the established order. The formal approval of the community, international or regional, for an act of one of its members or for a new situation, possesses great force. There can be little doubt that the Final Act of the 1975 European Conference on Security and Cooperation has bestowed legitimacy on the territorial arrangement brought about by the Second World War. Arguments that the document could not confer legitimacy because it did not have legal force were beside the point, though they might comfort domestic opinion. 'Legitimacy', as Kenneth Boulding points out, 'is a wider concept than the formal concept of law.' It is the acceptance of those concerned that a state of affairs has become part of the established order.[21] Equally, legal recognition may fail to reflect real acceptance. If a settlement is imposed on the defeated without regard for their views, it may become a source of unending dissension. Dr Kissinger's analysis of the post-Napoleonic settlement is equally applicable to the 1871 Treaty of Frankfort (after the Franco-Prussian War) and the 1919 Treaty of Versailles imposed on Germany: 'There exist two legitimacies in such cases: the internal arrangements among the victorious powers and the claims of the defeated.'[22] Legal means may be the most generally accepted path to acquiring legitimacy. But they cannot, demonstrably, ensure the viability of an unacceptable arrangement.

Post facto legitimization may sometimes be unavoidable, but clearly such a potentially contentious and unreliable procedure cannot be the primary vehicle for introducing peaceful innovation. Nor, as the Soviet Union would probably admit, is a wait of thirty years for the stamp of legitimacy to be recommended. In domestic society change acquires legitimacy by being implemented in conformity with procedures accepted as fit and proper for the purpose; legitimacy is a quality of conduct rather than of retrospective approval. Law is made by organs of legislation with defined and recognized functions. Changes of government are peacefully achieved in Western societies by the working of a predetermined mechanism of succession based upon law and tradition. In the international system special problems arise. Innovation cannot be legislated, for there is no legislature. Nor can it be derived from received principles of legitimate succession since there are none. The only way that rules can evolve in an acceptable manner, in the absence of any simple, agreed and invariable formula for change, is by negotiation. Instead of legitimizing an arrangement that has already been put into effect with all its associated complications, negotiation seeks to achieve compliance with innovation before it has been implemented. A freely negotiated agreement permits the implementation of change with, and not in opposition to, the wishes of the parties involved. Any aggressor can induce a change on the ground, though its durability is another matter. The task of diplomacy is to modify the existing order without incurring a free for all in which everyone stands to lose.

In the making of rules of the game, therefore, negotiation performs an indispensable function. It is true that in the limiting case of tacit agreement explicit negotiation may perform a negligible role in the transmission of expectations. Articulation of agreement may be unnecessary because the area of common interest is sufficiently highlighted by the logic of the situation. Or positions may simply be defined by declaration rather than a constructive exchange of views. Finally, instructions as to their actions may be dictated by the hegemonial power to its satellites. But for explicit agreement on rules of the game, whether verbal, nonbinding or binding, to be arrived at between free agents, some form of negotiation is indispensable.

At a minimal level negotiation may illuminate and permit the straightforward articulation of convergent goals and interests without the reconciliation of differences. Even this would be precluded by the absence of diplomacy. At a more subtle level negotiation may provide a mechanism for the adjustment of claim and counterclaim and bridge the gap between competing desires and conceptions, creating agreement where none would otherwise have existed. Obviously its capacity to reconcile divergent interests is limited (though it can sometimes engineer the trade-off of mutual concessions in different areas and thereby permit agreement). However, accepting that diplomacy does not take place in a vacuum and that its role can only be fully understood within the context of existing constraints, the give and take of negotiations can project constructive and innovative solutions to difficult problems. Diplomacy, in short, cannot perform miracles, but if there is a conceivable basis of agreement only dialogue has the prospect of bringing it to the fore.

The indispensability of diplomacy can be demonstrated by examining an improbable instance of its working: the role it played in relations between Nazi Germany and Fascist Italy. Both powers were openly contemptuous of its utility. Foreign policy, for Hitler and Mussolini, often seemed like a mere continuation of war by other means; the *fait accompli*, subversion and force substituted for negotiations and compromise. Yet the noteworthy point is that when they decided on a policy of mutual accommodation they naturally turned to the only feasible vehicle for achieving this – diplomacy.

Until his attack on Abyssinia in 1935 Mussolini maintained an alignment with Britain and France based on a traditional respect for British naval power in the Mediterranean and opposition to German ambitions in Austria. Involvement in Abyssinia, League sanctions and the perceived hostility of Britian and France, however, produced a reorientation in Italian policy. Ideology complemented interest to draw Italy towards Nazi Germany: Hitler was the self-admitted pupil of Mussolini; both states proclaimed a strident opposition to communism and a belief in the decline of the decadent democracies.

One serious obstacle to close ties between the two states was Austria. As recently as 1934 Austrian Nazis had been responsible for the murder of the Austrian Chancellor Dollfuss, and Mussolini had moved Italian troops to the Brenner Pass as a warning to Germany. However at the beginning of May 1936 Hitler decided to respond to Austrian signals of willingness to negotiate a settlement of points in dispute. With the prospect of an improvement in Austro-German relations the possibility of a *rapprochement* with Italy also increased. The visit of an Italian inter-Services delegation to Berlin in the first week of June provided a clear indication of growing Italian interest. It was admitted in Rome that the officers had been received by Mussolini before their departure.[23] By the beginning of July Austro-German negotiations were drawing to a successful conclusion.

Meanwhile three of the five signatories of the Locarno Agreements on Western security of 1925, Britain, France and Belgium were meeting in Geneva (without the presence of the other two signatories, Germany and Italy) to discuss the implications of recent changes in the international situation, including the German remilitarization of the Rhineland of the previous March. It was decided to call a meeting at an early date to which Italy, but not Germany, would be invited. On 7 July Italy was formally invited to a conference to be held in Brussels. The invitation was to mark the final failure of the Western powers to keep Italy and Germany apart.

When the German Ambassador in Rome met with Mussolini and Ciano on 11 July, therefore, the conversation concentrated on two primary topics of mutual interest: Austria and Locarno. The German Ambassador started the conversation on a positive note: Germany was prepared to recognize the Italian conquest of Abyssinia whenever the question should arise. This was a clear gesture of friendship. Von Hassell then went on to inform the Italians that the successful conclusion of the Austro-German Agreement was expected that evening. Mussolini expressed 'lively satisfaction over the event, which . . . would finally remove the last and only mortgage on German–Italian relations'.

Moving on to the issue of the forthcoming meeting in Brussels of the Locarno powers Von Hassell posed an important question: If Germany were not invited to the talks, would Italy also be prepared to stay away? Mussolini grasped the outstretched hand: he fully agreed with the German request. A note had already been drawn up rejecting the meeting unless Germany was invited and certain mutual assistance agreements, concluded by Britain and France with the smaller Mediterranean states during the Abyssinian War (and clearly directed against Italy) were declared invalid.[24] Mussolini stressed the need for Italo-German cooperation over the conference: 'parallel German and Italian interests required their not being too hasty in the matter'. Here, for the first time, we see the unmistakable emergence of an agreement to cooperate. On this occasion the issue was limited and specific. But the groundwork was being laid for a much wider partnership.[25]

Under the terms of the Austro-German Agreement Germany recognized the full sovereignty of Austria in return for Austrian acknowledgement that she was 'a German state'. Not published was the Austrian agreement to align herself with German foreign policy and to include representatives of the Nazi Party in the federal government.[26] Mussolini immediately declared his 'satisfaction' at the treaty.[27] Von Hassell reported home the 'profound impression' felt in Rome. Fear of an *Anschluss* had 'at least temporarily, been removed' and a burden on German–Italian relations lifted. He quoted Mussolini as saying 'that in the course of the last twelve months events had shown clearly enough the parallelism between German and Italian interests, which formed a much better basis for political cooperation than formal pacts or emotional attitudes'.[28]

From this point on, signs of growing German–Italian cooperation began to appear. When the Western powers conceded Italy's terms for the Brussels meeting, Italy and Germany announced their acceptance of the invitation in almost identical form after prior coordination. It was made clear that both countries were keeping each other fully informed.[29]

With the outbreak of the Civil War in Spain a further area for 'parallel' German–Italian action appeared. As cooperation extended it became increasingly important for the two sides to sit down and define in a more explicit way the rules of the game which were to govern their overall relations. On 23 September 1936 an important meeting took place between Mussolini and Hans Frank, German Minister without portfolio. Alongside a general review of the international situation, two cardinal principles of German–Italian relations were enunciated: German disinterest in the Mediterranean, notwithstanding support on ideological grounds for the Spanish rebels, and an assurance of strict German adherence to the Austro-German Agreement of 11 July 1936. Frank passed on the personal message of Hitler 'that he regards the Mediterranean as a purely Italian sea. Italy has a right to positions of privilege and control in the Mediterranean. The interests of the Germans are turned towards the Baltic'. He concluded by expressing the hope of 'increasingly close collaboration'.

For his part Mussolini associated himself absolutely with the Austro-German Agreement and claimed that he himself had made the initial suggestion to the Austrian Chancellor. He acknowledged that 'Austria was . . . a German country'.[30]

On the basis of the virtual spheres of influence understanding sketched out between Mussolini and Frank both Foreign Offices began work on a detailed protocol governing German–Italian relations. The document itself and the conversations which accompanied its final drafting provided a most exhaustive programme for future cooperation between the two countries in fields ranging from negotiations for a pact to replace Locarno, policy towards the League, policy towards communist propaganda, recognition of the Franco regime and joint military action in Spain, coordination prior to any international economic conference, and mutual support in such matters as German colonial aspirations, relations with Austria and Italian aims in Abyssinia.[31] On 1 November 1936 Mussolini announced the creation of the 'axis' in a speech in Milan.[32]

Irrespective, therefore, of the ideology of the participants, diplomacy provides the mechanisms and language of discourse necessary for states to work out their differences and arrive at agreement. The expedients of diplomacy, institutional, juridical and ceremonial, are usually taken for granted. But without the ambassador with the defined role, the gesture with the known weight and the document with the conventional significance, negotiation would be difficult if not impossible. This is true even for a Hitler or a Mussolini.

Declarations

Declaratory diplomacy involves the use of public channels of communication – the speech, media interview or statement – to define the limits of tolerance or extent of one's claim in a particular area. It may be chosen because the alternative of quiet diplomacy is precluded or because publication is intended to broadcast the irrevocability of one's position. A willingness to negotiate is usually accompanied by the recognition that the final outcome will reflect some kind of compromise. Publicity and flexibility are antithetical; therefore declarations on the whole hinder if not preclude negotiation.

The solemn warning, the declaration of commitment, the assertion of interest (or disinterest) are familiar weapons in the diplomatic armoury. Quite detailed propositions, such as Israel's offer to the Soviet Union in 1970 of a *modus vivendi* on the Suez Canal, have also come in declaratory form.[33]

A recent study by Herbert Dinerstein on the origins of the 1962 Cuban missile crisis permits some insight into the extent to which declaratory diplomacy is exploited as a device to manage expectations and thus, it is hoped, to control events – but also into its danger and ineffectiveness.[34] From July 1960 to the American discovery of the Soviet missiles in September 1962 the Soviet Union was engaged in a verbal exercise, carefully publicized by Soviet news agencies, to draw Cuba away from the sphere of legitimate American action and into that of the Soviet Union.

It all began with a speech made by Khrushchev on 9 July 1960 in which Soviet support of Cuba was given the totally new dimension of nuclear strength: 'It must not be forgotten that now the United States is not so inaccessibly distant from the Soviet Union as in the past. Figuratively speaking, Soviet artillerymen, in case of need, can with their missile fire support the Cuban people if the aggressive forces of the Pentagon dare begin intervention against Cuba.'[35] It is true that Khrushchev was talking 'figuratively' and said 'can' rather than 'will', but the point was well taken, not least by a satisfied Castro.

President Eisenhower responded immediately. He warned that the United States would never permit the establishment of a regime dominated by international communism in the Western Hemisphere, thus reaffirming in the face of Soviet probing that Cuba was to be still considered as falling within the American sphere of influence. Unfortunately Eisenhower went on to announce his determination to uphold the Rio Treaty, thus limiting himself to acting within the Organization of American States. Failing a two-thirds majority in that body, intervention in Cuba would expose the United States to the charge of violating the sovereignty of a sister American republic.[36]

The Soviet press now moved a stage further by publishing foreign comments on the Khrushchev speech in which the reservations had been excised from the originally conditional commitment.

Far from clarifying the attitude of his Government to this challenging trend President Eisenhower proceeded to add to the ambiguity. Asked by a reporter if the United States would permit a communist-dominated regime in Cuba, the President replied that if Cuba were in the position of a satellite state, very definite action would be called for. But if communism were freely established, he did not see how the United States could object or intervene. He did not believe that this was going to happen, however.[37]

By the autumn of 1960 the United States was approaching the climax of its presidential campaign. Both Nixon and Kennedy, the two candidates, made it plain that they thought Cuba was 'lost' and had to be 'freed'. To quieten consequent Cuban anxiety Khrushchev repeated his warning to the United States. He denied to a Cuban journalist on 22 October that he had spoken symbolically on 9 July and agreed that the threat would remain symbolic only if the imperialists did not convert their menaces into military actions. Khrushchev's comments were not couched in the clearest of language. Nevertheless he had reiterated and even reinforced his commitment to defend Cuba.[38]

So far there was no reason for the Soviet Union to assume that its claim to involvement in the affairs of South America had made any real dent in the historic principle of United States' hegemony on the American continent – a doctrine enunciated by President Monroe in 1823, effected by the defeat of Spain in 1898 and practised successfully for over half a century. The disastrous and half-hearted Bay of Pigs invasion and its aftermath were to change all this.

On 18 April 1961 the CIA-backed invasion of Cuba by Cuban exiles launched from Miami began its abortive course. The same day a Soviet Government statement on the invasion and a personal message from Khrushchev to Kennedy were delivered to the American Embassy in Moscow *before* the Soviet Government could have known whether or not the invasion had been abandoned by the United States. The official statement warned that the Soviet Union would not 'abandon the Cuban people in their plight' and that 'interference in Cuba's internal affairs must cease immediately'. Otherwise 'the peaceful lives of the population of the United States' would be placed in jeopardy.

The personal message was more explicit, though obviously less committal (which was presumably the purpose of the double-message device): 'As for the Soviet Union let there be no misunderstanding of our position: We will give the Cuban people and their government every assistance necessary to repulse the armed attack on Cuba.'

In his fateful reply to the Soviet note President Kennedy denied any intention of intervening militarily in Cuba, apparently yielding to the Soviet demand.[39] Whatever the weight given to Soviet threats within the American Government, the decision to leave the Cuban emigrés to their fate after they had been set up by the United States could only have appeared as a remarkable victory in Soviet eyes for their policy of deterrence. The episode had thus brought about an extraordinary reversal of the rules of the game between the superpowers. The Soviet Union had proclaimed, with apparent success, its 'right' to intervene in Cuba to protect the Castro regime; the United States had conceded the 'right' to intervene against a government inimical to its interests at the very moment when, with American prestige at stake, it could have been expected to do so.

On 19 April 1961 a Soviet journalist reported from New York that the American expectation of beating Cuba in a lightning stroke had miscarried and that the United States had failed to anticipate the Soviet offer of aid to Cuba. Khrushchev's warning to Washington showed that the gamble on isolating Cuba had failed.[40]

Any lingering doubts that Khrushchev may have had about the effectiveness of his threats or of the safety of supporting movements beyond the hitherto accepted peripheries of Soviet influence would have been dispelled by Kennedy's amazingly inept admission to him during their summit meeting at Vienna the following June that the Bay of Pigs had been a mistake.[41] Kennedy had made the inexcusable error for a national leader of confusing his personal wish to create a frank and friendly relationship with his Soviet counterpart with his official duty to represent and express in measured words the best interests of his country.

Having established, with such apparent success, its claim to intervene in Cuba, a state formerly a client of the United States, the Soviet Union could now move one further step forward to asserting a right to overseas bases. In a statement of 18 February 1962 on the Cuban problem the

Soviet Union denied the exclusivity of American rights to overseas bases, referring obliquely to the American Guantanamo base on Cuba:

If the United States threatens Cuba, then let it draw conclusions regarding countries where American military bases are located. Some people in the United States, still relying on the policy of 'positions of strength', continue to rattle weapons and threaten other peace-loving states; but this is a stick with two ends. If the United States seizes one end of the stick, then other states can take hold of the other end and employ it against those forces that the United States employs to threaten the Soviet Union and other peace-loving states.[42]

The United States failed to note this extension of Soviet pretensions and Herbert Dinerstein suggests that silence was taken to imply consent.[43]

For about a year and a half the Soviet bloc had been supplying Cuba with large-scale military assistance including MIG jet fighters.[44] In July and August 1962 several thousand Soviet 'technicians' and large quantities of military equipment began arriving on the island. In the face of mounting reports of the presence of missiles, albeit only of the short-range, defensive type, Attorney-General Robert Kennedy 'thought that maybe the President ought to issue some sort of warning statement to the Soviet Union so that it would know in advance that we would not tolerate the installation of long-range ballistic missiles'.[45]

On 4 September, therefore, President Kennedy publicly confirmed press reports of the presence on Cuba of anti-aircraft missiles but denied evidence of

any organized combat force in Cuba from any Soviet bloc country; of military bases provided to Russia; of a violation of the 1934 treaty relating to Guantanamo; of the presence of offensive ground-to-ground missiles; or of other significant offensive capability either in Cuban hands or under Soviet direction and guidance. *Were it to be otherwise, the gravest issues would arise.*[46]

The warning was repeated at a press conference on 13 September.[47] At long last, but too late, the United States had come out with its own firm and unambiguous declaration. Unfortunately the missiles were already being installed . . .

In the end the Khrushchev – Kennedy exercise in declaratory diplomacy proved disastrous. Intended to sketch out the bounds of permissible action on both sides, the result was absolute incomprehension and a mutual failure of anticipation. Both seriously miscalculated the effectiveness of communicating rules by declaration. The one fortunate outcome of the entire episode was a realization of the need to develop much clearer guidelines to permitted conduct and of more effective channels of communication.

The 1962 failure of signalling is by no means a unique one in the history of diplomacy. On the contrary, as a method of rule definition declaratory diplomacy has a consistently poor record. Grey's warning to France in 1895 against incursion into the Sudan was ignored: the result was the Fashoda crisis of 1898. Similarly, Chinese declarations to the

United States to keep clear of the Sino-Korean border in 1950 fell on deaf ears. As Chinese Foreign Minister Ch'en Yi recalled in 1962: 'At the time of the Korean War, we first warned against crossing the thirty-eighth parallel but America ignored the warning. The second time, we warned again, but America occupied Pyong-yang. The third time, we warned once again, but America aggressed close to the Yalu River and threatened the security of China.'[48] The result was China's entry into the Korean War.

Whether the difficulty with declaratory diplomacy is the inattention of the opponent, bureaucratic obtuseness or a temptation to use it for bluff, devaluing the credibility of this form of communication, declarations are plainly not excessively to be relied on. Words cannot substitute for a willingness to act, create capabilities where none exist, set up constraints which others do not believe can be maintained, or harmonize contradictory interests. They can only clarify, emphasize and reinforce a situation perceived by the opponent to exist in fact or in potential on the ground. Diplomacy, whether declaratory or silent, can only be effective if it matches the means of verbal persuasion at its disposal to concrete realities.

It follows from this that the way to mitigate the unreliability of declaratory diplomacy is to reinforce the verbal message with visible actions as an earnest of intent. In the October 1973 crisis the USSR signalled to the United States to restrain Israel from destroying the Egyptian Third Army on two complementary channels: in a letter 'leaving little to the imagination', as Senator Jackson put it, First Secretary Brezhnev placed before his American counterparts the alternative of joining in a joint Soviet–American force to impose a ceasefire or risk seeing the Soviet Union act alone by sending her own forces to the area. Alongside the verbal message came a set of blatant military indicators, including the alerting of Soviet airborne troops and preparations to implement the supply operation needed to support such a force.

Dr Kissinger's rejection of the Soviet proposals was no less emphatic. At a press conference on 25 October he spelled out the American refusal to any move which would 'transplant the great-power rivalry into the Middle East'. The United States, he warned, would 'oppose the use of threat by any country to achieve a position of predominance, either globally or regionally'. Simultaneously it was made known that United States forces, including troops and strategic nuclear forces, had been put in a state of 'standby alert'.

By the next day Israel had been persuaded to stop, the alert was cancelled and Secretary Brezhnev was speaking in more conciliatory tones; the confrontation was at an end.[49]

Warnings, like other verbal pronouncements in diplomacy, are most effective when coordinated with measures on the ground. The message is communicated together with the means for its accomplishment. Statements of threat or admonition, however adequate they may appear to the signaller, may be overlooked, suppressed or disbelieved by the audience to which they are directed. Words, after all, cannot in themselves change realities. For a message to be communicated both unmistakably and credibly it is well to demonstrate, for the benefit of doubters, the consequences of inattention.

Chapter eleven

Maintaining rules

Rules of the game are above all else a wasting asset. Unless renewed they are subject to a constant process of decay. Even where rules are expressed in binding legal form they are not immutable because although the text may be unaltered, expectations of the validity of that text continuously alter. That an agreement possesses formal status does not mean that it is exempted from the eroding effects of time and changing circumstances.

There are two reasons for the built-in obsolescence of rules of the game. The first reason is the basic assumption of actors, pointed out in chapter four, that this is the case. This may sound like circular reasoning. However it is simply a universal lesson of experience. No observer of foreign policy can conclude other than that time and changing circumstances inexorably erode the validity of prescriptions about international behaviour. Were rules of the game to lay down categorical moral imperatives, true for all actors and periods, the assumption of obsolescence would not hold. But rules of the game are not ethical axioms; they are arrangements, tacit or explicit, without any inherent, immutable value; they are instruments, not goals. States follow their prescriptions not because they are 'good' but because they are existential facts about the level of expectations in the international community at a given point in time.

Rules of the game, though, are facts of a particular kind: they are *conditional* propositions which only hold under assumed circumstances. As statements about expectations they rest on the confidence of the observer in the well-foundedness of his judgement. To the extent that conditions remain constant, that confidence is likely to be upheld. The more conditions alter, the lower one's confidence is likely to be. Included in the concept of conditions liable to change is a chain of contingent factors the constancy of any one of which may be crucial to confidence. In order better to grasp the role of confidence in the stability of rules of the game one has only to consider both the sensitivity and the consequentiality of the same factor in the economy; confidence is of the essence in the orderly working of financial institutions. Moreover the logic of mutual expectations may easily convert a shift in mood into a self-fulfilling prophecy: if others lose confidence in one's credit-worthiness or credibility, this may result in unmanageable pressure on one's commitments.

Among those central factors on which confidence in expectations is likely to be conditional are the following.

The identity of actors involved

A change in the leadership of a state calls into question the reliability of its commitment to the rule. One cannot assume that the new leadership will understand or accept the rule in the same way – if at all – as did its predecessor. Infringement of a promise casts doubt on the credibility of the one who gave his word. But the same kind of personal responsibility does not bind those not a party to the original contract. This is, of course, a psychological, not a legal point. Under international law treaties are supposed to bind states, not their agents. However, the repudiation of commitments is not confined to understandings nonbinding under international law, as is demonstrated by the rejection by successive British Governments of the terms of Britain's entry into the European Economic Community. History amply justifies the doubt cast by actors on the continuity of obligations from one regime to the next. At the very least a change of government is known to provide a timely and convenient pretext for a reappraisal of uncomfortable commitments. This is why a new government that does want to maintain continuity of obligations must actually say so. Clearly this is not something that can be otherwise taken for granted. Assurances of this kind have even been given by American Administrations.[1]

The interests of actors

Acceptance of an obligation or prohibition derives from a particular perception of the national interest at a certain point in time. But perceptions of interest are themselves subject to a host of independent and variable influences. As long as Britain was vulnerable only to invasion from the sea, her vital interests were associated with the independence of the Low Countries. The development of air power in the interwar period shifted Britain's defensive boundary, in Stanley Baldwin's words, 'from Dover to the Rhine'. After 1945 it shifted again to the West German border with the communist bloc. 'Isn't it better', a Ministry of Defence advertisement asked, 'to have our frontier on the Elbe than on Brighton beach?'[2] As interests change, so do the commitments that derive from them. Separate national interests, which converge at one moment permitting agreement, diverge as goals are achieved and new problems arise.

Actors' capability

Rules of the game reflect and are underpinned by a given configuration of power. That configuration can alter as a result of change in any one of the parameters of national strength such as technology, armament, economic viability, government stability, national will and so on. Or the distribution of power in a given area can shift as a result of the retreat or breakup of a previously dominant actor. Once his 'guarantee' is withdrawn, a new pattern of predominance will emerge and local actors will be obliged to redefine the normative structure of their relationships. In this context one could include .the British withdrawal from the Persian Gulf and that of the United States from Vietnam, with the far-reaching repercussions they set off.

The nature of the wider international environment

Autonomous developments in the natural, scientific and social worlds create new problems and conditions which old arrangements cannot solve and perhaps do not even cover. The outcome of the Vietnam War, the rise in the price of oil and the emergence of a 'third world' majority at the United Nations are dramatic developments of this kind which have overturned fundamental assumptions. Without an overall perspective on historical change – and this is not the place for it – it would be impossible to do justice to the complexity of this problem. Nevertheless even a rudimentary sketch is sufficient to draw attention to the precariousness of the factors underpinning confidence in existing rules of the game. It is hardly surprising that actors presuppose their inherent obsolescence. There is nothing discreditable about this. If circumstances did not change, there would be no need for rules of the game at all. It is precisely the unpredictability of the future which makes guides to expectations necessary in the first place.

A second reason for the obsolescence of rules, besides the fragility of the confidence of observers, relates to the psychology of rule acquisition. Rules of the game are expectations of behaviour derived from learning situations of a kind described in the previous chapter. Their tendency to continuous decay can be compared to that of other types of response. In the classic Pavlovian model of associative learning a conditioned response (salivation) is formed when a conditioned stimulus (a light) is repeatedly accompanied by an unconditioned stimulus (meat powder). However if the experiment continues and the reward (reinforcement) is omitted, then the amount of response gradually diminishes. This is known as a process of *extinction*.[3] Analogously, in international politics failure to maintain reinforcement of a particular expectation will lead, under the eroding influence of factors discussed above, to its gradual extinction. Thus the continuing validity of a given rule of the game can only be assured by its constant reinforcement. The burden of this chapter will accordingly consist of an examination of the ways in which actors reinforce rules of the game in order to maintain confidence in their validity.

The working of the process of extinction in international politics can be exemplified by the steady erosion in expectations, that took place throughout the summer of 1938, that Britain would fight for Czechoslovakia. Over the weekend of 21–22 May 1938 the British Government became convinced that rumours of German troop movements in Silesia and northern Austria indicated an imminent German attack on Czechoslovakia. The German Government were consequently warned in the most solemn terms. If a conflict should arise between Germany and Czechoslovakia, France would 'be compelled to intervene in virtue of her obligations' and 'in such circumstances His Majesty's Government could not guarantee that they would not be forced by circumstances to become involved also'.[4]

In the atmosphere of crisis and imminent expectation of war which had gripped the capitals of Europe the British declaration had a profound effect. It was believed to have saved the peace and finally, at long last, swung Britain behind efforts to contain German power. Ironically, the British Government had not anticipated the depth of this impression and hastily tried to retreat into their previous more neutral position. Efforts were at once made to correct the belief that a commitment had, in effect, been given to the security of Czechoslovakia. In Czechoslovakia itself, for instance, the warning 'acquired the highest significance. The fact that we acted at all, and at this precise moment, has made a deep impression. We are, naturally, regarded as having committed ourselves, morally at any rate, to intervene if there is a European war.'[5] The expectation had been conditioned; the May crisis, in effect, had acted as a test case of British purpose.

In the negotiations which followed throughout the summer of 1938 between the Sudeten Germans and the Czechoslovak Government – in which Britain, France and Germany became increasingly involved – the image of determination and the expectation of her intervention which Britain had acquired in May could have been of great help, not least in deterring Germany. However, far from exploiting this expectation to restrain German demands, which were becoming ever more strident, Britain steadily retreated from her original position. The German Government became increasingly confident that they would be able to press home their demands on Czechoslovakia (presented through the supposedly independent Sudeten German Party) without risk of British or French opposition.

A key role in the effacement of the original impression was played by the British Ambassador in Berlin, Nevile Henderson, who was convinced of Hitler's irrationality and that any repetition of the warning of 21 May would drive him to desperation. As early as 28 May the firmness of the British position was tested out by a high German official. How could the Czechs be exhorted to reason, he asked Henderson, while being promised 'that in the extreme resort they would after all receive assistance'? Henderson rose to the bait. If the Czechs were to commit 'unbearable provocation, then Britain would not support them, but would on the contrary leave them to their fate'. Henderson continued to minimize the significance of the British declaration and never lost an opportunity to express his personal bias in favour of the Sudeten Germans. On 6 August he went so far as to say 'that Great Britain would not think of risking even one sailor or airman for Czechoslovakia'.[6]

By midsummer Nazi agitation against Czechoslovakia had reached a new pitch of violence. Far from re-emphasizing previous warnings to Germany, Britain merely increased her onesided pressure on Czechoslovakia. In the Mediterranean, Mussolini, contrary to repeated solemn assurances, including an agreement signed with Britain in April, increased Italian intervention in the Spanish Civil War. Italian bombing of civilian targets continued; nor were British ships in Spanish waters immune. Between mid-April and mid-June 1938 twenty-two British-registered ships were attacked, of which eleven were either sunk or very seriously damaged. Twenty-one British seamen died. Passivity in the face of this kind of provocation could only call into question British willingness to stand by her interests. Sir Robert Vansittart admitted this on 11 August: 'May 21 had made a deep impression at the time but he thought it had largely been "effaced"; every fresh surrender in Spain had deepened the "effacement". He doubted whether there was now a single adviser to tell Hitler that he might soon be fighting a European war.' Jan Masaryk, the Czechoslovak Minister in London, agreed with Vansittart: 'Britain had done a good stroke on May 21 by making some of these Germans believe that she would be drawn in, and what was needed was something more now to confirm the impression, which had become weaker with time.'[7] Reporting from Berlin, French Ambassador François-Poncet corroborated these assessments: Germany now expected that Britain 'would remain passive' in the event of a German attack on Czechoslovakia. French Foreign Minister Bonnet accordingly instructed his representative in London to suggest that the British Government renew the warning already given to Germany. Lord Halifax disagreed, believing that quite enough had been said already.[8]

In Germany itself the impression made by the British *démarche* inevitably lessened with the passage of time just as western observers feared. At the end of 1937, in his famous conference of 5 November, Hitler had expressed the belief that Britain and France had 'tacitly written off the Czechs'. After the May scare he continued to rely on this intuition and indeed, in his rage at being humiliated by appearing to back down, registered his 'unalterable decision to smash Czechoslovakia'.[9] On the other hand he could now no longer overlook the *possibility* of Anglo-French intervention. Thus in a draft directive of 18 June 1938 it was affirmed that military action against Czechoslovakia would be decided upon only 'if . . . I am firmly convinced that France will not march and that consequently Britain will not intervene'.[10] In the middle of July Hitler instructed his adjutant, Wiedemann, to justify Germany's western fortifications by referring to the May episode: 'We saw on 21 May just what to expect of France and Britain.'[11] Any hesitations that may have resulted from the prospect of a war in the West were, however, soon dispelled. On 28 July Wiedemann was reported to have said that Hitler was still resolved on war even if the West intervened.[12]

Although Hitler (and Foreign Minister Ribbentrop) may have been prepared to run the risk of Anglo-French intervention, whatever the consequences, after 22 May army and government circles were very seriously concerned by the eventuality. Generals Beck and Jodl were both certain that France and Britain would interfere were Czechoslovakia attacked.[13] Gradually this certainty diminished. Writing on 20 June 1938, after several reassuring meetings with Henderson, von Weizsäcker, permanent head (State Secretary) of the German Foreign Office, cautioned Ribbentrop that Czechoslovakia could 'easily lead to conflict with the Entente'. The problem was 'not yet ripe enough for an immediate attack, which the Entente would watch passively'.[14] By mid-August 1938, as Vansittart and François-Poncet learned from their own sources of information, the initial German dismay at Hitler's seemingly suicidal policy had subsided. Hitler himself had regained his confidence that 'other powers would certainly not make any move'; Britain and France would not intervene.[15] In the absence of a repetition of British warnings, critics of Hitler inside the regime were devoid of all ammunition. Thus Britain was to embark on the final stage of the Czechoslovak crisis having dissipated the one sure asset with which she had entered the dispute.

Given the steady extinction or effacement of rules, the problem of their renewal becomes of central importance to the whole conduct of foreign affairs. A series of devices performs this task of reinforcement. In order of emphasis they are: (1) verbal reiteration; (2) symbolic repetition; (3) diplomatic reaffirmation; (4) active enforcement.

Verbal reiteration

In the first instance rules of the game are maintained by the platitudinous repetition of received principles. All relevant diplomatic declarations may be mobilized for this task, including communiqués, speeches and even after-dinner toasts. This constant repetition, tedious to casual observers, is not meant to impart new information but to reinforce a previously learned response. Diplomatic reiteration can be compared with learning by rote in the classroom; the response is conditioned by a repetitive drill; frequent revision keeps the lesson in mind. Peculiar to diplomacy is the expectation of observers that repetition of a principle is necessary, not only to condition the response, but also to demonstrate that the actor concerned is still interested in maintaining the rule. Should the reiteration cease this is likely to be interpreted as an indication of an underlying intention on the part of the actor to dissociate himself from the rule in question. Former US Secretary of State Cyrus Vance commented ruefully on the scrutiny to which his declarations were subjected:

You have to be damn careful. If you're loose with what you say you may have lost the case. I am dealing with a lot of nations who are watching. Don't think they don't dissect every word. Every time you vary one word or one clause from the standard formulation, you get a rocket from each of the parties saying you've changed the position of the U.S.[16]

Actually Vance was being slightly ingenuous here. With his wealth of experience he was a past master of edging away from a policy by gradual, and at each stage marginal, semantic changes.[17]

The role of declaratory reiteration can be well illustrated from the case of Soviet–Yugoslav relations. After the death of Stalin in 1953 Yugoslavia and the Soviet Union began to work on mending the rift which had occurred at the time of Yugoslavia's expulsion from the Cominform in 1948. In May 1955 a Soviet delegation at the highest level visited Belgrade. From the moment that he greeted this group at the airport Tito did not lose a single opportunity to set out the irreducible principles which he insisted were to govern future relations between the two states: equality, independence and non-interference in internal affairs. Such principles may not seem remarkable in themselves, but were of the highest significance in the light of previous relations and compared to those governing Moscow's ties with her East European satellites.

The Soviet Union was obliged to accept Tito's terms. The Belgrade Declaration (communiqué) of 2 June 1955, signed at a state and not party level in order to indicate the equality of the signatories, has provided, ever since, the authoritative text for the conduct of Yugoslav–Soviet relations. Among its provisions are the following: 'respect for sovereignty, independence, territorial integrity, and for equality between the states in their mutual relations;' peaceful coexistence between nations; 'mutual respect and non-interference in internal affairs for any reason;' a discontinuation of propaganda.[18]

These principles have not been abstract and empty phrases but have provided the operative rules for relations between the two states. Yugoslavia has tenaciously insisted on nothing less. To the extent that the Belgrade Declaration had been maintained, Yugoslavia has seen its relations with the Soviet Union as satisfactory; to the extent that the Soviet Union has tried to whittle away from these principles or to use them as a stepping-stone to the reabsorption of Yugoslavia in the Soviet bloc, Yugoslavia has fought with all her strength for their preservation. And in the background has been a Yugoslav willingness, in the final analysis, to oppose with armed force any attempt by Warsaw Pact forces to infringe upon her independence.

Following any period of tension or uncertainty in Soviet–Yugoslav relations it is to the text of the 1955 Declaration that Yugoslavia has insisted they look as a basis for a renewal of relations. When Tito and Khrushchev met in August 1957 for the first time after the Hungarian uprising the communiqué which followed their talks 'affirmed the momentous importance of the Belgrade and Moscow Declarations . . . and expressed their readiness to continue to implement the principles set forth in these Declarations'. So it was after a rift which lasted from 1958 to 1962, after the fall of Khrushchev in 1964 and in the wake of the gravest challenge to Soviet–Yugoslav relations posed by the Warsaw Pact invasion of Czechoslovakia in 1968.[19]

Together with a Yugoslav insistence on the terms of the 1955 Declaration has gone an equally firm resistance to any formula, declaration or even ritual which might indicate endorsement, tacit or formal, of Soviet pre-eminence or of Yugoslav inclusion in the Soviet sphere of influence. Thus at a meeting in Moscow in 1957, commemorative of the October Revolution, the Yugoslav delegation refused to put its signature to a joint declaration 'on the grounds that it revived the concept of a bloc in which one country was assigned a leading role'. In a similar light must be understood Tito's refusal to accept an invitation to a meeting of communist parties in Moscow in June 1969 since this might be thought to imply tacit approval to Soviet claims to pre-eminence.[20]

Since 1968 the Belgrade Declaration has continued to enjoy a prominent and invariant place in political pronouncements between the two states. This was the case after state visits in 1971, 1972 and 1973. By 1976, however, Yugoslav leaders were becoming worried by a seemingly deliberate and disquieting Soviet tendency to pass over the 1955 Declaration in silence. Suspicions, never far from the surface, began to re-emerge that Moscow might still regard Yugoslavia as within the Soviet sphere of influence and therefore subject to the iniquitous Brezhnev Doctrine invoked against Czechoslovakia in 1968. It was with obvious relief, therefore, that the communiqué which concluded a visit by the Soviet leader to Belgrade in November 1976 – his first in five years – was received. Once more the validity of the 1955 accord was reaffirmed. Equally significantly the term 'socialist internationalism', which had appeared innocuously in 1963 but which had acquired more sinister overtones in 1968, was dropped. Instead the communiqué introduced the obviously compromise formula of 'internationalist, comradely and voluntary cooperation', giving the Russians the opportunity to emphasize internationalism and the Yugoslavs to place the accent upon 'voluntary cooperation'.[21]

It is with such apparently trivial nuances that many diplomatic exchanges are concerned. But one should not be misled by appearances. Behind the nuance and the platitude lie substantive issues possessing far-reaching implications. Diplomatic texts provide, by convention, a recognized guide to the rules of the game governing relations between the signatories. Any change in Soviet–Yugoslav relations away from the 1955 Declaration and towards a text more favourable to the Soviet Union will be understood and will mean that Yugoslavia's long struggle to retain its independence has finally weakened.

Symbolic repetition

Rules of the game may be maintained, not only by the platitudinous repetition of verbal formulae but also, where appropriate, by the regular performance of a practice which, symbolically or directly, perpetuates an established rule of conduct. In the animal world the territory of the group or the individual creature is continuously marked out by activities such as the regular deposition of urine at certain points along the boundary, bird song, patrolling, visual signalling and, if necessary, active defence.[22] These practices are recognized by other members of the species as indicating possession. Their discontinuation signifies an end of possession.

Analogously, rules of the game in international politics may be preserved by ritual display. A good example of a practice regularly performed to demonstrate the continuing validity of a rule of the game is the United States' habit of sending a small squadron of frigates, once or twice a year, for a short cruise in the Black Sea. Throughout the postwar period the Soviet Union has sought to establish the principle, in opposition to the terms of the 1936 Montreux Convention, that the Black Sea is a *mare clausum*, that is, closed to all but Black Sea powers. Though not a signatory of the Montreux Convention, the United States has refuted the Soviet version and wished to maintain the accepted principle of freedom of transit and navigation through the Straits in accordance with appropriate international agreements. (The United States may also have been concerned to avoid the strategic asymmetry which would arise if, while Soviet warships enjoyed a free entry into the Mediterranean and access to the vulnerable coasts of Southern Europe, the Soviet Union's own Black Sea coastline possessed immunity from the fleets of the NATO powers.) If the United States were to cease the practice no one else would maintain it and the validity of the principle would lapse by dint of disuse.

Thus a regular pattern of visits has been established: in October 1963, September 1965, January 1966, November 1967, June and December 1968, June, August, September and December 1969, March, May, August and December 1970, April, July and November 1971 etc. For its part the USSR, pursuing a mirror-image policy, rarely neglects to protest at the American cruises which it condemns as provocative and illegal.[23]

A similar ritual of 'boundary renewal' has arisen from the concern of the Western allies to maintain the credibility of their commitment to the defence of West Berlin. Partly this requirement has been met by stationing troops in the city and punctiliously insisting on every detail of ritual and procedure laid down in the original occupation agreements. But since there is no way that the allied garrisons could actually withstand a determined onslaught their mere presence has been considered an inadequate warranty of Western political purpose.

One solution to this problem has been to arrange periodic visits to the city by prominent western leaders. In August 1961 Vice-President Johnson visited West Berlin, followed by President Kennedy in June 1963 (when he made his 'Ich bin ein Berliner' speech), Harold Wilson in March 1965, Queen Elizabeth II in May 1965, American Secretary of Defence Clark Clifford in October 1968, President Nixon in February 1969 and Vice-President Mondale in February 1977. Each one of these figures has represented and usually declared his country's commitment to the defence and independence of West Berlin. Paying the obligatory visit to Berlin in July 1978 President Carter declared: 'We consider an attack on Western Europe to be the same as an attack on the United States. Whatever happens, Berlin will remain free.'[24] Thus declaration and ritual combined to reinforce the learned response, and to convince observers that the United States was still prepared to make the effort of persuasion.

Diplomatic reaffirmation

When a rule is perceived to be at risk, because of others' disregard or their deliberate exploration of the validity of existing limits, declaratory and symbolic repetition may be felt to provide inadequate reaffirmation. At this point a courteous diplomatic reminder is called for. Between states enjoying correct or purportedly correct relations, routine diplomatic contact is the obvious initial recourse. If it succeeds, so much the better; if it fails, the nature of the challenge is confirmed and the need for more emphatic measures demonstrated. Indeed one of the purposes of prior understanding is to provide one with a legitimate basis for future claims and, if necessary, defensive counteraction.

As long as a state wishes to preserve the overall terms of some agreement or the friendly nature of a relationship it is bound to lend a sympathetic ear to the justified appeals of its partner. This is true irrespective of its underlying motives in concluding the agreement. Even the Polish–German Non-Aggression Pact of 1934, so brutally denounced by Hitler in 1939, functioned effectively in this regard for as long as Germany continued to be interested in maintaining proper relations with Poland. Up to the start of the rot at the end of 1938 Polish diplomacy successfully intervened on several occasions to protect its rights, basing its initiatives on the peaceful consultation clauses of the 1934 accord. In 1935, for example, the German Foreign Minister even anticipated an approach by the Polish Government and advised the Nazi President of the Danzig Senate in advance to avoid steps provocative to Poland since they might 'inevitably have an extremely harmful effect on German–Polish relations'. When friction did nonetheless ensue between Poland and the Danzig authorities over some issue of jurisdiction, Hitler received the Polish Ambassador with demonstrative consideration and immediately ordered urgent steps to be taken to settle that particular dispute in conformity with Polish wishes.[25]

Active enforcement

Ideally, in order to maintain the normative order, it should be sufficient to clarify unambiguously for the potential violator the bounds of the permissible and the consequences of an infringement of those bounds. How-

ever, should quiet diplomacy fail to parry others' attempts to extend existing limits, preservation of the rules of the game may well rest on one's
willingness and ability to ensure their enforcement. Thus the 'bottom
line' of the preservation of rules is the strength to stand firm on one's
interests; this is why rules of the game at any one time are contingent on
a given distribution of power. Rules that cannot be enforced run the risk
of being replaced by others reflecting more closely the interests of the
powerful at the expense of the weak. This is not to say that there is a
linear link between the unenforceability of a rule and its redundancy.
Reputation alone may be sufficient to maintain the credibility of a commitment for an indeterminate period. Or the validity of the rule may not
be put to the test. Conversely, a rule may cease to be enforced because of
a loss of nerve rather than a loss of power.

Understanding the link between power and rules of the game can help
to remove misconceptions about the plausibility of relying on states to
behave on a basis of voluntary self-restraint. Self-restraint may be exercised, but in a world of scarce resources and conflicting ideologies it
would be unwise to assume it. States can indeed resist everything except
temptation. The whole effort to create ground rules of coexistence between rivals rests on their ability and will to maintain their positions when
challenged. The absence of such ability and will, or a loss of confidence
in the existence of these factors, will inevitably lead to an unravelling of
existing restraints. If, in a ruthlessly competitive world, one's own weakness and irresolution are exploited, it is useless to shift blame on to the
shoulders of one's opponent. Accommodation between rivals cannot
replace one's own efforts. Where a power vacuum exists, it will be filled.
The logic of power has always been to take advantage of situations in
which one's opponent failed to reinforce restraints with countervailing
force. Richard Helms, former US Ambassador to Iran and Director of the
CIA, expressed neither surprise nor resentment at the Soviet invasion of
Afghanistan. Nor did he even see it as an irresponsible gamble, because
the United States had left itself completely vulnerable. 'What are we
going to do about it? We have no forces there, no bases. What can we do
for the time being but remonstrate?'[26] And mere remonstration or futile
menaces, in the face of accomplished facts, can achieve nothing. In the
end the plaintiffs will be obliged, however grudgingly, to resign themselves to the new reality.

Sometimes a demonstration of resolution will be sufficient to maintain
one's principle. Western access to Berlin, threatened for years by communist harassment until the improvement in atmosphere engendered by
the 1972 Quadripartite Agreement, was only preserved by the stubborn
enforcement of established practice. In 1958, when Khrushchev
demanded an end to four-power occupation of the former German capital,
the United States demonstrated the continued viability of western access
by sending through an army convoy from West Germany. A more serious
test arose the following February when Soviet border guards detained a
US army truck convoy heading back to Marienborn in West Germany.

After two tense days and vigorous American protests the convoy was finally allowed through without inspection.[27]

In 1961 a new confrontation occurred with the closing on 12 August of the border between East and West Berlin as a prelude to the construction of the Berlin Wall. Western passivity to the move, except for a belated formal protest, demonstrated that here was one change in the rules that no one was prepared to oppose. Willy Brandt, then Mayor of West Berlin, bitterly called for 'political action' and not just words, fully understanding that the formal protest, when changes were taking place on the ground, implied tacit consent. On the other hand the strict limits of that compliance were indicated on 18 August when President Kennedy ordered a battle group of 1,500 troops to move along the autobahn from West Germany to West Berlin. An accompaniment of 250 vehicles including two bulldozers signalled the message that any obstruction would be determinedly pushed aside.[28]

Since 1961 Western army convoys have continued to move in and out of West Berlin as a matter of routine, without incident. Very occasionally reports of these transits have reached the inside pages of the press as a reminder that the Western powers are still in Berlin. Otherwise the event, by its very regularity, has ceased to warrant attention.

In the final analysis, enforcement of a rule may require armed resistance. If this is the case rules of the game will clearly have ceased to serve as an agreed focus of restraint but they will at least provide legitimacy for defensive counteraction. It may be of interest in this context to conclude this chapter with an eye-witness account of the situation in July 1973 at the island of Chenpao/Damansky on the Sino-Russian border, which had been the scene of such fierce fighting in 1969.

The border dispute in this area arose, it will be recalled, from the contradictory claims of the two sides. Whereas China argued that the border ran down the centre of the river, putting the island under Chinese sovereignty, Russia claimed full possession of the river up to the Chinese bank and any islands in midstream. After the fighting in 1969 a very strong impression was created by Russian statements that Chinese troops had been forced to retreat and that the fighting had left the island firmly under Soviet control.

Neville Maxwell discovered in July 1973 that the reality on the ground was quite different from the picture presented by Russian propaganda:

The present situation around Chenpao is quiet, but not relaxed. The Chinese do not patrol on the Soviet side of the island during the winter, and the Russians have made no attempt since March 1969 to approach the island. There has been no firing since September 1969. As I noticed on my own trip down the Ussuri to Chenpao, Chinese patrol boats steer down the middle of the main channel; and they experience only occasional harassment, the Chinese say, from Soviet gunboats.[29]

It is true that the Sino-Soviet border dispute is as far away as ever from resolution. There has been no Soviet recognition of China's position on the ground. On the contrary, no one can guarantee against the outbreak of further hostilities. Nevertheless the Chinese have maintained their claim in the face of severe Soviet pressure. That they have done so is only because they stood their ground. When all other mechanisms for maintaining rules have failed, the ability and willingness to use force remain the final expedient.

Chapter twelve

Breaking rules: the act

To replace an established rule actors can either seek, directly or indirectly, the prior consent of other parties involved or they can act unilaterally to impose their will. In either case their behaviour is influenced by the prior existence of a set of rules governing the issue or relationship in question to which other parties are committed. It is true that in some cases the actor may infringe rules unintentionally and only become aware of the misdemeanour when faced with the outcry of the injured party. On the whole, though, actors do have a very good idea when they are approaching the limits of the permissible. It is this foreknowledge which both demonstrates the existence of rules and also determines the strategy to be adopted to achieve the change. Rule change is unlikely to go by default; it can occur either with the compliance, tacit or explicit, of others or in the face of their resistance. The difference between strategies of consent and strategies of infringement is that whereas the former aim to overcome opposition before the change of rules, the latter seeks to do the reverse: to change the rules first and answer questions afterwards.

For this reason strategies of rule infringement will be combined with tactics intended to mitigate or overcome the anticipated opposition. Once a breach of the rules has been committed, the victim must be persuaded to resign himself to the new reality. Rarely will states take kindly to changes put into effect without consultation or consent, however desirable the change in itself. And a change which is implemented in the face of the opposition of parties who are in a position to block its consolidation, is unlikely to be successfully incorporated into the 'canon' of rules. In any assessment of the likelihood of success or failure of an attempt to impose a unilateral change of rules the ability to maintain the innovation at an acceptable cost is bound to be a potent consideration.

In this chapter I shall consider two strategies of rule infringement: the *fait accompli* and incremental change. The related problem of legitimizing the infringement has already been touched on in chapter ten in the context of the discussion on rule-making.

The strategy of the *fait accompli*

The classic tactic for altering the situation unilaterally is by means of the *fait accompli* – the creation of an accomplished fact. According to this method the opponent is faced with an irreversible change which he cannot revoke whether he wants to or not. With the passage of time, it is hoped, he will be obliged to reconcile himself to the new reality. As Bülent Ecevit, the Turkish Prime Minister, put it, following the Turkish invasion of Cyprus in 1974: 'Let no one think or speak as if nothing new has happened in Cyprus and nothing has changed there. A lot has changed in Cyprus since the morning of July 20 1974. A lot has changed irrevocably.'[1] This was precisely the reason for the invasion: to transform the situation, once and for all, on the ground.

Grasp of this principle equally underlay Arab policy towards Israeli occupation of Arab territory after the 1967 war. President Nasser's first gesture on the very day, 9 June, that Israeli troops reached the Suez Canal, was to declare that the main task facing the Arab people was to 'remove the traces of this aggression'. The practical alternatives were set out by President Boumédienne of Algeria: One was 'the road of submission and of accepting the *fait accompli*'; the other was 'the road of continuing the battle'.[2] Thus, from as early as 2 July 1967 onwards, small-scale commando raids and artillery bombardments were launched by Egypt on Israeli positions on the east bank of the Suez Canal. Nasser's motives were presumably the same as those given at the time of his launching of the War of Attrition in 1968: That the front must not be allowed to freeze; for that, he was convinced, would be the end of everything.[3] The *fait accompli* would become part of the established order.

Where the opponent does comply with the innovation, his powerlessness to do anything may stem from a number of causes:

1. *The change entails the irreversible transformation of some part of the physical world*. Into this category come acts such as the bombardment and immobilization of the French Fleet at Mers-el-Kabir by the British Admiral Somerville in July 1940. A ship once sunk remains sunk. Another example would be the Israeli policy of creating 'facts on the ground' in the territories occupied after the 1967 war, such as the building of housing estates to encircle the reunited city of Jerusalem and constructing a direct road from Tel Aviv to Jerusalem. Israel had not set up settlements in the 'areas', Foreign Minister Dayan pointed out, in order to shift them around later like 'flower-pots'. (At the same time he recognized that new settlements would not *determine* final borders: beyond a certain minimum point, Israel's power of resistance would not be limitless.)[4]

2. *By presenting the opponent with an accomplished fact the onus of whether or not to initiate the use of force is shifted on to his shoulders*. The infractor calculates that the inhibition against using force is greater than the value of the lost asset. In the nuclear age this is thought to be an especially potent consideration between the superpowers. Will the victim of a *fait accompli* risk nuclear suicide in order to restore something

already lost? Soviet assaults, from the Berlin Blockade to the invasion of Afghanistan, have clearly rested on the judgement that the West would not think the issue at hand worth a war. In 1967 President Nasser probably made the same calculation when he decreed the Straits of Tiran closed to Israeli shipping.

3. *The balance of force is distributed clearly and decisively to the advantage of the infractor, hence opposition would be futile.* When the Indian Army moved into Portuguese Goa in December 1961 forcibly to incorporate the colony into the Indian Union, it did so at the cost of only a single soldier wounded. After the Turkish invasion of Cyprus in 1974 Greek Prime Minister Karamanlis was obliged to admit that: 'Armed opposition to the Turks in Cyprus was made impossible by reason of distance and also by reason of the accomplished facts ... it could not be attempted without the risk of weakening the defence of Greece itself.'[5]

4. *Although the opponent does possess the potential to retaliate against the* fait accompli *he requires an excessive length of time for his military preparations.* As time goes by he loses the initiative and the delay makes it increasingly difficult to overcome the inertia and opposition in the way of an attack. French military unpreparedness and British sympathy for German claims made it possible for Hitler to send his army into the Rhineland in March 1936 (the area had been demilitarized by the Treaty of Versailles) and then deflect opposition by a spurious 'peace offensive'. Every day that passed lessened the incentive to react and increased the understanding of the British public for the German move.

According to Mohamed Heikal it was precisely this reasoning which encouraged President Nasser to nationalize the Suez Canal in 1956. Nasser believed that Britain, under Anthony Eden, had to intervene immediately if at all: 'It must appear as a direct reaction. If Eden delays, the pressure against him will increase.' Thus the peak danger time for Egypt would be 80 per cent at the beginning of August, one week after the nationalization, 'decreasing each week through political activities'. By the end of September the danger of British intervention would have been reduced to 20 per cent. Since Nasser estimated that the British could not intervene for at least two months, the chances of success seemed encouraging.[6]

5. *Because of unavoidable constraints (such as public opinion) on his freedom of action, an actor may be unable voluntarily to consent to a given change in the* status quo *although he may not be opposed to it in principle.* A *fait accompli* will free him from his dilemma and enable him to plead *force majeure* – that he has no alternative but to accept the change since it has already gone into effect. In April 1941 the governor of South Greenland refused to accept an agreement concluded by the United States and Danish Governments to establish American defence facilities in Greenland. Accordingly he informed the US consul that he

would only be prepared to accept it as inevitable 'when faced with the *fait accompli*'. US coastguard cutters obliged, and established the facility without the governor's consent.[7]

Similarly, Field-Marshal Montgomery is reported to have been convinced that Britain and France should have carried out the Suez operation in two days and not dragged it out to ten, thus avoiding American opposition. President Eisenhower, whose administration had applied the pressure which obliged the Anglo-French withdrawal, later privately agreed: 'Had they done it in two days I would have accepted it. But what the hell do you want me to do when you drag it out?'[8]

One of the great problems with the strategy of the *fait accompli* is that, unless the operation is self-evidently of a limited nature contained within recognizable bounds, there is the danger that the infringement will be perceived as a threat to the entire system. Having overthrown one set of restraints, what guarantee is there, others wonder, that the infractor will voluntarily accept new rules of the game? Hence the *fait accompli*, far from being accepted as a 'one off', containable, alteration of the *status quo*, may be seen as merely the first step in an overall programme of aggression aimed at bringing down the existing structure of relations in its entirety. In the next chapter I shall enlarge on this analysis.

Failure of actors to anticipate the gravity with which an infringement of the rules may be viewed over and above the immediate issue at stake is a common prelude to international crisis – and worse. For those who are perceptive enough to recognize this danger but nonetheless decide to go ahead with their *fait accompli* it will be necessary, should they wish to avoid an escalation of the conflict, to persuade their opponent of the limited nature of their objectives. To use a surgical image, to prevent haemorraging, the area of the operation must be sutured off from the rest of the system.

No one in diplomatic history showed greater consciousness of the need to contain and limit change without provoking the wider involvement of third parties in the dispute – posing the threat of an uncontrollable breakdown of international order – than Bismarck. In 1866, after the great Prussian victory over Austria at Sadowa, Bismarck was faced with the classic dilemma of the victor: whether to keep to the modest aims laid down before the war – Prussian hegemony in Germany north of the Main – or to give in to the pressure of the King and the generals for territorial annexation and a triumphant march through the Austrian capital. For William I Austrian opposition to Prussian objectives, which had resulted in war, deserved moral opprobrium and consequent punishment. Bismarck, expressing the realist rather than the moralist view of politics, told his King: 'Austria was no more in the wrong in opposing our claims than we were in making them.'[9]

Most important, Bismarck believed that only studied Prussian restraint could prevent the intervention of other European powers. In his famous Nikolsburg Memorandum of 24 July 1866 he placed these arguments before the King: thanks to Prussian acceptance of French proposals before the war the danger of active French participation had been eliminated; but unless 'present concessions' were 'not quickly converted into fact, then there would be a new *volte-face*'. In Russia, Prussian conditions of peace were viewed with alarm. Even in England it could only be 'assumed' that the Goverment would 'recognize the *faits accomplis*'. Having declared, therefore, that it would accept Prussia's original aims, Austria should be brought to 'a speedy settlement'. 'It would be a political blunder to put the whole outcome in jeopardy by attempting to wrest from Austria a few more square miles of territory or a few more millions of war payments, and expose it to the risk of a prolonged war or negotiations in which foreign intervention could not be excluded.' If the King accepted these arguments then the necessary legal measures could be taken to extend the boundaries of Prussia in north Germany. The whole acquisition could then be presented 'as a *fait accompli* which, as it will have had Austria's recognition and France's agreement, cannot be contested by anyone who could endanger it.'[10]

In more recent history the art of 'knowing where to stop' finds its best, if least understood, demonstration in Chinese diplomatic management of the Indo-Chinese War of 1962. During the 1950s the Indian and Chinese Governments had been unable to arrive at an agreed delineation of the boundaries between them. In the absence of a settlement China had begun, discreetly but unilaterally, to create facts on the ground in the way of roads and emplacements to establish her version of the border.

Once the Indian Government woke up to this strategy it was decided not to make a public issue of the dispute but to answer Chinese moves by a corresponding Indian 'forward policy' which would stake out on the ground the area claimed by India. By 1962 China had decided that it could no longer permit the situation to drag on. Neville Maxwell argues that military action was decided on to bring India to the negotiating table and to show her that any attempt 'to achieve a settlement on her own terms, by moving into Chinese-held territory, was futile. But failing that, it would suffice if India were made to accept that the *status quo* had to be left alone until she was prepared to embark on general boundary negotiations.'[11]

To produce a decisive effect China would have to launch a large-scale attack capable of achieving rapid success. The difficulty would then be to demonstrate to the world that Chinese aims were strictly limited in scope and that there need be no fear of the situation deteriorating into an all-out war aimed at the invasion and total defeat of India. Outside perceptions of unlimited Chinese aims could lead to incalculable consequences and the danger of intervention by either, or both, of the superpowers.

On 20 October 1962 the Chinese launched their attack. Their advance was rapid and the Indian Army was powerless to contain it. Indian Government sources expressed the assessment that China's goal was not only to wrest control of the border mountains from India but also to bring direct threat to bear on Assam itself.[12] In diplomatic and military circles it was taken for granted that 'China will simply occupy as much Indian frontier territory as she can seize before winter conditions halt fighting'.[13] Observers had no possible way of knowing at this stage that Chinese objectives were strictly limited. Chinese diplomacy, therefore, had the task of making this clear.

On 24 October, in coordination with the initial success of their military offensive, still only three days old, the Chinese Government came forward with their first signal of restraint. It was proposed that both sides affirm that the dispute must be settled peacefully, that India agree to respect the *line of actual control* and withdraw her armed forces 20 kilometres from that line. In a further note of 4 November Chou En-lai emphasized that China had no wish to acquire gains beyond the border as of November 1959 – the 'line of actual control' – and that his Government's sole purpose was to achieve Indian recognition of the border existing before the onset of the forward policy.

It is worth quoting the relevant sentences of this crucial document:

The 'line of actual control' mentioned in the proposal is basically still the line of actual control as existed between the Chinese and Indian sides of 7 November 1959. . . . The fact that the Chinese Government's proposal has taken as its basis the 1959 line of actual control and not the present line of actual contact between the armed forces of the two sides is full proof that the Chinese side has not tried to force any unilateral demand on the Indian side on account of the advances gained in the recent counter-attack in self defence.[14]

On 21 November, lest any doubt remain about the limited nature of Chinese aims, a unilateral ceasefire was declared involving a withdrawal of Chinese forces 20 kilometres back from the line of actual control. The next day fighting ceased. *The Times* well expressed the reaction of the world: 'Astonishment alone blots out relief at the sudden Chinese decision.'[15]

China had carried off a remarkable success by the complete subordination of her military moves to a prior political strategy. The first arrivals of Soviet and American military assistance to India at the time of Chinese withdrawal indicated just how well-judged Chinese restraint had been.

All too often states fail either to communicate the limits of their aims credibly or to contain the extent of their ambitions. A classic example of this kind of loss of control is provided by Nasser's mismanagement of the May 1967 crisis which resulted in the Six Day War between Israel and Egypt. Against a background of growing tension on the Syrian–Israel border, a build-up of Egyptian troops and armour in Sinai and the expulsion of the United Nations Emergency Force on 19 May from Egyptian soil, President Nasser ordered the reoccupation of the strategic position of Sharm el-Sheikh. On 22 May he declared the Straits of Tiran closed to Israeli ships: 'Under no circumstances will we allow the Israeli flag to pass through the Gulf of Aqaba. The Jews threaten war. We tell them you are welcome, we are ready for war.'

According to testimony at the subsequent trial of the then Egyptian

Minister of War, Shams ad-Din Badran, Nasser had decided on a *fait accompli* before the imminent arrival in Cairo of UN Secretary-General U Thant, who would doubtless try to exert a calming influence on the course of events. Most analysts of Middle East affairs are satisfied that Nasser did not actually want to go to war with Israel at this time. By the last week in May he had achieved a considerable degree of success, having seized the initiative, reasserted his leadership of the Arab world and seemingly reduced Israel to a state of indecision and demoralization. During the following days this impression could only have been reinforced. Israeli diplomacy failed to gain anything other than verbal support from the West to restore freedom of passage for Israeli shipping through the Straits of Tiran, and was warned against the use of force to restore the situation. The prospects of terminating the crisis through diplomatic means could not be ruled out. Nasser personally suggested that the issue of navigation through the Straits be taken to the International Court of Justice, which would not have solved Israel's problem but presented a dignified way of conceding defeat.

Unfortunately Nasser did not know when to stop or to curb his inflammatory and menacing rhetoric. Instead of stressing the limited and 'legitimate' nature of his aims and unambiguously signalling his willingness to call a halt to the spiral of tension and bellicosity – all of which would have increased the difficulty for an initially divided Israeli Government in deciding on a military response and would have contributed to Israel's diplomatic isolation – Nasser did just the opposite.

Whatever may have been his hidden intentions he now defined his objectives in extravagant terms. In a speech to Arab trade unionists on 26 May and in a press conference on 28 May he argued that the real problem was not passage through the Straits of Tiran but Israel's very existence: 'Israel's existence, by itself, is aggression'; 'We accept no kind of co-existence with Israel'; 'The Arabs are determined to regain the rights of the Palestinians.' Regaining Palestine had always been, Nasser declared, only a question of timing. 'Recently we feel we are strong enough, that if we were to enter a battle with Israel, with God's help we could triumph.' If war came 'it will be total and the objective will be to destroy Israel. We feel confident that we can win, and we are now ready for a war with Israel.'[16]

On 30 May King Hussein of Jordan arrived in Cairo to sign a defence agreement with President Nasser under which the Egyptian Chief of Staff would command both Jordanian and UAR forces in the event of war. Even if the rhetoric could be overlooked – and it did, in fact, add greatly to tension in Israel – this military pact looked very much like a tightening of the noose, to use Golda Meir's graphic image.[17] It was to meet this perceived threat that Israel launched her attack on 5 June.

The outbreak of the Six Day War stands as a grim warning against all but the most calculated exercises of the *fait accompli*. It very much bears out James Cable's analysis of the conditions necessary for the success of the strategy.[18] These are:

(1) that the act or threat of force should possess a definite purpose of which the extent is apparent to both sides (my point about the need to signal the limit to the initiative);
(2) that the purpose of the initiative must be 'tolerable' to the victim – that is, not worth a war: this was barely true of the closing of Sharm el-Sheikh and blatantly untrue when Nasser began talking of the destruction of Israel;
(3) that sufficient force be used to attain the defined objective so that the victim can only acquiesce or retaliate after the fact, but that excessive force be avoided to preclude an 'irrational' reaction:

In one sense Nasser succeeded, in that Israel did have to fire the first shot. On the other hand Arab troop concentrations and military consultations did have the effect of pushing the crisis over the brink of political manoeuvre into the abyss of full-scale war.

The strategy of incremental change

In contrast to the risks posed by the strategy of the *fait accompli*, decision-makers often prefer the safer and less irrevocable strategy of incremental change, popularly known as 'salami' tactics. Instead of confronting the opponent with the provocation of an accomplished fact, change is achieved over a period of time and via a series of intermediate and, it is hoped, digestible steps. In essence the strategy involves a mutual process of learning. For his part the initiating party seeks to accustom his opponent to the change both by persuasion and by demonstration of its harmlessness. Familiarity, it is reasoned, will reconcile the opponent to the evolving situation where a sudden shock might be perceived as threatening. Conversely the initiator is also given the opportunity of learning from the reactions of the victim of the limits of his tolerance.

Where the issue at stake is perceived to be far-reaching enough, even a marginal change will be vigorously resisted. This was indeed the reaction of the Western allies when the Soviet Union attempted to impose new restrictions on Western freedom of access to Berlin in the 1958–61 period. The very issue of the continued presence of the Western occupying powers in a city which was generally understood to be a test case of Western resolution was correctly perceived to be at stake. By focusing initially on comparatively marginal rights the communist side was able to assess the will of its opponent. When it became clear that submission could not be expected, then the initial, cautious advance left the way open for a quiet and honourable retreat.

Alternatively, the initiator may decide that adjustments are called for in the pace and style of his strategy: for instance, that certain kinds of persuasion are more effective than others, that greater reassurance is required to sugar the pill or that a more cautious approach is called for. Finally he is put in a position to evaluate the risks and utilities of his overall course of action in the light of the opponent's responses. By providing himself with greater information about the behaviour of his opponent the initiator widens the range of alternative options available to him and lowers the likelihood of unexpected conflict. As George and Smoke put it: 'The initiator may rely on feedback either to perfect his utility calculations, to condition his opponent to the forthcoming challenge, or to gauge and control the risk of an overreaction to the challenge by the opponent.'[19]

A skilful recent example of this strategy is provided by the Syrian intervention in the Lebanon during the course of 1976. Over a period of little more than six months the Syrian Government was successful in overcoming Israeli and American objections to the involvement of Syrian forces in the Lebanese Civil War; so much so that by the end of the year there was a large force of Syrian troops in the country giving Syria virtual control over the future course of political developments and turning Lebanon into a Syrian protectorate in all but name. First, in order to bypass an Israeli prohibition on Syrian intervention, units of the Syrian-controlled but Palestinian-manned Palestine Liberation Army, estimated to number between 1,000 and 3,000 troops, were sent into the Lebanon from Syria on 19–20 January 1976. At a second stage, in April, after demonstrating that the initial and limited intervention had been insufficient, Syrian armoured units occupied a border post three miles inside the country. A restrained Israeli reaction and overt United States approval permitted Syrian forces to take up further positions in the eastern and northern border areas of the Lebanon up to a depth of about fifteen miles. The final stage of Syrian intervention came at the beginning of June 1976. Additional troops, estimated to number between 2,000 and 3,000 men, supported by armour, crossed into the Lebanon and moved to occupy northern areas of the country. An offensive in the autumn against Palestine guerrilla groups brought Syrian Forces to all parts of the Lebanon except for a buffer zone along the Israel border. At the end of the year a ceasefire had been imposed and was holding.[20]

A year before it would have been hard to believe that Syria could attain for herself this degree of freedom of manoeuvre. Certainly any attempt to achieve this other than by a series of cautious and graduated stages, at each of which care was taken to avoid alienating the United States or posing a direct threat to Israel, would have been highly dangerous. The success of Syrian intervention in the civil war may or may not have been based on a predetermined plan to take over the Lebanon. Most likely it was hoped that each discrete step would be sufficient to resolve the situation and the following step was only taken when the previous one was observed to have failed. In this lay the strength of the approach. At any given point Syria retained control of the future extent of her involvement while demonstrating to other interested parties that she was exhausting all possibilities before proceeding to widen her intervention.

Legitimization of the intervention was obtained by Syria with equal skill. By creating an accomplished fact other Arab states were faced with a situation they could do nothing to alter. Explicit acknowledgement of the Syrian presence came in October 1976 at a summit meeting in Riyadh of the parties principally involved, where it was agreed that the Lebanese ceasefire should be policed by a pan-Arab peacekeeping force including Syrian troops. It soon became clear that the contingents from other Arab countries had a mainly symbolic function; the overwhelming majority of the peacekeeping force was made up of Syrian soldiers who had been in the Lebanon all along and now simply changed the colour of their helmets. Saudi officials in Cairo were reported as admitting that the Riyadh agreement could be regarded as a *post facto* legitimization of the Syrian position in the Lebanon. In Damascus the outcome of the summit was seen as a major diplomatic triumph which effectively endorsed Syrian policy in the Lebanon and also tacitly recognized Syria's primary responsibility for controlling the ceasefire and supervising a settlement.[21]

Turning from the Lebanon to the final stages of the Vietnam War we are faced with an incremental strategy whose final objective – the defeat of South Vietnam and the introduction of a communist regime – had certainly been determined from the outset. Nevertheless, by deciding on a step-by-step approach to widening the war in the south, as opposed to a classic all-out invasion on the lines of the North Korean attack on South Korea in 1950, North Vietnam assured for herself the same kind of advantages enjoyed by Syria in the Lebanon: the option of regulating the extent and rate of her involvement in conformity with the observed reactions of other interested parties and especially the United States.

According to Van Tien Dung,[22] the North Vietnamese general in charge of the offensive against the South, the decision to invade South Vietnam was taken in principle at the twenty-first session of the congress of the Vietnam Workers' Party in October 1973 and put into operational form at top-level meetings of the political and military leadership in the spring of 1974. Extensive infringements of the ceasefire had (according to Western sources) taken place almost without interruption from the day the Paris Peace Accords were signed in January 1973 and American forces had begun their final withdrawal. American allegations in a note of 20 April 1973 to North Vietnam of violations of the agreement did not affect the completion of the withdrawal of United States forces from South Vietnam. Alongside various serious infringements of the accords over 30,000 Vietnamese troops were claimed to have infiltrated into the South. The tasks of re-equipment and stockpiling, and augmenting North Vietnamese troop strength were reported to have continued throughout the year, still without any reaction, other than diplomatic, from the United States.[23]

During the course of 1974, according to Van Tien Dung, preparations for an offensive accelerated: a 1,000 kilometre-long highway was constructed and an immense pipeline and telecommunications system laid deep into the South. From April to October 1974 the North Vietnamese Army engaged the opponent in a series of small-scale test encounters. By October 1974 the North Vietnamese Politburo and military high command had concluded that the Thieu Government was weakening and that

Washington was entangled amidst insurmountable internal and international obstacles: divisions among the leadership, Watergate and the 'economic' (energy?) crisis would prevent an American re-entry into the war.[24] Dr Kissinger was himself to admit that the Saigon Government had received only enough money for fuel and ammunition – not for spare parts and replacement weapons.[25]

On 14 December 1974 the North Vietnamese 7th Division, supported by Vietcong forces and about forty tanks, overran the district town of Duc Phong. Within a short time the whole of Phuoc Long province, to the north of Saigon, was in North Vietnamese hands. American failure to respond to these defeats signalled a green light to the North Vietnamese offensive and was to determine the final outcome of the war.

In their public statements on the crisis the United States Government put a brave face on things. On 11 January 1975 a stern note was addressed by the United States to the guarantors of the Paris Peace Accords (under the Declaration of the International Conference on Vietnam of 2 March 1973) accusing North Vietnam of persistent violation of the agreement. Warning that North Vietnam 'must accept the full consequences of its actions' the note went on, in an admission of impotence, to urge the guarantor powers to 'call upon the Democratic Republic of [North] Vietnam to halt its military offensive and join the Republic of [South] Vietnam in re-establishing stability and seeking a political solution'. The State Department made it known that the United States felt itself released from any of the constraints imposed by the 1973 accords.

In practice there was nothing that President Ford could do to reverse the situation. His hands were tied by a Congressional ban on United States military activity in or near Indo-China. Even a special request to Congress for 300 million dollars in additional military aid met with strong opposition and was finally rejected by the Senate majority Democratic caucus. In Van Tien Dung's version: 'Ambassador Martin [in Saigon] and Dr Kissinger protested, but left it at that. The *thoi co* – the opportune moment – had arrived.' On 4 March 1975 the final North Vietnamese offensive was launched on the Central Highlands, which was to result in the collapse of South Vietnamese resistance and the fall of Saigon.[26]

That North Vietnam chose to implement a step-by-step strategy for the invasion of the South should come as no surprise. The approach was a natural corollary to the patient philosophy of a prolonged, shifting, people's revolutionary war developed first by Mao Tse-tung and adopted by Vo Nguyen Giap. As Giap had written of the tactics employed at Dien Bien Phu in 1954:

We came to the conclusion that we could not secure success if we struck swiftly. In consequence, *we resolutely chose the other tactic: to strike and advance steadily*. In taking this correct decision, *we strictly followed this fundamental principle of the conduct of a revolutionary war: strike to win, strike only when success is certain; if not, then don't strike.*[27]

Successful implementation of the incremental strategy can be seen to depend on two key factors: alertness to the responses of the opponent and a careful calculation at each stage of the balance of advantage and risk. Both are found in the North Vietnamese and Syrian cases. An example of a failure based on neglect of these factors is the Indian 'forward policy' of 1960–62 which ended in the Chinese victory of October–November 1962.

At the beginning of 1960 the Indian Government conceived the idea of adopting a strategy of gradual military incursion into contested border areas as a way of undermining Chinese control and of establishing the Indian claim on the ground. There would be no attacks on Chinese positions but Indian patrols would penetrate the spaces between them gradually setting up a network of outposts. Eventually, without any need for violence, India would simply overwhelm the Chinese presence, as an antibiotic smothers a microbe.

Thus, in the words of Indian Defence Minister Krishna Menon; 'We started moving gradually from the areas we occupied and I think we more or less began to control 4,000 square miles of territory some of which China would contest as theirs, the line of control moving nearer and nearer to the present line each year.'[28] From the outset the Indian Government seemed to take it for granted that China would not react violently to the forward policy or that the Indian Army, faced with insuperable logistic problems and a superior opponent, might not be walking into a trap.

In November 1961 the Indian Government decided to intensify activity on its borders and orders were given to this effect. The Chinese, however, were far from acquiescent and submitted a vigorous warning: 'The Chinese Government has been following with great anxiety the Indian troops' steady pressing forward on China's borders and cannot but regard such action of the Indian side as an attempt to create new troubles and to carry out its expansion by force in the . . . border areas.' If Chinese border guards had not been under orders to avoid conflict, the note went on, India's 'gross violations of China's territory and sovereignty' would have had very serious consequences. 'The Chinese Government deems it necessary to point out that it would be very erroneous and dangerous should the Indian Government take China's attitude of restraint and tolerance as an expression of weakness.'

Unfortunately this is precisely what the Indian Government did do. In its reply it asserted that the Indian patrols were moving into their own territory and rejected the protest as unwarranted interference in India's internal affairs.[29] Thus India had received, in the clearest possible language, a warning that China would not passively reconcile herself to the forward policy. Despite this and later warnings, and a deteriorating military situation, nothing was done to alter the scope or rate of Indian advance. On the contrary, Chinese restraint was taken as compliance with the changing situation.

In May and July 1962 Indian forward positions were invested by Chinese troops in far superior numbers. When these threatening dispositions were not followed up by the use of force it was concluded that China had backed down in the test of wills. **The** *Hindu* commented in July that the Chinese withdrawal 'in the face of the determined stand of the small Indian garrison' confirmed the basic logic of the forward policy.[30] Encouraged by its apparent success the Indian Government refused to compromise on its demand for prior Chinese withdrawal as a precondition for talks.

By August 1962 firing on both sides had become commonplace. Though 'outnumbered and outgunned by an adversary with immense advantages of mobility and tactical situation', Indian troops pressed ahead with the strategy of their Government. Prime Minister Nehru seemed oblivious to the risk involved. He told Parliament:

> It is true that these posts are in constant danger of attack with large numbers. Well, it does not matter. We have taken the risk and we have moved forward, and we have effectively slowed their forward march. . . . If [the Chinese] want to they can overwhelm some of our military posts. That does not mean we are defeated. We shall face them with much greater problems and face them much more stoutly.[31]

It was as though the Indian Government somehow believed its forces to be exempt from normal strategic considerations and its forward posts immune from enemy fire. Far from consolidating at one point and then, after careful evaluation, moving forward, the Indians pressed ahead regardless.

As August passed into September, the Chinese protests became more threatening. 'Shooting and shelling are no child's play and he who plays with fire will eventually be consumed by fire', Peking wrote in mid-September. 'If the Indian side should insist on threatening by armed force the Chinese border defence forces . . . and thereby rouse their resistance, it must bear the responsibility for all the consequences arising therefrom.'[32]

On 20 September an armed clash broke out between the Indian and Chinese troops. Within a month, after public and private Chinese warnings of the most explicit kind had failed to halt Indian probing or to bring about negotiations, the People's Liberation Army launched its coordinated offensive.

In view of the extensive range of threatening messages transmitted by the Chinese Government the Indian failure to appreciate the dangerous consequences of its forward policy is indeed puzzling. Different explanations have been put forward to account for Indian obtuseness, including most of the elements familiar to students of surprise attack: rigid adherence to an inflexible and inaccurate conception of the opponent; poor communications between the front and the political leadership in the rear; wishful thinking; self-righteousness; the malfunctioning of intelligence agencies. It has also been argued that the Chinese Government failed to transmit comprehensible signals: the over-use of similar signals in the past and China's generally 'aggressive terminology' made it difficult to draw the correct conclusions on the eve of the war.[33] One lesson, at least, can be extracted from the sorry episode: that if a state actively sets out to implement a policy for unilaterally changing the *status quo*, it cannot hope to carry this through without the most meticulous attention to the responses and signals of the opponent and without very careful evaluation indeed of the balance of risks, values and capabilities involved at each and every stage of the operation.

Chapter thirteen

Breaking rules: perception and crisis

One consequence of attempts to infringe (alter unilaterally) rules of the game, may well be a perception of threat on the part of the opponent. There is no necessary connection between the two phenomena: not all infringements of rules induce perceptions of threat and not all perceptions of threat follow infringements of rules. On the one hand the circumstances and degree of the infringement, as well as the importance attached by the opponent to the issue at stake and his vulnerability to the aggressor will all affect whether or not threat is perceived. On the other hand threat is patently perceived under conditions other than infringements of rules of the game, for instance, because of paranoid-like features in the personality of the decision-maker. Nevertheless, previous research by the author into a range of historical case-studies suggests that there is, indeed, a significant correlation between the two phenomena.[1]

Several writers have also pointed out that the perception of threat is a central element in international crisis,[2] something which is again borne out by my own research. In fact I would go so far as to argue that threat perception is a necessary condition of crisis. If it is absent there can be no crisis; hence the occurrence of surprise attack, when the victim, having failed to appraise the situation correctly, is assaulted without the opportunity for countermeasures. Conversely, threat may be perceived, even though one's reading of the opponent's intentions is mistaken.

But whatever the objective danger, the perception of threat gives rise to a series of events characteristic of crisis; in the language of social psychology these are called *coping process*, measures to meet the anticipated danger. These include: a tremendous increase in the flow of information – to and from observers in the field, across the desks of decision-makers, within departments and in the communications media; a process of intensive consultation within the Government of the state under threat, to evaluate the situation and arrive at possible alternative responses; heightened diplomatic activity – at the United Nations, perhaps, in missions to enlist the support of allies and neutral parties, and in contacts with the Government of the offender, to learn more of his intentions, to warn him of the consequences of his actions and to attempt to defuse the crisis through diplomatic means; finally, the mobilization of defensive resources appropriate to meet the anticipated danger. These may be military, if the threat is perceived to be directly to national security. Equally, they may be diplomatic, economic or clandestine, depending on the situation. The to-ing and fro-ing associated with such a sustained burst of government activity, to the extent that it is visible to outside spectators, is one way in which the press and television first learn of the crisis situation.

Often in the past international crisis has been a decisive intermediate stage on the road to a period of disruptive international tension and even war. Both world wars were preceded by series of crises, of longer or shorter duration, which in the end escalated out of hand. Modern techniques of crisis management, by which opponents attempt to tread the precarious path between realizing their political aims – offensive or defensive – without losing control over the situation and lurching into unwanted war, have not obviated the risks attached to crisis. (And, notwithstanding remarkable advances in the technology of communication, it is not certain that they are an improvement on the diplomatic mechanisms current in the nineteenth century.) Thus it is particularly important to try and clarify the logic behind threat perception and the reasons why such an appraisal tends to lead on to a willingness to resort to countermeasures of a far-reaching kind which may possess critical implications for the stability of the international system.

As a point of departure, let us consider the very fundamental connection between the violation of a territorial border and the perception of a direct threat to the security of the injured state. If a neighbour will not respect the limits of your territorial sovereignty, then what will he respect? As Thomas Schelling has cogently argued, to cross a border is to challenge symbolically, as well as physically, the territorial integrity of the victim 'and to demonstrate or at least to imply an intention to proceed'. After the border 'there is just no other stopping place that can be tacitly acknowledged by both sides'. Hence acceptance of the incursion would be tantamount to admitting that the rest of one's territory was fair game to the enemy.[3] Hardly surprising, therefore, that a border violation or its prospect should arouse such far-reaching anticipations and responses on the part of the victim.

Schelling's analysis of the symbolic significance of territorial penetration can be reinforced historically. After the Ottoman occupation in 1906 of certain posts in the Sinai peninsula (claimed by the British Government to come under Egyptian administration) the most alarmist prognoses were offered by British officials. Lord Cromer, British Consul-General in Cairo, discerned in the move a potential 'menace to the liberty of Egypt and to freedom of transit through the canal'. Even the sacrosanct route to India might be endangered by torpedo-boats lurking in the Gulf of Aqaba. In the face of this perceived threat to the British Empire, a ten-day ultimatum was delivered in Constantinople and the Mediterranean Fleet steamed eastwards . . . On the tenth day the Sultan Abdul Hamid capitulated.

On the face of it the British reaction seems exaggerated, to say the least. It only makes sense in the light of the far-reaching implications attributed to territorial violations in the Schelling analysis. In fact Sir Edward Grey put forward a very similar argument: 'Unless Abdul Hamid intended a serious encroachment on Egypt, it was not worth his while to trouble the Sinai peninsula at all.'[4] In other words, in a dialectic of mutual expectations, since he must have known that his incursion would not be viewed as a merely limited step, but would be forcefully opposed, he would only have initiated the move if he had intended from the first to throw down a challenge to the entire British position in the area. Why otherwise risk war for a few desert outposts?

Analogous perceptions may well have underlain the 1969 border incidents between China and Russia. Previous negotiations had broken down when Chinese claims for minor border adjustments produced a rigid and hostile Soviet reaction: the threat of military defeat was held out to China if it persisted in seeking territorial revision.[5] On 2 March 1969 a violent clash occurred between Soviet and Chinese troops on the disputed island of Chenpao Damansky. Two weeks later an even fiercer engagement was fought. A series of small-scale clashes culminated in an incident on 13 August on the Sinkiang border, in which China was reported to have suffered heavy losses. Both sides at this point began to make the most serious and intensive preparations for all-out war.

But at the brink of the abyss both sides held back. At a meeting held on 11 September between Kosygin and Chou En-lai the basis of a truce was agreed upon including a mutual withdrawal of troops.[6] For a definitive analysis of the motives and perceptions of China and the Soviet Union one would have to have access to documentary sources which are simply not available. Nevertheless, in the absence of such material the development of the situation on the ground indicates that each saw, in the attitude of the other, a threat of the gravest magnitude. Can all this, one wonders, have possibly arisen out of a border dispute in a farflung area of frozen wasteland? The only possible explanation, of course, is that the issues perceived to be at stake went far beyond immediate questions of border delineation and demarcation. As Neville Maxwell argues, the Russians had convinced themselves that the Chinese were bellicose, expansionist and reckless,[7] while the Chinese concluded that Soviet troop concentrations were a prelude to an attempt to wrench from China vast areas of her northern provinces.[8] Mutual public accusations of 'expansionist ambitions' and 'aggressive designs' may have been more than simply rhetoric.

The logic of exaggeration reflected in the examples given above is characteristic of the reasoning underlying cases in which an ostensibly limited disagreement over borders has escalated into a major issue of war and peace. In the period 1945 to 1970, three-quarters of the principal external wars involved frontier disputes of one kind or another. In most of these cases 'territorial conflicts have usually concerned relatively restricted frontier areas'. Between the benefit of marginal frontier rectification and the cost of full-scale war there would seem to be a complete absence of proportion. Simply attributing these disputes to national pride and honour is to beg the question.[9]

Although the connection between territorial violation and threat perception is clear enough, a less obvious link has been suggested by D.G. Pruitt between rule infringement and the latter. He argues that: 'The sign from which an intention of threat is inferred consists of *stepping over* a "boundary" on a conceptual dimension.'[10] As in many territorial disputes, the immediate trigger to the crisis often appears relatively trivial in the light of subsequent perceptions and reactions. The crisis of March 1939, which precipitated the breakdown in Polish–German relations and the British guarantee to Poland, was set off by the German occupation of the rump of Czechoslovakia, although Polish policy had been openly hostile to Czechoslovakia (and had hoped to benefit from its break-up) and Britain had already acquiesced in a long line of German violations of the Versailles Treaty and accepted the detachment of the Sudetenland from Czechoslovakia at the Munich Conference. The Cuba crisis resulted from the emplacement of a few, albeit nuclear, missiles on Cuba, even though they could not have affected massive American strategic superiority. The United States would still have retained at least a two-to-one advantage over Soviet missile strength and its second-strike capability would not have been threatened. Secretary of Defence McNamara actually admitted that it made 'no great difference whether you are killed by a missile from the Soviet Union or from Cuba'.[11] Only the latest example was the extreme American reaction to the despatch of Soviet troops to Afghanistan. Afghanistan had been well and truly within the Soviet bloc since the communist coup of March 1978 and the Soviet–Afghan Friendship Treaty of December 1978, and for months several thousand Soviet military and civilian advisers, jets and helicopter gunships had been helping the local Government to subdue its dissidents.

How can one account for the seemingly exaggerated, even hysterical, responses of observers in these and other cases? Why all the fuss? In each one of these examples the significance of the precipitating event lay in the appraisal that a serious infringement of existing rules of the game had occurred and that as a result the entire structure of relations between the rivals was in jeopardy. In a way closely paralleling the appraisal of victims of territorial violation, the encroachment itself, however limited, was perceived to be the precursor of an encompassing programme of aggression and expansion.

In the crisis of March 1939 it is instructive to examine perceptions from the perspective of three capitals: London, Warsaw and Rome. An appraisal of threat was common; but in each case the normative principles at stake were different. It is useful to bear this in mind when one comes to consider the divergent perceptions of, say, NATO allies in different crises. Threat is not an objective and invariant attribute of particular situations but is a function of the particular, bilateral rules of the game between the actors involved.

The Prague crisis, March 1939

The crisis of March 1939 came about as the result of the entry of German troops into Czechoslovakia and the declaration of German protectorates over Bohemia, Moravia and Slovakia. In the view of the British Government the final dismemberment of Czechoslovakia was, first and foremost, a massive breach of faith. The cession of the Sudetenland by Czechoslovakia to Germany at Munich had not been seen as an end in itself. The whole point of the appeasement policy was to clear away obstacles in the path of a general settlement of differences. The achievement of Munich, seen in this light, was therefore the declaration, signed by Hitler and Chamberlain, that: 'We are resolved that the method of consultation shall be the method adopted to deal with any other questions that may concern our two countries, and we are determined to continue our efforts to remove possible sources of differences, and thus to contribute to assure the peace of Europe.'[12] Events of 14–15 March 1939 combined to make a mockery of this pledge. In Lord Halifax's words at the first Cabinet meeting on the crisis, 'Germany's attitude in this matter was completely inconsistent with the Munich Agreement. Germany had deliberately preferred naked force to the methods of consultation and discussion.'[13]

A second assurance, made by Hitler in September and broken the following March, was the personal promise made to Chamberlain and then proclaimed to the world, that the acquisition of the Sudetenland was his last territorial ambition in Europe and that he had no wish to include non-Germans in the *Reich*.[14] Indeed it was the conviction that German aims were essentially limited to the 'just' goal of achieving self-determination for German minorities outside the *Reich* that underlay British responsiveness to German claims. When Hitler based his arguments on the right of self-determination he was aiming at the Achilles heel of British moral assumptions.

Imagine, then, the shock of the British Government to find that Germany had overstepped the bounds of legitimate grievance and, all promises to the contrary, was finally to rule over Czechs as well. 'This was the first occasion on which Germany had applied her shock tactics to the domination of non-Germans', Halifax told his colleagues. 'It was important to find language which would imply that Germany was now being led on a dangerous path.'[15]

Since Germany had so brutally violated the rules of the game, British policy-makers began to wonder whether there were any limits at all to German ambitions. In what direction, the German Ambassador was rhetorically asked, were 'the next adventures' to be framed? It seemed as if Germany were seeking to 'dominate Europe and, if possible, the world' by force. Halifax could only conclude that the German absorption of Czechoslovakia had clearly shown that Germany had 'resolved to go beyond its hitherto avowed aim of consolidation of [the] German race. They have now extended their conquest to another nation and if this should prove to be part of a definite policy of domination *there is no state in Europe which is not directly or ultimately threatened.*'[16]

The view from Warsaw was equally menacing, though the assumptions on which Polish–German relations were based were quite different. Poland had not been a party to the Munich Agreement and it was not to the violation of this agreement that she objected. It was not the destruction of Czechoslovakia as such that was perceived as a threat to Poland. The German invasion of 15 March produced only concern in foreign ministry circles at the failure to consult or notify. As far as Polish Foreign Minister Beck was concerned, German actions had not yet overstepped the bounds of the permissible.

All this changed when the German Government first declared a protectorate over Slovakia and then, on 21 March, demanded the reincorporation of the Baltic port of Danzig into the *Reich*. Beck now accepted the seriousness of the situation and began referring to Germany as 'the enemy'. The limits beyond which Poland would not go, Beck told his officials, had been defined and included an infringement of Polish territory and the unacceptability of an imposed solution in Danzig. Besides its objective importance, Danzig was a symbol. 'This means that, if we join that category of eastern states that allow rules to be dictated to them, then I do not know where the matter will end.'[17]

By the declaration of a protectorate over Slovakia Germany infringed an explicit verbal assurance given to Poland recognizing the latter's special interest in the area. On 24 August 1938 Polish Ambassador Lipski had discussed, among other things, the future of Czechoslovakia with Göering. Following instructions, Lipski argued that his Government did 'not believe the present Czech creation can exist any longer'. He then went on to stress Poland's close ties with Slovakia and her wish for Slovak autonomy. 'Goering eagerly confirmed that this is a necessity. He added that Germany is fortunately in such a position that these matters are of no concern to it.'[18]

The infringement of this disclaimer of German interest and implicit recognition of Polish priority was a red light for the Polish Government. Lipski complained on the 21 March to Ribbentrop that it was bad enough that there had been no understanding between their two Governments on the Czech question. 'But in regard to Slovakia the position was far worse.' Emphasizing Polish cultural affinity with Slovakia – as he had in August – and their long common frontier, Lipski protested that the German protectorate was 'directed against Poland' and 'a serious blow' to Polish–German relations.[19]

The final straw as far as those relations were concerned was the renewal of German demands for an alteration in the status of Danzig. On this point there could be no question about Polish rights, which were laid down in the 1919 Treaty of Versailles and had been emphatically acknowledged by Hitler both in public and in private. In a speech of 20 February 1938, for example, he declared that the way to Polish–German 'friendly cooperation' had been successfully paved with an understanding 'beginning with Danzig'.[20] To call this understanding into question could only, in the opinion of the Polish Government, be a deliberate provocation.

It may be surprising to learn that the break up of Czechoslovakia was received with almost the same disquiet in Rome as in London and Warsaw. Indeed the appraisal of the Italian Government, as reflected in the pages of the diary of Count Ciano, was remarkably close to the British view of the situation. Though he did his best to conceal it from the diplomatic community in Rome, the Italian Foreign Minister was given very little forewarning of German plans. He wrote:

> The thing is serious, especially since Hitler had assured everyone that he did not want to annex one single Czech. This German action does not destroy the Czechoslovakia of Versailles, but the one that was constructed at Munich and at Vienna. What weight can be given in the future to those declarations and promises which concern us more directly? It is useless to deny that all this worries and humiliates the Italian people . . . [German] hegemony begins to be disturbing.[21]

The first Italian objection was therefore that Germany had violated the nationality principle – the right to national self-determination – which Hitler had so fervently affixed to his own banner. Mussolini, despite his own political cynicism and annexation of Ethiopia (non-white races did not count), had sincerely believed that Nazi aims were limited to redressing the nationalist grievances of Versailles. Worse, he had publicly committed himself to this position in an open letter to the British mediator, Lord Runciman, at the height of the crisis of the previous September. Mussolini had written:

> If Hitler were claiming to annex three million and more Czechs, Europe would be right to be disturbed, and to take action. But Hitler is not thinking of doing so. I who am writing you this letter am in a position to tell you – in confidence – that if he were offered more than three million Czechs as a present, Hitler would politely but firmly decline the gift. The *Führer* is concerned and preoccupied with the three million and more Germans and with them only. No one can contest such a right.[22]

The second sore point was that Mussolini's full collaboration with Hitler at the Munich Conference (and later in the Vienna Awards which had settled Polish and Hungarian claims to Czechoslovak territory) had not prevented him from feeling fully committed by the outcome of that conference. After all, the meeting had taken place as a result of Mussolini's personal mediation and the memorandum which had formed the basis for the Munich Agreement had been put forward by the Duce. The result of the conference had been acknowledged as a triumph for Mussolini the peacemaker. Later he had boasted to Fascist leaders that for the first time in seventy years Italy had taken a preponderant and decisive share in international politics.[23]

Now all that had been shattered without so much as a gesture of consultation. From Berlin Ambassador Attolico warned that Italy should draw the necessary conclusions from the events of the last few days. The

German Government with one stroke had annulled the agreements of Munich and Vienna, without any regard for the principal architect of these treaties and their only potential ally.[24]

Italian conclusions were therefore pessimistic. Ciano wrote that 'the events of the last few days have reversed my opinion of the *Führer* and of Germany; he, too, is unfaithful and treacherous and we cannot collaborate with him.' Mussolini agreed. Briefly, the idea of an anti-German coalition to 'check German expansion' was picked up. There was no doubt in Italian minds that 'Prussian hegemony' had been established in Europe and further expansion in central and south-eastern Europe could be expected. Fears were expressed of a German drive into the Balkans, Italy's back door. Reassured by hurried German disclaimers, Mussolini eventually concluded that he had no choice but to reconcile and accommodate himself to the new reality of German power.[25]

The Cuban missile crisis, 1962

In the Cuban missile crisis of 1962 one finds American perceptions shaped by the same judgement that Soviet actions threw off existing constraints and were a challenge to the fabric of international order. The key text for understanding American perceptions is the dramatic address given by President Kennedy over radio and television on 22 October 1962 in which he publicly revealed for the first time the news of the emplacement of Soviet missiles on Cuba.[26] Kennedy saw Soviet behaviour as a violation of existing rules of conduct in a number of ways.

First, he described it as a 'flagrant and deliberate defiance' of international law, namely, the Rio Pact of 1947 and the Charter of the United Nations. This may well have been the sincere conviction of President Kennedy. On the other hand we have the evidence of the legal adviser at the time to the State Department that it was not felt that a strong case could be made on legal grounds alone because it was hard to demonstrate legally that an aggressive act was involved.[27] We may consider this, therefore, to be a formal argument inserted to prove that law was on the side of the United States – a familiar device in international and especially American discourse.

More substantive was the argument that the build-up infringed an informal understanding that offensive missiles should not be stationed on Cuba. The terms of this understanding, according to the President, were signalled by the United States in public warnings of 4 and 13 September and accepted, in both public and private statements, by the Soviet Union. In Kennedy's own words, 'only last month, after I had made clear the distinction between any introduction of ground-to-ground missiles, and the existence of defensive anti-aircraft missiles, the Soviet Government publicly stated on September 11 that, and I quote, "the armaments and military equipment sent to Cuba are designed exclusively for defensive purposes" . . .' That assurance had been reiterated only the previous Thursday by Soviet Foreign Minister Gromyko: the Soviet Government, he had promised, would never become involved in rendering offensive assistance to Cuba.

The third American objection was that the Soviet move was a blatant act of trespass into 'an area well known to have a special and historical relationship to the United States and the nations of the Western Hemisphere, in violation of Soviet assurances, and in defiance of American and hemisphere policy'. It is interesting that Kennedy declined to make any reference to the Monroe Doctrine of 1823, which first proclaimed United States preponderance on the American continent, perhaps feeling that it would lack resonance for a contemporary audience.[28] However, he cited in the broadcast a Congressional resolution of 20 September 1962 which did specifically recall the Monroe Doctrine. But legal justification apart, mutual recognition of the other's sphere of influence was a fundamental and hitherto uncontested groundrule of superpower relations.

Thus the 'sudden, clandestine decision to station strategic weapons for the first time outside of Soviet soil', Kennedy concluded, was 'a deliberately provocative and unjustified change in the *status quo* which cannot be accepted by this country, if our courage and our commitments are ever to be trusted again by either friend or foe'. Mr Macmillan agreed. Acquiescence, he told the House of Commons, 'would throw doubt on America's pledges in all parts of the world and expose the entire free world to a new series of perils'.[29]

The Afghanistan crisis, 1979–80

A final example of threat perception is provided by the 1979–80 Afghanistan crisis. The same pattern noted in previous examples was present here: the appraisal that a violation of the rules had taken place jeopardizing overall relations, and that it was not simply the precipitating act in itself that constituted the danger, but the normative implications of what was seen as a departure from established practice.

During the course of 1979 the USSR had steadily widened its involvement in the counter-insurgency campaign of the Afghanistan Government to a level, at the beginning of December, of about 4,000 military advisers in Afghan uniforms or civilian clothes (which in itself suggests that they had something to hide). Another 4,000 civilian experts were also at work. Several hundred Soviet troops were known to be on security duty at an airbase near Kabul. Repeated American warnings and appeals for restraint were ignored. At the end of November regular Soviet forces, which had been stationed on the border for some months, were reported to have crossed over and joined in the fighting. On 5 December a *Tass* commentator declared that the Afghan Government could count on Soviet help in the fighting. Meanwhile a battalion of what looked like garrison troops was being introduced. Concern was expressed by the State Department but no action was taken. Thus on the eve of the crisis

Afghanistan was scarcely nonaligned: she was allied by a friendship treaty to the Soviet Union and thousands of Soviet advisers and some troops were already in the country.[30]

The crisis itself was precipitated by a quantum jump in Soviet involvement. Starting on Christmas Day 1979 tens of thousands of troops and a massive airlift of military equipment poured into Afghanistan. The President was replaced in a coup and he and members of his family executed. In his address to the nation on 4 January 1980 President Carter described the situation as the invasion of a 'sovereign nation' by 'fifty thousand heavily armed troops' and the installation of a 'new puppet leader'. As a result an 'extremely serious threat to peace' now existed.

The list of American grievances was a long one. First, President Carter characterized 'the overthrow of the established government and the execution of the President of that country' as a 'gross interference in the internal affairs of Afghanistan . . . in blatant violation of accepted rules of behaviour'. Second, although it was not the first time that the Soviet Union had invaded a neighbour, it was 'the first such venture into a Muslim country' since the occupation of Iranian Azerbaijan in 1946.[31] Third, for the first time Soviet forces had been used against a country not hitherto 'an occupied satellite of the Soviet Union'.[32] Indeed this was the point most heavily emphasized: by invading Afghanistan the Soviet Union had moved outside its Warsaw Pact sphere of influence. It was 'unprecedented', Carter complained, for the Soviets *themselves* to attack 'a nation that was not already under their domination, that is, a part of the Warsaw Pact neighbourhood. They have used surrogate forces, the Cubans, to participate in other countries, like Angola or Ethiopia.'[33] (In itself this seemed to be an admission that the United States would not have had the same objection to the use of proxy forces for which precedents did exist.) Finally, President Carter expressed his personal dismay that Brezhnev should have lied to him in a conversation over the hot line to explain the reasons for the Soviet invasion.[34] (Brezhnev had claimed that his forces were invited into Afghanistan by the deposed President to help against an outside threat.)

On the basis of the appraisal that there had been a 'blatant violation of accepted rules of behaviour' and that 'a new threshold' had been crossed, Washington concluded that 'a grave threat to peace existed' and that Soviet action had given rise 'to the most fundamental questions pertaining to international stability'.[35] It was argued, with a familiar logic, that the invasion 'could be a stepping stone to some broader aim, perhaps to their historic interest in a warm water port, perhaps to their interest in oil'.[36] Carter himself talked of 'the threat of further Soviet expansion into neighbouring countries', especially Iran and Pakistan, and an attempt to seek 'control over much of the world's oil supplies'. He added, in an encompassing image of menace:

If the Soviets are encouraged in this invasion by eventual success, and if they maintain their dominance over Afghanistan and then extend their control to adjacent countries, the stable, strategic and peaceful balance of the entire world will be changed. This would threaten the security of all nations including, of course, the United States, our allies, and our friends.[37]

Rules and their violation

Here, then, are three cases in which a perception of threat and a subsequent international crisis were clearly connected in the minds of decision-makers with infringements of rules of the game. In the examples given the danger perceived was of a political rather than military kind. Official concern was no less profound for that. After the initial uproar had subsided, however, public opinion tended to lose interest. 'What on earth does it have to do with us?' wondered Enoch Powell in *The Guardian* after the invasion of Afghanistan. Talk of a Russian threat stemmed from misuse of a small scale map; in reality, Teheran, Qatar, Riyadh and Dover were an immense distance from Kabul.[38]

In Western democracies foreign policy-making is burdened during periods of crisis by a grave disadvantage: the difficulty of mobilizing public support in response to political threats without distorting the nature of the issues involved. The result is a peculiar disparity between official hysteria and public indifference. When national leaders begin to talk of 'credibility' and the 'balance of power', incomprehension and even incredulity only deepen. During the Cuba crisis President Kennedy warned that if the Soviet move were tolerated it would 'change the balance of power' in the entire Cold War.[39] President Carter said much the same thing. But when observers, as they were invited to, evaluated the strategic balance in the aftermath of the encroachment, it was far from obvious that either Cuba or Afghanistan made very much difference.

Arguments to the balance of power are misleading. International equilibrium is precisely what was believed to be at stake in the crises examined, but not in the old-fashioned sense of a balance of forces based on the counterpoise of opposing alignments of equal military strength. Implied, rather, was order in the sense of a stable structure of relations, grounded in a mutually reinforcing network of normative expectations.

Why infringements of the rules should raise, in Carter's words, 'the most fundamental questions pertaining to international stability', can be answered by considering the function of rules of the game as described in chapter three.

The boundary function

Rules of the game, I have argued, help to obviate conflict by setting limits on states' permitted scope of action. By demarcating the area of the permissible from that of the forbidden, rules enable actors to proceed with their own affairs without fear of collision. Not only geographical frontiers, but also spheres of influence and conceptual prohibitions on, for instance, interference in others' internal affairs, perform this delineatory role. As we have seen, a physical border sets the one and only agreed limit on a state's jurisdiction and freedom of access at any given time. Similarly, a conceptual limit uniquely restricts, in a manner generally understood by the parties involved, a state's political freedom of action. Just as there is no other border beyond the border violated, there is no other rule to replace straightaway that rule which has been broken. Loss of a boundary makes it very difficult to improvise a substitute at short notice or to insulate the broken rule from others still intact. You cannot simply choose the rule which suits you; there can be no selective observance. In Chamberlain's words of March 1939: 'If it is so easy to discover good reasons for ignoring assurances so solemnly and so repeatedly given what reliance can be placed upon any other assurances that come from the same source?'[40] When one rule is flouted, all rules tend to be discredited.[41] And how can order be preserved in a world without restraints on conduct? The fabric of international society would disintegrate in a free-for-all of unbridled competition.

The signpost function

A rule, like a signpost, permits actors to coordinate their behaviour when direct communication is precluded. Travellers journeying apart are able to meet at a common destination by following the signs. Neither needs to know the precise route of the other. When signposts are removed, this kind of coordination is ruled out. Violations of the rules knock down existing signposts. Relationships without the guidance of rules become like landscapes without landmarks or common points of reference. Even should one wish to cooperate, means of coordination are unavailable. When an actor infringes the rules he is making a general statement about his reliability, or lack of it, for every violation (except in circumstances recognized to be exceptional) is a precedent for the future. Confidence is lost in one's ability to harmonize one's actions with an actor whose future conduct has ceased to be predictable. The situation in March 1939 was serious, Josef Beck argued, because one of the central elements in the definition of Poland's situation – Germany – had 'lost its calculability'.[42] With tacit coordination ruled out, international relations are reduced to a dialogue of the deaf. Order is more than a mere absence of conflict. It also entails cooperation. Those interested in preserving a particular order are invariably interested in working together to enforce barriers against those who are not. And even if cooperation to achieve shared goals is sometimes too much to expect, rivals will rarely be able to prevent collision without a joint effort to remove objects of dissension.

The tripwire function

Finally, it can be seen that violations of the rules give rise to deep concern about the viability of the existing international order, because this is precisely their function. Rules are intended to provide an early warning network to raise the alarm at the prospect of impending danger. Since the burglar, just as well as the jeweller, understands the purpose of the plate glass window, its deliberate breaking can only be interpreted as a declaration of intent to steal the contents. Where rules were not expressly set up as an alarm system they may still, in the event, perform a warning function. Defenders of the Munich Agreement pointed out that it was only after Germany had violated agreements voluntarily entered into that one could arrive at the true nature of Nazi ambitions. President Carter clearly felt very much the same way when he commented that the Afghanistan invasion had drastically changed his opinion of the Russians and he now had serious doubts about Moscow's ultimate foreign policy goals. [43]

Rules of the game provide indispensable support for the structure of international order. Like the scaffolding supporting a building, each section is held in place by the others in a mutually reinforcing lattice. To flout the rules is like damaging a section of the scaffolding. First scaffolding and as a consequence building threaten collapse. This is why the act of infringement implies more than a limited attempt to achieve immediate gain, but is perceived to be a warning of impending danger to the entire structure of orderly relations.

Chapter fourteen

Conclusion: rules reviewed

The collectivity of states would seem, on the face of it, to be subject to irresistibly disintegrative forces: scarce and inequitably distributed resources; cultural, ethnic and linguistic divisions which set nation against nation and breed fear and mistrust; ideological rivalry and competing visions and ambitions. And yet, for all this, much of the time states are at peace. Why this should be so and how peace can be reinforced are questions that have puzzled students of international politics. Traditional solutions to the puzzle, such as the balance of power, the working of international law or the existence of great power condominium, have proved partial or unsatisfactory. It is true that in domestic society cross-cutting institutional, bureaucratic and social balances, law and authoritative government do help to maintain order (though with an underpinning of coercive power not possessed by any organ of the international community). Yet the essential fabric of social order, the precondition for the establishment of all other mechanisms, is woven from the thread of social norms, the often unconscious ties by which the individual acknowledges the primacy of the community. So pervasive and deeply ingrained are they that they are taken for granted and tend only to be noticed when infringed or absent.

The thesis of this book is that an analogous role in the preservation of international order is played by international norms, called here rules of the game. Like social norms, they tend often to be overlooked by observers. Unlike social norms, however, as a result of the quite different spatial problems of the international community, bilateral norms – rules of conduct between a state and its neighbours and associates – are likely to predominate. Regional and universal norms certainly exist but are of less operative significance. Law, in the form of treaties and legal norms, is thought of here more as a special case of rules of the game than as something *sui generis*. It is noteworthy in this respect that agreement and accommodation between political entities reach far back into history and predate by millennia the emergence of any kind of comprehensive or organized body of international law. The great powers, which have often been seen, in the shape of the European Concert or the Security Council, as the guardians of international order, may at times impose their will on the collectivity. But this does not exempt them from the need to regulate relations among themselves by a network of rules. *Quis custodiet ipsos custodes*? Finally, the balance of power is a central factor in the working and maintenance of rules – not as an end in itself, as the unique guarantor of order, but as a condition of the viability and nature of the code of conduct at a given point in time. The balance of power is like the distribution of stress in a bridge; a stable structure depends on an even dispersal of the load, but the latter is a point of departure for the overall design, not its constructional objective.

Rules of the game themselves, it is stressed, are abstractions. The border, the treaty or the declaration are not the restraint but the sign of its existence, the instrument of its publication. Rules of the game are expectations of correct conduct, deviance from which is expected to incur sanction or loss. They are not natural laws, one-off orders or categorical moral imperatives. They are not necessarily the basis of correct prediction and do not seek to advance human welfare in terms of values existing outside the requirements of political order (though of course some would attribute very great value to the avoidance of war and suffering as a result of international anarchy). Whether or not they actually work in practice is a contingent fact dependent on circumstances, the interests of participants and the capacity and willingness for enforcement. This means that rules of the game, like social norms, can be quite conceivably infringed but, on the other hand, do tend, most of the time, to be reliable guides to action.

The need for rules of the game in the first place arises from the logic of the sovereign existence of independent states. In a world consisting of separate, wilful entities, the behaviour of each one of which is inherently unpredictable, an uncertain future holds out not only the risk of repeated collision but also obviates the possibility of constructive planning. Like primitive man in an uncontrollably hostile environment, the energies of states in these circumstances are absorbed by the pressing dictates of a precarious survival. Rules of the game serve to reduce this dangerous uncertainty by prescribing a system of normative principle – prohibitions, permissions and obligations – to guide states in their conduct. Such principles, serving as landmarks in an otherwise featureless landscape, act as a focal point around which states are able to coordinate their expectations of others' behaviour and hence harmonize their mutual actions. Rules of the game function in an analogous way to social conventions; they prevent embarrassment or confusion by laying down predetermined patterns of behaviour available for individuals to follow in problematic social situations. However for the international system rules are more than a convenience, they are a prerequisite of orderly existence. By inserting predictability into the behaviour of states, the risks of collision are greatly reduced; by permitting reliance on others' complementary courses of action, cooperation is also facilitated; and by lessening the danger of constantly imminent conflict, states are freed to progress beyond the bare dictates of survival.

A useful way to look at rules of the game is as a form of communication, a sort of language. Like a language, rules allow states to transmit information and bridge their atomic separation. Rules can then be thought of as having a grammar and a vocabulary which in turn generate the propositions which are the rules themselves. The grammar determines what does or does not make sense in the language, how propositions are formed and communicated, how rules relate to each other and so on. For instance the principle that no information in the international system is *a priori* redundant directs attention to the possibility that any action or articulation, whether deliberately directed at an external audience or not, may be used by observers as evidence of the state of expectations at a particular point in time. This particular principle has consequences for the vocabulary of rules of the game and helps to account for some features of diplomatic discourse. Extreme care in diplomatic formulation derives from the assumption shared by speaker and audience that every feature of a diplomatic text has its due meaning. The stylized forms and the studied courtesy of diplomatic intercourse also have their significance when it is appreciated that any departure from the norm will be seen as a meaningful act. The non-redundancy principle further implies that alongside linguistic utterances a whole range of acts of state possess communicatory significance, including leadership gestures, protocol and military moves. All these devices, verbal and nonverbal, can pass on information about the attachment of a state to its commitments, the acceptable limits of an opponent's freedom of action, one's position on the pretensions of a third party to extend the scope of his influence and so on.

The remarkable features of the 'language' by which rules of the game are expressed are first its subtlety and second its universality. On the one hand this has the great advantage of permitting communication between states of different cultures and languages, and is, therefore, a condition of the existence of an international community of even the most rudimentary kind. On the other hand it imposes on governments the need for the most discriminating and carefully controlled use of information. A lack of coordination between different organs of foreign policy and the transmission of contradictory and misleading messages complicate the task of diplomacy and may inadvertently create more uncertainty than they clear up.

Rules of the game, I go on to argue, can be considered as existing along a spectrum of formality from, at the one end, tacit rules, via the spirit of agreements and nonbinding agreements, to, at the other end, rules expressed in the form of international treaties.

Tacit rules are set out neither by a written document nor in a verbal promise, States concerned prefer them to remain unarticulated for various reasons, including the wish to avoid embarrassment and the expectation that publicity would be harmful. Wartime might be thought to provide a suitable occasion for restraints of this kind but in fact the experience of both world wars suggests the extreme fragility of tacit rules and their rapid obsolescence. Espionage and other forms of clandestine activity appear to provide more successful scope for their functioning. The reasons for this are surely that it is in the interest of rivals to maintain such practices with the minimum of publicity; retaliation by one side will only reverberate on the welfare of its own citizens on the territory of the opponent. On the whole, though, the most fertile areas for tacit accommodation are those in which serious opponents are obliged to maintain a minimum level of restraint in their relations. Both superpower relations and relations between enemies in the Middle East are kept within some kind of bounds by tacit rules of the game. Rules are not maintained for sentimental reasons; on the contrary, if opportunities at low cost present themselves to score a point off the opponent, they will be gratefully accepted. Nor is a normative structure, totally unacceptable to one of the rivals, likely to last very long. But as long as both sides maintain the capacity for mutual deterrence they are likely to perceive it in their interests to avoid situations promising minimal benefit at maximal cost.

The spirit of an agreement is the tacit dimension of a formal accord and includes those aspects of the agreement which seemed 'self evident' at the time or, indeed, constituted the very philosophical basis of the accord. The textualist approach which holds that only the letter of the text counts, ignores an entire dimension of international understanding. Looking at treaties from the wider perspective of their spirit is important, first, because, as a matter of fact, it is an element of international relations; second, because conduct which ignores the spirit of an agreement is likely to dispose of that agreement in a very short time. Behaviour which, by its strict and narrow adherence to the letter of the accord in fact violates its formal spirit, may be technically legitimate but should be recognized for its wider, uncooperative nature. It is understandably difficult for jurists to admit the relevance of something as amorphous as the spirit of an agreement; after all, one of the very points of a treaty is to have available a definitive text. Nevertheless, the defensibility of a particular act in a court of law is less important than whether it serves the shared interest in accommodation which underlay the original agreement. The problem of defining the spirit of an agreement in legal terms should not prevent us from recognizing its operative significance.

Nonbinding agreements are another aspect of diplomatic practice which have not received the attention they deserve from international lawyers. Two kinds of understanding come under the heading of 'nonbinding agreement'. The first is the oral promise or 'gentlemen's agreement'. On the whole oral promises serve short term purposes and facilitate the conduct of ongoing contacts. There are, notwithstanding, notable examples of international agreements which have taken oral form. Usually this has been to avoid the risks and possible controversies associated with a formal document requiring ratification, publication and justification before allies and third parties.

The second form taken by the nonbinding agreement is the written document not possessing legal force. One example is the communiqué. A vital instrument in the conduct of diplomacy, the communiqué is a record of the 'state of play' at a given point in time and can give a revealing insight into the signatories' perception of the rules of the game governing their relations. Precisely because it conventionally lacks legal force, states can use it as a guide to expectations without the inhibitions attached to a fullblown accord. It can be replaced if and when necessary. The Belgrade and Shanghai Communiqués demonstrate, in contrast, that impermanence is not a necessary attribute of the device where circumstances favour its durability.

It is sometimes thought that legally binding agreements are the only ones of importance or interest to the student of international politics. Although this is incorrect it is still true that international treaties and norms have a prominent place in the definition of rules of the game. The reasons for this prominence include: ancient practice; the wish to buttress an agreement with the weight of international law, and therefore legitimacy; the need to ensure precision and obviate misunderstanding in the drafting and interpretation of agreements; the symbolic weight of the formal compact; and finally, as an authoritative textual guide to a perhaps obtuse bureaucracy. It can be seen from this list that purely legal considerations are not necessarily paramount in the preference for a legally binding text. Rather, that long tradition has lent the treaty such evocative political, cultural as well as legal associations that it is transformed from just 'a scrap of paper' into a document carrying a historical weight of significance and dignity. For this reason treaties of various kinds – peace, friendship, arms control – often act as turning points in international relationships with a resonance going beyond the ostensibly limited provisions of the formal text. By removing contentious and destabilizing issues they may clear the way for later more far-reaching accommodation or cooperation. Nevertheless, for all this the treaty, as a device setting out the mutual obligations of the signatories, performs the same regulatory functions and is subject to the same 'grammatical' principles as other, albeit less formal, modes of rule definition.

In a constantly changing world rules of the game reflect and regulate the shifting pattern of relations between states. Unlike domestic society, the international community cannot rely on legislation or executive decision for making rules acceptable to the community, that is, possessing legitimacy. In the absence of such authoritative processes of rule-making and change, rules of the game are made along two vectors, by actions intended to create realities on the ground and through diplomatic means. The former category includes expectations generated by trends of policy – the ongoing give and take of relations between states; as a result of the outcome of setpiece test cases that function as constitutive experiences for the future; and by the deliberate signalling of claims of various kinds by nonverbal indicators. Although established practice is a common and effective way to generate rules, it lacks the certainty of legitimacy, because there is always the possibility that a state of affairs which has not acquired others' formal consent will be overturned in the future. Diplomatic means cannot achieve absolute certainty, but they do ensure, ahead of time, the compliance of those concerned with contemplated innovations. Hence negotiation is the central mechanism by which states, through a dialogue of claim and counterclaim, can peacefully adjust the normative framework of their relations. Declaratory diplomacy falls somewhere between rule making by practice and negotiation. By articulating claims in advance it seeks to achieve the prospective, practical acquiescence of others with the wishes of the innovator. Unfortunately it has often been a source of misunderstanding and subsequent contention since it does not actually elicit the formal approval of other parties; at best it acquires their tacit compliance, at worst their helpless resentment. Failing resort to quiet diplomacy, declaratory diplomacy can be effectively reinforced by nonverbal signals of intent. In the light of past failures to grasp or take seriously warning declarations, moves on the ground can ensure against misunderstanding.

As a result of the volatility of the international system there is a continuous erosion in the expectation of the validity of existing rules of the game. Changes in leadership, technology, interests and the distribution of power undermine rules whether formal or informal. Those that are not renewed lapse by dint of disuse. In order to maintain the validity, where desired, of existing rules, states have evolved a series of mechanisms suited for this purpose. These include the platitudinous verbal repetition of accepted principles, the repetition of symbolic acts understood to assert the commitment of the actor to some arrangement or established practice and reaffirmation through diplomatic channels. In the final analysis, should these communicatory expedients fail to achieve the desired effect, the actor may be obliged to fall back on the threat or exercise of forcible persuasion to preserve the given state of affairs. This is why the factor of relative power is central to the maintenance of international order. Expectations of a state's inability or unwillingness to stand on its rights are likely to encourage those dissatisfied with the *status quo* to explore the possibility of obtaining advantage. Importance is attached to credibility – as one government's perception of others' confidence in its reliability – because its loss, it is feared, will encourage opponents to probe for points of weakness.

If rules are 'made to be broken' the problem of the infractor is somehow to obtain the benefit of his infringement without toppling the overall structure. The art is not simply how to do it; it is how to get away with it. Two strategies have been favoured: The strategy of the *fait accompli* aims to alter the situation on the ground before the victim has time to react. He is then presented with the uncomfortable alternatives of compliance by resignation to the change or resistance in unfavourable circumstances. (Judicial resort presents an honourable variant of the first alternative which may be attractive in combining protest with inaction.) Public opinion, the international community and the inertia of bureaucracy and military all conspire to oppose the counteruse of force. As time passes, any reaction other than diplomatic or legal recourse, futile in the face of an accomplished fact, becomes increasingly difficult. The infractor becomes the new defender of the *status quo*; the victim now bears the iniquity of seeking to disturb international equilibrium.

The trouble with the *fait accompli* is that the victim cannot always be counted on to react 'rationally'. All too often what looks like a successful *coup* turns out to be the first stage in a rapidly deteriorating situation. For this and other reasons the strategy of incremental change has much to commend it. Avoiding the risks associated with a sudden initiative, the infractor in this case aims to alter the situation by a carefully gradated series of adjustments. If at any stage the initiative threatens to develop unpredictably, a line of retreat is available. Conversely, if the victim shows no sign of being able or willing to resist the encroachment, the initiator is in a position to move forward at an appropriate rate to his final goal. Like the *fait accompli*, incremental change does not always work out in practice. What looks like tacit compliance, or resignation, may be merely the hesitation that precedes painful resistance. Moreover the Western democracies, which have often in the past been faced by the challenge of ruthlessly expansionist dictatorships, tend to be both mis- leadingly long-suffering but correspondingly ferocious when pushed just that bit too far.

The general disadvantage of rule infringement is that violations of par- ticular rules tend not to be seen as isolated, containable incidents, but as premeditated attempts to undermine the overall normative structure gov- erning relations between the parties involved. Whether the normative principle at stake is geographical or conceptual, its violation, it is feared, is merely the thin end of an aggressive wedge aimed at toppling the estab- lished order. This is why even minor territorial violations and encroach- ments on the *status quo* have so often given rise to vigorous condemna- tion and violent counteraction. The issue perceived to be at stake by the victim is that of the equilibrium of the system itself; compliance threatens to lead to the unravelling of all other restraints hitherto limiting the aggressor's freedom of action. In the subsequent crisis, which arises all too often from the unexpectedly vehement reaction of parties concerned, the risks of a breakdown of order and the outbreak of hostilities do indeed become acute. On the outcome of the confrontation may well hang the continuing viability of the existing system, whether this was the intention of the infractor or not.

The question that the reader may find troubling him is whether rules of the game really do govern the conduct of states. Surely, he will argue, the wars of the past, the Hitlers and the Afghanistans, make a mockery of the claim that international relations are anything more than an unprinci- pled struggle for power. Reliance on anything other than preponderant power to preserve international order may seem dangerously futile. Other readers may dispute the view contained here on the grounds that it is too complacent: only a revolution in international practice away from 'power politics' holds out any hope for the survival of mankind in the nuclear era.

Although the purpose of this book has been analytical rather than didactic, it seems to me that both the 'realism in terms of power politics' and the radical schools give insufficient weight to the inherent inhibitions which the international collectivity imposes on its members. Nor do they do full credit to the constructive possibilities held out by the wise management of this mechanism of control. Of course states seek to increase their wealth, military capability and influence. Of course expansionist ideologies and paranoid nationalisms will drive states to foreign adventures. History is indeed littered with violent and disorderly episodes.

But none of these unpleasant realities disproves the validity of the concept of rules of the game, just as the occurrence of crime, antisocial behaviour and even civil disorder do not contradict the idea of social norms. What they do is to demonstrate the limitations and occasional fragility of rules without invalidating them as such. Nevertheless it is worth reiterating some of the arguments in favour of the existence of rules of the game.

1. First of all, the principle of rules of the game is not subject to the voluntary choice of states, to be taken up or discarded as and when convenient. Rules are simply a relational necessity arising from the existence of separate political entities which impinge on each other, most obviously in terms of their geographical proximity, but also along other dimensions of international life. It is surely no coincidence that other animal and human collectivities obliged to organize some kind of communal life also resort to various generalized principles of order having the same role as rules of the game. That states reject particular rules or even entire normative structures is a quite separate point. As a propaganda statement of the Togo Ministry of Information, calling for the cession of the Volta region of Ghana, explained it: 'The principle that the frontiers inherited from colonialism are sacrosanct undoubtedly prevents Africa tearing itself apart, but general principles have never ruled out consideration of individual cases.[1]

2. Nor do violations of rules affect the basic concept. If states never sought advantage, rules would not be needed. It is because states live in a ruthlessly competitive world that rules are required. It is inevitable in such circumstances that rules of the game, like social norms, are sometimes violated. The idea of a rule presupposes the possibility of its infringement. Not violation of rules, in fact, but indifference to the existence of rules would seriously count against my thesis. It is when rules are violated that their presence becomes most ostensible; crises arise as a result of the perception that the infractor wishes to undermine the existing structure of rules; strategies of rule violation are required because the infractor is fully aware that his intrusion is likely to meet with opposition and that this must therefore be neutralized or bypassed.

3. Finally, and this is surely the decisive point, the Brezhnevs of this world do not seek to *abolish* rules of the game as such. Indeed the Soviet leaders are great sticklers for rules from which they derive benefit or which are invulnerable to their gnawing. Khrushchev was insistent on the need for 'peaceful coexistence'. It may be that the

Soviet Union seeks to modify existing norms to its advantage and perhaps even dreams of replacing the present world order by a system more conducive to the realization of its objectives, whatever they may be in ideological, national or economic terms. A hegemonic system, dominated by the Soviet Union, would seem no less feasible, judging by past examples of such systems, than the present multilateral system in which the independence of members is preserved. Such a system need not be anarchic. On the contrary, relations between members of the Soviet bloc are very finely regulated by the full spectrum of normative controls described in this book, not by any means always to onesided Soviet benefit. They are, of course, underpinned by the reality of Soviet power and would be quite different were they based wholly on consent rather than coercion.

Notwithstanding the force of these arguments, there is no doubt that the international system is passing through an age of dislocation in which decisive shifts in the distribution of power have occurred not yet fully reflected in existing rules; the result has been continuing structural stress. The USSR, a dynamic force on the scene, acquiring new strength and confidence, seeks (whether deliberately or as the result of internal pressures is unimportant) the influence and position commensurate with its power. In opposition stand the defenders of the *status quo*. In this kind of situation, when dissatisfied or ambitious states are continually pushing at the limits of existing rules, exploring opportunities for unilateral gain as they arise, the concept of a rule-governed order may fall into disrepute. After Munich the admitted errors of Anglo-French diplomacy became confused with the very idea of trying to reach accommodation with the dictator powers. In view of later events the attempt to reach a general settlement with Germany can hardly be criticized in itself. Similarly, after disappointments in relations with the Soviet Union in recent years, voices have been raised in the West deprecating the principle of accommodation with the Soviet Union.

Here is not the place to consider in detail the effectiveness of East–West 'détente' in its various manifestations over the years. There have been areas and periods of greater and lesser success. In Europe strategic equilibrium has made possible the weaving of an intricate fabric of ties between the two halves of the continent. In Africa and Asia the Soviet Union never concealed, nor did the United States fail to recognize, that in the ideological field the superpowers remained, in President Nixon's words, 'totally dedicated competitors'.[2] At the very height of détente, in the summer of 1973, *Pravda* insisted on the indivisibility of restraint and competition: 'In conditions of incipient easing of tensions, the Soviet Union continues to take the side of all those who are fighting against social, national and racial aggression.'[3] This has meant, not surprisingly, that where the opportunity has arisen of obtaining advantage at low risk, the USSR has gone ahead. Western disappointment is more the result of self-deception than Soviet duplicity. The Soviet Union may be a ruthless and dedicated rival of the West; it is neither foolhardy, impercipient, nor unrealistic. Faced by an equally realistic and determined opponent, willing and able to define, communicate and stand on its interests, there is no reason why a structure of peaceful accommodation should not be maintained.

Whatever the occasional disappointments, there is surely no alternative in the nuclear age but for rivals to persist in their attempt to weave a fabric of coexistence. Fantasies of omnipotence at one extreme and disengagement at the other cannot wish away the inescapable need to sustain the normative basis of international order. Rules of the game are far from being a panacea. They are not self-enforcing and the wisdom of their management cannot be taken for granted. Equally, they are not an optional extra to be taken up and discarded at will. They are a structural fact of life of the international community. If rules of the game, favourable to one's interests, are neglected or mismanaged, others less advantageous will simply take their place. Correctly understood and managed they can provide a mechanism for restraint and mutually beneficial cooperation. In the absence of any practical alternative that is more than a utopian vision rules of the game look like the only instrument available for the attempt to hold off catastrophe.

References and further reading

Chapter 1: Rules as a mechanism of international order

1. **Singer, J.D.** and **Small, M.** (1972) *The Wages of War 1816–1965*, Wiley, New York, 374.
2. **Bull, H.** (1977) *The Anarchical Society*, Macmillan, London, 16–19.
3. **Falk, R.A.** (1972) Zone II as a world order construct, in Rosenau, J.N. Davis, V. and East, M. (eds), *The Analysis of International Politics*, Free Press, New York, p. 191.
4. **Morgenthau, H.J.** (1967) *Politics Among Nations* (4th edn), Knopf, New York, 197–205.
5. **Aron, R.** (1966) *Peace and War*, Weidenfeld and Nicolson, London, 130–1.
6. *The Anarchical Society, op. cit.*, Ch. 6.
7. **McWhinney, E.** (1964) *Peaceful Coexistence and Soviet-Western International Law*, A.W. Sythoff, Leyden, 24–5; see also **Falk, R.A.** (1968) *Legal Order in a Violent World*, Princeton University Press.
8. **Albrecht-Carrié, R.** (1968) *The Concert of Europe*, Harper, New York, 21–2; **Medlicott, W.N.** (1956) *Bismarck, Gladstone, and the Concert of Europe*, Athlone Press, London, 18.
9. Falk, Zone II as a world order construct, *op cit.*, 188.
10. **Rapoport, A.** (1966) What is information, in Smith, A.G. (ed.) *Communication and Culture*, Holt, Rinehart and Winston, New York, 53–5.

Chapter 2: The nature of rules

1. **Ganz, J.S.** (1971) *Rules: a systematic study*, Mouton, The Hague and Paris, 14.
2. **Andrews, B.** (1978) Social rules and the state as a social actor, *World Politics*, **20**, 524–5.
3. Ganz, *Rules, op. cit.*, p. 16.
4. *Ibid.*, 74.
5. **Goldmann, K.** (1969) International norms and governmental behaviour, *Cooperation and Conflict*, **3**, 172.
6. Ganz, *Rules, op. cit.*, pp. 77–9.
7. **Wittgenstein, L.** (1953) *Philosophical Investigations*, Macmillan, New York, 85.
8. **Kratochwil, F.V.** (1978) *International Order and Foreign Policy*, West-

view Press, Boulder, Colorado, 115; Andrews, Social rules and the State as a social actor, *op. cit.*, 527–8.
9. **Quinn, M.S.** (1975) Practice-defining rules, *Ethics*, **86**, 76–86.
10. **Vaz, E.W.** (1978) Institutionalized rule-violation and control in professional hockey, *Sociological Abstracts*, **26**, 78SO8755.
11. **Black, M.** (1962) *Models and Metaphors: studies in language and philosophy*, Cornell University Press, Ithaca, New York, 119.
12. **Hart, H.L.A.** (1961) *Concept of Law*, Clarendon Press, Oxford, 54–5; Goldmann, International norms and governmental behaviour, *op. cit.*, 173.
13. *Ibid.*, 176–7.
14. **United States Department of State**, *Bulletin*, 26 June 1972, 894.
15. **Hume, D.** (1739) *A Treatise of Human Nature*, (1911 edn), Vol. II Dent, London, 195.
16. **Cohen, R.** (1979) *Threat Perception in International Crisis*, Wisconsin University Press, Madison, Wisconsin, 24.

Chapter 3: The logic of rules

1. *The Times*, 28 Jan. 1977.
2. **Kissinger, H.A.** (1979) *The White House Years*, Weidenfeld and Nicolson and Michael Joseph, London, 716.
3. See **De Jouvenel, B.** (1967) *The Art of Conjecture*, Weidenfeld and Nicolson, London.
4. **United States Department of State**, *Bulletin*, 23 July 1973, 144.
5. Hume, *A Treatise of Human Nature*, Vol. II, 195–6 (see ref. 15, Ch. 2).
6. **Schelling, T.C.** (1960) *The Strategy of Conflict*, Harvard University Press, Cambridge, Mass., Ch. 3.
7. **United States Department of State** (1950) *Foreign Relations of the United States 1933*, Vol. II, 782–8.
8. Falk, Zone II as a world order construct, 187 (see ref. 3, Ch. 1).
9. **Ribbentrop, J.** (1954) *The Ribbentrop Memoirs*, Weidenfeld and Nicolson, London, 112.
10. **Anderson, M.S.** (1970) *The Great Powers and the Near East 1774–1923*, Edward Arnold, London, 75 (emphasis in original).
11. *The Sunday Telegraph*, 13 Jan. 1980.
12. Kratochwil, *International Order and Foreign Policy*, 4, (see ref. 8, Ch. 2).
13. **Dilks, D.**, (ed.) (1971) *The Diaries of Sir Alexander Cadogan 1938–1945*, Cassell, London, 161.
14. **Grey of Fallodon, Viscount** (1925) *Twenty-Five Years, 1892–1916*, Vol. II, Hodder and Stoughton, London, 6.
15. Kissinger, *The White House Years*, *op. cit.*, 574–5.
16. **Carlyle, M.**, (ed.) (1953) *Documents on International Affairs 1949–1950*, Oxford University Press, London, 103–5.
17. **Gladwyn, Lord** (1972) *The Memoirs of Lord Gladwyn*, Weybright and Tulley, New York, 228.

Chapter 4: The language of international politics: grammar

1. Hume, *A Treatise of Human Nature*, Vol. II, 224 (see ref. 15 Ch. 2).
2. *Ibid.*, 195.

3.   **Gould, W.L**, and **Barkun, M.** (1970) *International Law and the Social Sciences*, Princeton University Press, 193.
4.   Kissinger, *The White House Years*, 689 (see ref. 2. Ch. 3).
5.   **Bourne, K.** (1970) *The Foreign Policy of Victorian England 1830–1902*, Oxford University Press, London, 356.
6.   **Wilson, K.M.** (1975) The British Cabinet's decision for war, 2 August 1914, *British Journal of International Studies*, **1**, 151.
7.   **Bismarck, O.** (1898) *His Reflections and Reminiscences*, Vol. II, Smith, Elder, London, 280–1.
8.   **Jakobson, M.** (1969) *Finnish Neutrality*, Praeger, New York. 11.
9.   **Eban, A.** (1979) *An Autobiography*, Futura, London, 342–3, 399.
10. **Schelling, T.C.** (1963) The threat of violence in international affairs, *Proceedings of the American Society of International Law*, **57**, 108; **Halperin, M.** (1963) *Limited War in the Nuclear Age*, Wiley, New York 29.
11. Bourne, *The Foreign Policy of Victorian England*, *op. cit.*, 219.
12. **Beck, J.** (1957) *Final Report*, Speller, New York, 43.
13. **Franck, T.M.** and **Weisband, E.** (1972) *World Politics: verbal strategy among the superpowers*, Oxford University Press, New York, 129–31, 138.
14. **Watt, D.C.** (ed.) (1970) *Documents on International Affairs 1962*, Oxford University Press, London, 227–8.
15. *The Times*, 3 May 1977.
16. *The Guardian Weekly*, 6 Mar., 12 June 1977.
17. **Avon, Lord** [Anthony Eden] (1962) *Facing the Dictators*, Cassell, London, 476.
18. **Murphy, R.** (1965) *Diplomat Among Warriors*, Pyramid, New York, 322–3.
19. *The Times*, 4 Feb. 1976.
20. *Ibid.*, 6 Apr., 13 Apr. 1977.
21. *Newsweek*, 25 July 1977, 11; *The Guardian Weekly*, 30 Oct. 1977.

Chapter 5: The language of international politics: vocabulary

1.   Kissinger, *The White House Years*, 698–9 (see ref. 2, Ch. 3).
2.   Murphy, *Diplomat Among Warriors*, 314 (see ref. 18, Ch. 4).
3.   **Gilbert, F.** (1971) Ciano and his ambassadors, in Craig, G.A. and Gilbert, F. (eds) *The Diplomats 1919–1939*, Atheneum, New York, 522–4.
4.   **Feltham, R.C.** (1977) *Diplomatic Handbook* (2nd edn), Longman, London, 128–34.
5.   Kissinger, *The White House Years*, 692 (see ref. 2, Ch. 3).
6.   **Brown, G.** (1972) *In My Way*, Pelican, London, 226–7.
7.   **Robertson, T.** (1965) *Crisis*, Atheneum, New York, 253.
8.   *The Guardian Weekly*, 23 Mar. 1980.
9.   **Nicolson, H.** (1969) *Diplomacy* (3rd edn), Oxford University Press, London, 123.
10. *The Guardian Weekly*, 31 July 1977.
11. Kissinger, *The White House Years*, 783 (see ref. 2, Ch. 3).
12. *New York Times*, 13 Aug. 1978; see also *The Times*, 13 Dec. 1977.
13. *New York Times*, 9 Oct. 1977.
14. *Time*, 17 Oct. 1977, 20.

15. For example, Morgenthau, *Politics Among Nations*, 70–5 (see ref 4, Ch. 1); **Burton, J.W.** (1969) *Conflict and Communication*, Macmillan, London 54; **Cable, J.** (1971) *Gunboat Diplomacy*, Chatto and Windus, London, 63; **McClelland, C.A.** (1969) Action structures and communications in two international crises: Quemoy and Berlin, in Rosenau, J.N. (ed.), *International Politics and Foreign Policy*, (rev. edn), The Free Press, New York, 473–82; **Bell, C.** (1971) *The Conventions of Crisis*, Oxford University Press, London; **Bell, C.** (1974) The October Middle East war; a case study in crisis management during détente, *International Affairs*, **50**, 535–8.

16. **Jervis, R.** (1970) *The Logic of Images in International Relations*, Princeton University Press, 18–40; **Goffman, E.** (1970) *Strategic Interaction*, Oxford University Press, London.

17. **Ekman, P.** and **Friesen W.V.** (1969) The repertoire of nonverbal behavior; categories, origins, usage and coding, *Semiotica*, **1**, 75.

18. *The Inskip Diaries* (unpublished) 8 Sept. 1938.

19. **Barthes, R.** (1972) *Mythologies*, Hill and Wang, New York, 117, 143.

20. **Davies, J.E.** (1943) *Mission to Moscow*, Pocket Books, New York, 280–2, 295–6.

21. Ekman and Friesen, The repertoire of nonverbal behavior, *op cit.*, 60.

22. *Ibid.*

23. **Austin, J.L.** (1961) *Philosophical Papers*, Clarendon Press, Oxford, 220–39, quoted in Jervis, *The Logic of Images in International Relations*, *op. cit.*, 37.

24. Morgenthau, *Politics Among Nations*, *op. cit.*, 73.

25. Avon, *Facing the Dictators*, 589, 597 (*see ref. 17, Ch. 4*).

26. **Ciano, G.** (1953) *Ciano's Hidden Diary 1937–1938*, Dutton, New York, 86.

27. **Churchill, W.S.** (1950) *The Gathering Storm*, Reprint Society, London, 315–16.

28. **Waldheim, K.** (1973) *The Austrian Example*, Weidenfeld and Nicolson, London, 65.

29. Kissinger, *The White House Years*, 52 (*see ref. 2, Ch. 3*).

30. **Gathorne-Hardy, G.M.** (1950) *A Short History of International Affairs 1920–1939*, Oxford University Press, London, 486.

31. **Churchill, W.S.** (1950) *Grand Alliance*, Cassell, London, 22.

32. Cable, *Gunboat Diplomacy*, *op. cit.*, 196, 199.

33. **Lorenz, K.** (1966) *On Aggression*, Methuen, London, 111–12.

34. **Barker, A.J.** (1964) *Suez: The seven day war*, Faber, London, 90–1.

35. **Thomas, H.** (1965) *The Spanish Civil War*, Penguin, London, 564–5.

36. *Keesing's Contemporary Archives* (1969–70) XVII, 23544.

37. *Ibid.* (1952–54) IX, 13677; **Eden, A.** [Lord Avon] (1960) *Full Circle*, Cassell, London, 134–5.

38. **Argyle, M.** (1975) *Bodily Communication*, Methuen, London, 362.

39. Jervis, *The Logic of Images*, *op. cit.*, 38.

40. Schelling, *The Strategy of Conflict*, Ch. 2 (see ref. 6, Ch. 3).

41. Jervis, *The Logic of Images*, *op. cit.*, 123–30.

42. *New York Times*, 26 Feb.–2 Mar. 1977; *African Diary* (1977) XVII, 8417.

43. **Vagts, A.** (1956) *Defence and Diplomacy*, King's Crown Press, New York, 235, quoted in Jervis, *The Logic of Images*, *op. cit.*, 135.

44. **Wilson, H.** (1971) *The Labour Government 1964–1970*, Weidenfeld and Nicolson and Michael Joseph, London, 178–83; *Keesing's Contemporary*

Archives (1965–66) XV, 21136, 21175.

45. *Ibid*. (1957–58) XI, 15563.
46. Schelling, *Strategy of Conflict*, 195–9 (see ref. 6, Ch. 3); **Schelling, T.C.** (1966) *Arms and Influence*, Yale University Press, New Haven.
47. *The Times*, 11 July 1967.
48. **Watt, D.C.** (1965) *Survey of International Affairs 1961*, Oxford University Press, London, 604–6.
49. Cable, *Gunboat Diplomacy, op. cit.*, 142; *Keesing's Contemporary Archives* (1967–68) XVI, 22586–7.
50. **Sorensen, T.C.** (1966) *Kennedy*, Bantam Books, New York, 326–46; **Thomas, H.** (1971) *Cuba or the Pursuit of Freedom*, Eyre and Spottiswoode, London, 136–8.

Chapter 6: Tacit rules

1. **Ashworth, A.E.** (1968) The sociology of trench warfare 1914–1918, *British Journal of Sociology*, **19**, 407–23.
2. **Race, J.** (1972) Mutual self-limitation in civil war: the case of Vietnam, *Southeast Asia*, **2**, 211–30.
3. **Luttwak, E.** and **Horowitz, D.** (1975) *The Israeli Army*, Allen Lane, London, 316 fn.
4. *The Spectator*, 3 Jan. 1969, 9; **Webster, C.** and **Frankland, N.** (1961) *The Strategic Air Offensive Against Germany 1939–1945*, Vol. I, HMSO, London, 113.
5. **Quester, G.H.** (1966) *Deterrence Before Hiroshima*, Wiley, New York, 108, 114.
6. See **Trumpener, U.** (1975) The beginnings of gas warfare in World War I, *Journal of Modern History*, **47**, 460–80, and **Art, R.J.** (1973) The influence of foreign policy on seapower: new weapons and Weltpolitik in Wilhelminian Germany, *Sage International Studies Series*, Vol. II.
7. The example is suggested by **Whaley, B.** (1973) *Codeword Barbarossa*, MIT Press, Cambridge, Mass., 32.
8. *Documents on German Foreign Policy 1918–1945* (1962) Series D, Vol. XII, HMSO, London, 602–3, 1061–3.
9. **Weinberg, G.L.** (1954) *Germany and the Soviet Union 1939–1941*, E.J. Brill, Leiden, Appendix III.
10. **Sonntag, R.J.** and **Beddie, J.J.** (eds) (1948) *Nazi-Soviet Relations 1939–1941*, Government Printing Office, Washington, DC, 329.
11. *The Washington Post* in *The Guardian Weekly*, 10 Sept. 1978, 15.
12. Falk, Zone II as a world order construct, 190–3 (*see ref. 3, Ch. 1*).
13. *Time*, 30 Sept. 1974.
14. **Kaufman, E.** (1976) *The Superpowers and their Spheres of Influence*, Croom Helm, London, Ch. 1.
15. Kissinger, *The White House Years*, 1180 (*see ref. 2, Ch. 3*).
16. *Time*, 14 Jan. 1980.
17. **Williams, P.** (1976) *Crisis Management*, Martin Robertson, London, 101–13.
18. Eban, *An Autobiography*, 535–6 (*see ref. 9, Ch. 4*); **Kalb, M.** and **Kalb, B.** (1974) *Kissinger*, Little, Brown, New York, Ch. 18.
19. **Bar-Siman-Tov, Y.** (1980) *The Israel–Egyptian War of Attrition 1969–*

1970: a case-study of limited local war, Columbia University Press New York.
20. **Heikal, M.** (1976) *The Road to Ramadan*, Fontana, London, 84.
21. **Nixon, R.** (1978) *RN: the memoirs of Richard Nixon*, Sidgwick and Jackson, London, 479.
22. Kissinger, *The White House Years*, Ch. 14 (*see ref. 2, Ch. 3*).
23. *The Jerusalem Post*, 4 Feb. 1976.
24. *New York Times*, 21 Sept. 1975.
25. *Ibid.*, 30 and 31 Oct. 1975.
26. *Ibid.*, 31 Oct. 1975.
27. *Ibid.*, 24, 26, 27 Jan. 1976.
28. *Ma'ariv* (Hebrew) 14 Apr. 1976.
29. *The Jerusalem Post*, 3 June 1976.
30. *Hearing Before the Committee on International Relations House of Representatives*, 17 June 1976, US Government Printing Office, Washington, DC, 28.
31. *Ha'aretz* (Hebrew) 25 July 1976.

Chapter 7: The spirit of agreements

1. **Brownlie, I.** (1973) *Principles of Public International Law* (2nd edn), Clarendon Press, Oxford, 604–11; **Parry, C.** (1968) The law of treaties, in Sorensen, M., (ed.), *Manual of Public International Law*, St Martin's Press, London, 210–14.
2. **McDougal, M.S., Lasswell, H.D.** and **Miller, J.C.** (1967) *The Interpretation of Agreements and World Public Order*, Yale University Press, New Haven, 50.
3. **Gooch, G.P.** and **Temperley, H.**, (eds) (1936) *British Documents on the Origins of the War 1898–1914*, Vol. X, Pt. 1, HMSO, London, 550.
4. *Ibid.*, 596.
5. **Schreiner, G.A.**, (ed.) (1921) *Entente Diplomacy and the World*, Allen and Unwin, New York, 531, 574.
6. **Heald, S.**, (ed.) (1939) *Documents on International Affairs 1937*, Oxford University Press, London, 87.
7. *Documents on German Foreign Policy 1918–1945* (1951) Series D, Vol. III, 183–4, (*see ref. 8, Ch. 6*).
8. *Foreign Relations of the United States 1936* (1954) Vol. 2, Government Printing Office, Washington, DC, 618.
9. **Avon,** *Facing the Dictators*, 432–3 (*see ref. 17, Ch. 4*).
10. *Documents Diplomatiques Français 1932–1939* (1967) 2e série (1936–1939), Vol. IV, Imprimerie Nationale, Paris, 404.
11. **Vayrynen, R.** (1972) *Conflicts in Finnish-Soviet Relations*, Tampereen Yliopisto, Tampere: 32–3.
12. **Singleton, F.** (1974) Finland, Comecon and the EEC, *The World Today*, **30**, 64–8.
13. Jakobson, *Finnish Neutrality*, 78–9 (*see ref. 8, Ch. 4*).
14. *Keesing's Contemporary Archives (1961–1962)* XIII, 18485.
15. Jakobson, *Finnish Neutrality*, 78–9 (*see ref. 8, Ch. 4*).
16. **Singleton, F.B.** (1978) Finland between East and West, *The World Today*, **34**, 323.

Chapter 8: Rules established by nonbinding agreements

1. **Chayet, C.** (1957) Les accords en forme simplifiée, *Annuaire Français de Droit International*, **3**, 3–13.
2. See **Reuter, P.** (1972) *Introduction au Droit des Traités*, Armand Colin, Paris, 44.
3. **Schachter, O.** (1977) The twilight existence of nonbinding international agreements, *American Journal of International Law*, **71**, 296–304.
4. **Fawcett, J.E.S.** (1954) The legal character of international agreements, *The British Year Book of International Law*, **30**, 398–400.
5. Eden, *Full Circle*, 150 (*see ref. 37, Ch. 5*)
6. **Woodward, L.** (1971) *British Foreign Policy in the Second World War*, Vol. 2, HMSO, London, 178–9.
7. *Keesing's Contemporary Archives* (*1978*) XXIV, 28989; **Ayoob, M.** (1979) The superpowers and regional 'stability': parallel responses to the Gulf and the Horn, *The World Today*, **35**, 203.
8. **Dugdale, E.T.S.**, (ed.) (1929) *German Diplomatic Documents 1871–1914*, Vol. 2, Harper, New York, 169.
9. Reuter, *Introduction au Droit des traités, op. cit.*, 44.
10. **Churchill, W.S.** (1954) *The Second World War*, Vol. 6, *Triumph and Tragedy*, Cassell, London, 198.
11. Woodward, *British Foreign Policy in the Second World War*, Vol. 2, *op. cit.*, 138, 140; **Feis, H.** (1967) *Churchill, Roosevelt, Stalin*, Princeton, University Press, 448–50.
12. **Schwarzenberger, G.** and **Brown, E.D.** (1976) *A Manual of International Law*, (6th edn), Professional Books, London, 122.
13. **United States Department of State**, *Bulletin*, **66**, 20 Mar. 1972, 427. For the text see **Grenville, J.A.S.** (1974) *The Major International Treaties 1914–1973*, Methuen, London, 524–7.
14. Kissinger, *The White House Years*, 1086, 1091 (*see ref. 2, Ch. 3*).
15. Anderson, *The Great Powers and the Near East*, 71–5 (*see ref. 10, Ch. 3*).
16. **Henderson, G.B.** (1947) The Seymour conversations, 1853, in *Crimean War Diplomacy and other Historical Essays*, Glasgow University Press, 1–11.
17. **Chay, J.** (1968) The Taft-Katsura Memorandum reconsidered, *Pacific Historical Review*, **37**, 321–6; text of the document in **Link, A.S.** and **Leary, W.M.** (eds) (1970) *The Diplomacy of World Power: the United States 1889–1920*, Edward Arnold, London, 100–1.
18. **Esthus, R.A.** (1959) The Taft-Katsura Agreement – reality or myth, *Journal of Modern History*, **31**, 49.
19. **Pratt, J.W.** (1955) *A History of United States Foreign Policy*, Prentice-Hall Englewood Cliffs, New Jersey, 444.

Chapter 9: International treaties and norms

1. **Myers, D.P.** (1957) The names and scope of treaties, *American Journal of International Law*, **51**, 575.
2. **O'Connell, D.P.** (1970) *International Law*, Vol. 1, Stevens and Sons, London, 195–204.

3. Grenville, *The Major International Treaties*, 7, (*see ref. 13, Ch. 8*).
4. See **Pritchard, J.B.** (1955) *Ancient Near Eastern Texts Relating to the Old Testament*, Princeton University Press.
5. **Couve de Murville, M.** (1971) *Une Politique Étrangère*, Plon, Paris, 257.
6. **Macmillan, H.** (1973) *At the End of the Day 1961–63*, Macmillan, London, 462.
7. See **Chayes, A.** (1974) *The Cuban Missile Crisis*, Oxford University Press, London, Ch. 4; **Henkin, L.** (1968) *How Nations Behave*, Praeger, New York, Ch. 4.
8. *Yediot Ahronot* (Hebrew) 11 Apr. 1979.
9. **Mattingly, G.** (1965) *Renaissance Diplomacy*, Penguin, London, 157–9.
10. **Lewis, A.** (1979) The peace ritual and Israeli images of social order, *Journal of Conflict Resolution*, 23, 686.
11. **United States Department of State** *Bulletin*, 72, 12 May 1975, 609.
12. **Merrills, J.G.** (1976) *Anatomy of International Law*, Sweet and Maxwell, London, 64.
13. Couve de Murville, *Une Politique Étrangère, op. cit.*, 256.
14. **Adams, L.J.** (1974) *Theory, Law and Policy of Contemporary Japanese Treaties*, Sijthoff, Leiden, 67–8, 71.
15. **Triska, J.F. and Slusser, R.M.** (1962) *The Theory, Law and Policy of Soviet Treaties*, Stanford University Press, 5, 47, 228, 231.
16. **Fisher, E.** (1949) On boundaries, *World Politics*, 1, 196–222.
17. **Webster, C.** (1931) *The Foreign Policy of Castlereagh 1812–1815*, G. Bell, London, 268.
18. **Dugdale, E.T.S.** (ed.) (1928) *German Diplomatic Documents 1871–1914*, Vol. 1, Methuen, London, 144–8.
19. See **Lowe, C.J.** and **Dockrill, M.L.** (eds) (1972), *The Mirage of Power*, Vol. 3, Routledge and Kegan Paul, London, 631; Gooch and Temperley, *British Documents on the Origins of the War*, Vol. X, Pt. 1, 898–9 (*see ref. 3, ch. 7*).
20. **Dilks, D.** (ed.) (1971), *The Diaries of Sir Alexander Cadogan 1938–1945*, Cassell, London, 167.
21. Dugdale, *German Diplomatic Documents*, Vol. 1, *op. cit.*, 369–71.
22. For example see **Vital, D.** (1972) Czechoslovakia and the powers, September 1938, in Gatzke, H.W. (ed.) *European Diplomacy Between Two Wars 1919–1939*, Quadrangle Books, Chicago, 194–5.
23. **Roberts, H.L.** (1971) The diplomacy of Colonel Beck, in Craig, G.A. and Gilbert, F. (eds) *The Diplomats 1919–1939*, Atheneum, New York, 594–8.
24. Jakobson, *Finnish Neutrality*, 89 (*see ref. 8, Ch. 4*).
25. *Documents on German Foreign Policy 1918–1945* (1959) Series C. Vol. II, No. 77, 139–41 (*see ref. 8, Ch. 6*).
26. **Glahn, G. von** (1976) *Law Among Nations*, (3rd edn), Macmillan, New York, 421.
27. See **Olorurtimehin, B.O.** (1969) The Treaty of Niagassola 1886: an episode in Franco-Samori relations in the era of the Scramble, *Journal of the Historical Society of Nigeria*, 4, 601–13.
28. *Documents on German Foreign Policy 1918–1945* (1962) Series C, Vol. IV, No. 275, 587–8 (*see ref. 8, Ch. 6*).
29. **Sorensen, T.C.** (1966) *Kennedy*, Bantam, New York, 834.
30. **Brandt, W.** (1978) *People and Politics*, Collins, London, 189.
31. Triska and Slusser, *Soviet Treaties, op. cit.*, 25, 29; **Falk, R.A.** (1968)

Legal Order in a Violent World, Princeton University Press, viii-ix, 111–12.

32. **Buckley, W.F.** (1975) *United Nations Journal*, Michael Joseph, London, 188; Eban, *An Autobiography*, 494, 499–500, 558 (*see ref. 9, Ch. 4*).
33. Kissinger, *The White House Years*, 156–8 (*see ref. 2, Ch. 3*).

Chapter 10: Making rules

1. **Johnston, D.H.N.** (1965) *Rights in Air Space*, Manchester University Press, 27.
2. **Penson, L.M.** (1961) Obligations by treaty: their place in British foreign policy 1898–1914, in Sarkissian, A.O. (ed.), *Studies in Diplomatic History and Historiography in Honour of G.P. Gooch*, Longman, London, 88.
3. **Bourne, K.** (1970) *The Foreign Policy of Victorian England 1830*–1902, Clarendon Press, Oxford, 479, 481.
4. **Howard, M.** (1974) *The Continental Commitment*, Penguin, London, 46.
5. *Ibid.*, 48.
6. **Williamson, S.R.** (1969) *The Politics of Grand Strategy*, Harvard University Press, Cambridge, Mass., 320, 322.
7. **Trevelyan, G.M.** ((1937) *Grey of Fallodon*, Longman, London, 139–40.
8. **Wilson, K.M.** (1977) To the Western Front: British war plans and the 'military entente' with France before the First World War, *British Journal of International Studies*, **3**, 152–5.
9. Dugdale, (1928) *German Diplomatic Documents*, Vol. 4, 324–7 (*see ref. 8, Ch. 8*).
10. **Lowe, C.J.** and **Dockrill, M.L.** (eds) (1972) *The Mirage of Power*, Routledge, and Kegan Paul, London, 492.
11. **Wilson, K.M.** (1975) The British Cabinet's decision for war, 2 August 1914, *British Journal of International Studies*, **1**, 150–1, 156–7.
12. *Foreign Relations of the United States 1948* (1973) US Government Printing Office, Washington, DC, Vol. 2, 887.
13. **Clay, L.D.** (1950) *Decision in Germany*, Doubleday, New York, 359.
14. *Foreign Relations 1948, op. cit.*, Vol. 2, 890–1.
15. **George, A.L.** and **Smoke, R.** (1974) *Deterrence in American Foreign Policy*, Columbia University Press, New York, 125.
16. **Millis, W.** (ed.) (1952) *The Forrestal Diaries*, Cassell, London, 174.
17. **Petersen, C.C.** (1979) Showing the flag, in Dismukes, B. and McConnell, J.M. (eds) *Soviet Naval Diplomacy*, Pergamon Press, New York, 91, 93.
18. **Cohen, R.** (1979) *Threat Perception in International Crisis*, Wisconsin University Press, Madison, 48–52, 155–6.
19. **Remmek, R.B.** (1979) The politics of Soviet access to naval support facilities in the Mediterranean, in Dismukes and McConnell, *Soviet Naval Diplomacy, op. cit,*, 372–3, 385–6.
20. See, for instance, **Abba Eban** in *Ha' aretz* (Hebrew) 5 June 1970.
21. **Boulding, K.** (1967) The impact of the draft on the legitimacy of the nation state, in Tax, S. (ed.) *The Draft*, University of Chicago Press, 191.
22. **Kissinger, H.** (1974) *A World Restored*, Gollancz, London, 139.
23. *Documents on German Foreign Policy 1918–1945* (1966) Series C, Vol. V, 775 fn (*see ref. 8, Ch. 6*).
24. For the text of the Italian note see **Heald, S.**, (ed.) (1937) *Documents on International Affairs 1936*, Oxford University Press, London, 218.

25. *Documents on German Foreign Policy 1918–1945* (1949) Series D, Vol. I, 283–5 (*see ref. 8 Ch. 6*).
26. *Ibid.*, 278–82
27. **Toynbee, A.J.** (1937) *Survey of International Affairs 1936*, Oxford University Press, London, 451.
28. *Documents on German Foreign Policy 1918–1945* (1966) Series C, Vol. V 774–6. (*see ref. 8, Ch. 6*).
29. *Ibid.*, 849–51; **Muggeridge, M.** (ed.) (1948) *Ciano's Diplomatic Papers*, Odhams Press, London, 22; *Documents on International Affairs 1936*, op. cit., 219–20.
30. *Ciano's Diplomatic Papers, op. cit.*, 43–5.
31. *Documents on German Foreign Policy 1918–1945* (1966) Series C, Vol. V 1136–8 (*see ref. 8, Ch. 6*); *Ciano's Diplomatic Papers, op. cit.*, 52.
32. *Ibid.*, 60.
33. Bar-Siman-Tov, *The Israel–Egyptian War of Attrition*, 153–4 (*see ref. 19, Ch. 6*).
34. **Dinerstein, H.S.** (1976) *The Making of a Missile Crisis: October 1962*, Johns Hopkins University Press, Baltimore.
35. *Ibid.*, 82.
36. *Ibid.*, 86.
37. *Ibid.*, 90–2, 95–6.
38. *Ibid.*, 101–4.
39. *Ibid.*, 130–1.
40. *Ibid.*, 132.
41. *Ibid.*, 136.
42. *Ibid.*, 166–8.
43. *Ibid.*, 234–6.
44. **Watt, D.C.** (ed.) (1971), *Documents on International Affairs 1962*, Oxford University Press, London, 189–91.
45. Chayes, *The Cuban Missile Crisis*, (see ref. 7, Ch. 9).
46. *Documents on International Affairs 1962, op. cit.*, 194 (my emphasis).
47. *Ibid.*, 203–5.
48. **Whiting, A.S.** (1975) *The Chinese Calculus of Deterrence*, University of Michigan Press, Ann Arbor, 206.
49. Bell, The October Middle East War, *op. cit.*, 535–8 (*see ref. 15, Ch. 5*).

Chapter 11: Maintaining rules

1. See *Daily Telegraph*, 5 Nov. 1976.
2. Howard, *The Continental Commitment*, 94, 109 (*see ref. 4 Ch. 10*); **Muir, R.O.** (1975) *Modern Political Geography*, Macmillan, London, 144.
3. **Hilgard, E.R.** (1962) *Introduction to Psychology* (3rd edn), Harcourt, Brace, New York, 254–6.
4. *Documents on British Foreign Policy 1919–1939*, 3rd Series, Vol. I, 331–2, 334–5.
5. *Ibid.*, 409.
6. *Documents on German Foreign Policy 1918–1945 (1966)*, Series D, Vol. II, 352, 536 (*see ref. 8 Ch. 6*).
7. **Thomas, H.** (1965) *The Spanish Civil War*, Penguin, London, 678–9; **Crozier, W.P.** (1973) *Off the Record*, Hutchinson, London, 84, 87.

8. *Documents Diplomatiques Français 1932–1939* (2nd series) Vol. 10, 776–7, 815.
9. **Bullock, A.** (1962) *Hitler: a study in tyranny*, (rev. edn), Penguin, London, 369.
10. *Documents on German Foreign Policy 1918–1945 (1966)*, Series D, Vol. II, 358, 475 *(see ref. 8, Ch. 6)*.
11. **Irving, D.** (1978) *The War Path*, Michael Joseph, London, 121.
12. **Robertson, E.M.** (1963) *Hitler's Pre-War Policy and Military Plans 1933–1939*, Longmans, London, 135fn.
13. *Ibid.*, 129; Bullock, *Hitler, op. cit.*, 450.
14. *Documents on German Foreign Policy 1918–1945 (1966)*, Series D, Vol. II, 421 *(see ref. 8, Ch. 6)*.
15. *Ibid.*, 593; Irving, *The War Path, op. cit.*, 124, 125.
16. *Time*, 24 Apr. 1978.
17. See **Cohen, R.** (1978) Israel and the Soviet-American statement of October 1, 1977, *Orbis*, **22**, 622, 626–8.
18. **Clissold, S.** (ed.) (1975) *Yugoslavia and the Soviet Union 1939–1973*, Oxford University Press, London, 255.
19. *Ibid.*, 274, 289, 293, 300.
20. *Ibid.*, 71, 79.
21. **Cviic, K.F.** (1976) Yugoslavia after Tito, *The World Today*, **32**, 128; *The Times*, 13 Nov., 18 Nov. 1976.
22. See Lorenz, *On Aggression*, 26–30 *(see ref. 33, Ch. 5)*; **Ardrey, R.** (1967) *The Territorial Imperative*, Atheneum, New York.
23. **Howard, H.N.** (1974) *Turkey, the Straits and U.S. Policy*, Johns Hopkins University Press, Baltimore, 275; *New York Times*, 7 Jan., 4 Sept. 1966, 7 Dec. 1968, 6 June 1969, 10 Mar. 1975.
24. *Time*, 24 July 1978.
25. *Documents on German Foreign Policy 1918–1945 (1966)*, Series C, Vol. IV, 531, 541 *(see ref. 8, Ch. 6)*; **Jedrzejewicz, W.** (ed.) (1968) *Diplomat in Berlin 1933–1939: papers and memoirs of Jozef Lipski, Ambassador of Poland*, Columbia University Press, New York, 216.
26. *Time*, 7 Jan. 1980.
27. *New York Times*, 3–5 Feb. 1959.
28. *Ibid.*, 13–21 Aug. 1961; *Keesing's Contemporary Archives (1961)* XIII, 18275–7; **David, A.E.** (1975) *The Strategy of Treaty Termination*, Yale University Press, New Haven, 65.
29. **Maxwell, N.** (1973) The Chinese account of the 1969 fighting at Chenpao, *The China Quarterly*, **56**, 739.

Chapter 12: Breaking rules: the act

1. *Keesing's Contemporary Archives (1974)* XX, 26709.
2. **Dishon, D.** (ed.) (1971) *Middle East Record Vol. 3, 1967*, Israel Universities Press, Jerusalem, 256, 257.
3. **Heikal, M.** (1976) *The Road to Ramadan*, Fontana, London, 54.
4. *Jerusalem Post*, 8 Nov. 1977.
5. *Keesing's Contemporary Archives (1974)* XX, 26710.
6. **Heikal, M.** (1972) *Nasser: the Cairo documents*, Mentor, London, 88–90.
7. Cable, *Gunboat Diplomacy*, 202 *(see ref. 15, Ch. 5)*.

8. *The Guardian*, 14 Sept. 1976.
9. **Taylor, A.J.P.** (1965) *Bismarck: the man and the statesman*, Mentor, London, 68.
10. **Medlicott, W.N.** and **Coveney, D.K.** (1971) *Bismarck and Europe*, Edward Arnold, London, 52–4.
11. **Maxwell, N.** (1970) *India's China War*, Cape, London, 348.
12. *The Observer*, 28 Oct. 1962.
13. *Sunday Times*, 28 Oct. 1962.
14. **Watt, D.C.** (ed.) (1970) *Documents on International Affairs 1962*, Oxford University Press, London, 792–3.
15. *The Times*, 21 Nov. 1962.
16. Dishon, *Middle East Record 1967, op. cit.*, 198; **Churchill, R.S.** and **Churchill, W.** (1967), *The Six Day War*, Heinemann, London. 47.
17. **Meir, G.** (1976) *My Life*, Futura, London, 301.
18. Cable, *Gunboat Diplomacy*, 27–31 (*see ref. 15, Ch. 5*).
19. George and Smoke, *Deterrence in American Foreign Policy*, 120 (*see ref. 15, Ch. 10*).
20. **Avi-Ran, U.** (1976) Hame'oravut Hasurit Bemeshber Halevanoni, *Ma'arakhot* (Hebrew) Oct., 25–31; '**Dani**', (1977) Haplisha Hasurit Lelevanon, *Ma'arakhot* (Hebrew) June, 7–16.
21. *Financial Times*, 21 Oct. 1976.
22. *Le Monde*, 30 Apr. 1976.
23. *Keesing's Contemporary Archives (1973)* XIX, 25885, 26018; *The Guardian*, 7 Nov. 1973.
24. *Le Monde*, 30 Apr. 1976.
25. *Keesing's Contemporary Archives (1975)* XXI, 27105.
26. *Ibid.*, 27102–5; *Le Monde*, 30 Apr. 1976.
27. **Giap, V.N.** (1974) *People's War People's Army*, Foreign Languages Publishing House, Hanoi, 191–2 (emphasis in original).
28. **Brecher, M.** (1968) *India and World Politics*, Oxford University Press, London, 168.
29. Maxwell, *India's China War, op. cit.*, 225–6.
30. *Ibid.*, 237–9.
31. *Ibid.*, 253–4.
32. *Ibid.*, 255.
33. **Vertzberger, Y.** (1978) India's border crisis with China, *The Jerusalem Journal of International Relations*, **3**, 117–38.

Chapter 13: Breaking rules: perception and crisis

1. Cohen, *Threat Perception in International Crisis (see ref. 18, Ch. 10)*.
2. **Hermann, C.F.** (1969) International Crisis as a situational variable, in Rosenau, J.N., (ed.) *International Politics and Foreign Policy* (2nd edn), Free Press, New York, 409–21; **Brecher, M.** (1977) Towards a theory of international crisis behavior. *International Studies Quarterly*, **21**, 39–74.
3. Schelling, *The Strategy of Conflict*, 259 (*see ref. 6, Ch. 3*).
4. Grey, *Twenty-Five Years*, I, 123–5 (*see ref. 14, Ch. 3*); see also Cd 3006 (1906) *Correspondence respecting the Turco-Egyptian frontier in the Sinai Peninsula*, HMSO, London.
5. **Hinton, H.C.** (1971) *The Bear at the Gate*, American Enterprise Institute

for Public Policy Research, Washington, 17–18.

6. *Keesing's Contemporary Archives (1969)*, XVII, 23313, 23641–5.
7. **Maxwell, N.** (1970) Russia and China: the irrepressible conflict, *Pacific Community*, **1**, 551–63.
8. **Possony, S.T.** (1971) The antagonism between Russia and China, *Politische Studien*, **22**, 169–82.
9. **Luard, E.** (1970) Frontier disputes in modern *International* relations, in Luard, E. (ed.) *The International Regulation of Frontier Disputes*, Thames and Hudson, London, 7–9.
10. **Pruitt, D.G.** (1965) Definition of the situation as a determinant of international action, in Kelman, H.G. (ed.) *International Behavior*, Holt, Rinehart and Winston, New York, 403.
11. Chayes, *The Cuban Missile Crisis*, 3 *(see ref. 7, Ch. 9)*.
12. **Feiling, K.** (1946) *Life of Neville Chamberlain*, Macmillan, London, 381.
13. PRO, Cab. 23/98, 15 March 1939.
14. *House of Commons Debates*, 5th ser., vol. 339, col. 22; **Curtis, M.** (ed.) (1943) *Documents on International Affairs 1938*, Vol. 2, Oxford University Press, London, 259.
15. PRO, Cab., 23/98, 15 March 1939.
16. *Documents on British Foreign Policy*, 3rd series, IV, 271, 400 [my emphasis].
17. Jedrzejewicz, *Diplomat in Berlin*, 503 *(see ref. 25, Ch. 11)*.
18. *Ibid.*, 384–5.
19. **Republic of Poland, Ministry for Foreign Affairs** (1940) *Official Documents 1933–1939*, HMSO, London, No. 61.
20. *Ibid.*, Nos. 34, 37.
21. *Ciano's Diary 1939–1943*, 45–6 *(see ref. 26, Ch. 5)*.
22. *Documents on International Affairs 1938*, *op. cit.*, II, 207.
23. **Smith, D.M.** (1976) *Mussolini's Roman Empire*, Viking Press, New York, 132.
24. **Kirkpatrick, I.** (1964) *Mussolini*, Odhams Books, London, 372.
25. *Ciano's Diary 1939–1943*, 47–53 *(see ref. 26, Ch. 5)*; **Muggeridge, M.** (ed.) (1948) *Ciano's Diplomatic Papers*, Odhams Books, London, 276–9.
26. *Documents on International Affairs 1962*, *op. cit.*, 207–8.
27. Chayes, *The Cuban Missile Crisis*, 18–19, 23–4 *(see ref. 7, Ch. 9)*.
28. *Ibid.*, 23.
29. *Documents on International Affairs 1962*, *op. cit.*, 224.
30. *Facts on File 1979*, 232–3, 284, 368, 443, 580, 666, 966; *The Washington Star*, 13 Dec. 1979.
31. *Weekly Compilation of Presidential Documents*, 31 Dec. 1979, 2287.
32. *Ibid.*, 11 Jan. 1980, 25.
33. **United States Department of State**, *Bulletin*, **80**, 29.
34. *New York Times*, 1 Jan. 1980.
35. *Weekly Compilation of Presidential Documents*, 31 Dec. 1979, 2287; United States Department of State, *Bulletin*, **80**, 4.
36. *Ibid.*, 7.
37. *Weekly Compilation of Presidential Documents*, 11 Jan. 1980, 25–6.
38. *The Guardian Weekly*, 8 June 1980.
39. **Sorensen, T.C.** (1965) *Kennedy*, Harper and Row, New York, 678.
40. *The Government Blue Book*, (1939) Penguin, London, 46.
41. Schelling, T.C. (1963) The threat of violence in international affairs, *op. cit.*, *(see ref. 10, Ch. 4)*.

42. Jedrzejewicz, *Diplomat in Berlin*, 503 (*see ref. 25, Ch. 11*).
43. *The Times*, 3 Jan. 1980.

Chapter 14: Conclusion: rules reviewed

1. *The Times*, 28 Jan. 1977.
2. *Keesing's Contemporary Archives* (*1972*) XVIII, 25316.
3. *Current Digest of the Soviet Press*, 26 Sept. 1973, XXVI, 9.

Index